MORAL ACTION
IN YOUNG ADULTHOOD

RALPH L. MOSHER
DAVID CONNOR
KATHERINE M. KALLIEL
JAMES M. DAY
NORMA YOKOTA
MARK R. PORTER
JOHN M. WHITELEY

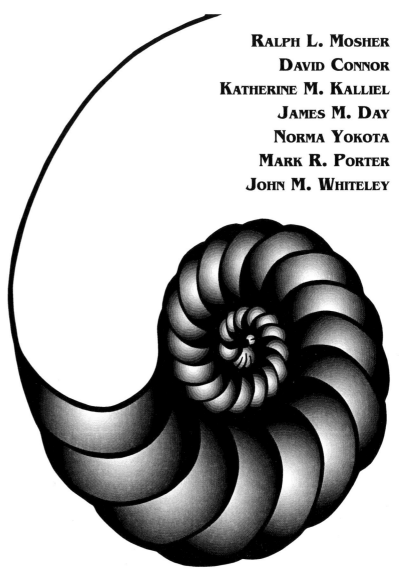

NATIONAL RESOURCE CENTER FOR THE FIRST-YEAR EXPERIENCE & STUDENTS IN TRANSITION

Additional copies of this book may be ordered at $40 each from the National Resource Center for the First-Year Experience and Students in Transition, University of South Carolina, 1629 Pendleton Street, Columbia, SC 29208. Telephone (803) 777-6029. Telefax (803) 777-4699.

Special gratitude is expressed to Randolph F. Handel, Corinna McLeod, and Tracy Skipper, Assistant Editors, for editing, design, and layout of this book; to Dr. Betsy Barefoot, Co-Director for Publications and Research; and to Dr. Dorothy Fidler, Senior Managing Editor.

ISBN Number: 1-889271-26-8

Dedication

James B. Craig
who, for over 20 years, has kept
the Sierra flame alive

Daniel G. Aldrich, Jr.
who nourished an atmosphere where
the Sierra work could grow

Ralph and Jessica Mosher
whose courage in adversity has given us
inspiration

ABOUT THE COVER

Students in the Sierra Project were nearly unanimous in reporting that they would not be who they had become if it were not for the college experience, especially on dimensions of thinking about moral issues. They did make one important qualifier: They had not *changed* as much as they had *developed*.

As we struggled to understand their meaning in using "developed" in contrast to "change," it seemed to us that they were expressing that the core of who they were had remained the same. It was their stance in relation to those choices which had become more acute and sensitive, and this was considered by them to be development. The chambered nautilus (*N. Pompilius, Linn.*) represents an appropriate visual metaphor, for it symbolically illustrates the student conception of the growth process as they experience it.

The actual cover sketch of the chambered nautilus is the original inspiration of Vivian Chang of the Publications Office at the University of California, Irvine in 1982. She read portions of *Character Development in College Students, Volume I* in its manuscript form and subsequently prepared a series of sketches from which this cover was selected.

The chambered nautilus is a member of the class Cephalopoda which contains the nautili, octopods, squids, and cuttlefish. Cephalopoda are the most highly organized of all mollusks and have attained the largest size of any invertebrates. In contrast to the occupants of "ordinary shells" whose bodies fill the entire shell cavity, the animal of the nautilus uses only a small portion of the shell or outer chamber; and builds pearly partitions behind its body through all the partitions, thus forming an anchor or mooring to the shell (Verrill, 1936, p. 150).

Several stanzas of a poem by Oliver Wendell Holmes on the Chambered Nautilus describe the growth of the Nautilus and parallel the growth which we have hoped to inspire in the character development of college students.

> Year after year beheld the silent toil
> That spread his lustrous coil;
>
> Still, as the spiral grew,
> He left the past year's dwelling for the new,
> Stole with soft step its shining archway through,

Built up its idle door;
Stretched in his last-found home, and knew the old no more . . .
Build thee more stately mansions, O my soul,
As the swift seasons roll!

Leave thy low-vaulted past!
Let each new temple, nobler than the last,
Shut thee from heaven with a dome more vast,

Till thou at length are free,
Leaving thin outgrown shell by life's unresting sea!

(Holmes, 1950, pp. 97-98)

References

Verrill, A. H. (1936). *Strange sea shells and their stories.* Boston: L. C. Page & Co.

Holmes, O. W. (1950). *The works of Oliver Wendell Holmes, Vol. I.* New York : Houghton Mifflin.

MORAL ACTION IN YOUNG ADULTHOOD
TABLE OF CONTENTS

From the Executive Director xi

John N. Gardner

From the President of The University of South Carolina
Ovid's Plea, Our Responsibility xiii

John M. Palms

FOREWORD
Sierrans Revisited Research: A Rationale xvii

Ralph L. Mosher

INTRODUCTION
From Character in College to Moral Action in Young Adulthood xxvii

John M. Whiteley

SECTION 1
Origins and Results of the Original Sierra Project

CHAPTER ONE
Nevitt Sanford on Community and Concern with
Moral Values in Higher Education 3

Nevitt Sanford

CHAPTER TWO

The Aims of the Sierra Curriculum:
"On Leaping Tall Buildings In A Single Bound" 13

Ralph L. Mosher

CHAPTER THREE

Character Development Over Four Years of Undergraduate Study 25

John M. Whiteley and Norma Yokota

SECTION 2

Theoretical Underpinnings of the Sierrans Revisited Research

CHAPTER FOUR

Young Adulthood in the Life Cycle 53

CHAPTER FIVE

Doing the Right or Good Act: Theories of Moral Action 69

CHAPTER SIX

Further Theoretical Perspectives on
Making Moral Choices 83

Molly Patterson

SECTION 3

Narrative Insights into Moral Action in Young Adulthood

CHAPTER SEVEN

Moral Dilemmas from Young Adulthood 109

CHAPTER EIGHT

Moral Dilemmas in Interpersonal Relationships 125

CHAPTER NINE

Moral Dilemmas in the Workplace 135

CHAPTER TEN
Exemplary Sierrans: Moral Influences 145

SECTION 4

Research Conclusions and Future Directions for Promoting Moral Action

CHAPTER ELEVEN
Moral Dilemmas of Everyday Life: Voices of the Sierrans 157

CHAPTER TWELVE
Exceptional Moral Behavior 175

CHAPTER THIRTEEN
Strength of Character and Moral Agency 183

CHAPTER FOURTEEN
Toward Promoting Moral Action in Young Adulthood 197

APPENDIX A
Moral Action Interview 209
Katherine M. Kalliel

APPENDIX B
Moral Behavior Interview 215
David Connor

APPENDIX C
The Moral Influence Interview 223
James M. Day

CONTENT AND AUTHOR INDEXES
.... 225

FROM THE
EXECUTIVE DIRECTOR

It is with great pleasure that I introduce this book which is co-authored by John Whiteley and his Sierra Project Revisited colleagues: Ralph Mosher, David Connor, Katherine Kalliel, James Day, Mark Porter, and Norma Yokota. John Whiteley is the educator who helped us launch this Center and this publications series. As the title implies, this volume is about moral action in young adulthood. It significantly widens the scope of the original moral and character development study involving a population of first-year college students which was performed in the Sierra Residence Hall at the University of California, Irvine in 1975.

It is my belief that nothing could be more important as an outcome of the first college year in American higher education than promoting the moral and character development of our students. The very creation of the course, University 101, which we have been offering to first-year students at the University of South Carolina for 26 years, was based on the exercise of moral and social activism of our students. Specifically, in May of 1970, approximately 1,000 of them gathered to protest the Cambodian invasion. These students were confronted by the South Carolina National Guard, and this confrontation resulted in a student riot and takeover of the Administration Building. The University's President, who was barricaded in his office for a period of 24 hours, emerged from that experience committed to the creation of a humane, student-centered environment; the centerpiece of that environment was the University 101 first-year seminar. Helping students explore and become committed to a reasoned system of values has been one of the primary goals of this course since it was first offered in 1972.

With this as personal and historical context, I commend this book to you and express my deep appreciation to John Whiteley and his colleagues for providing us this landmark study. We recognize the inherent difficulties in implementing any curriculum which is seen as an addition to traditional academic fare. But we hope that these extraordinary findings will spur you, our readers, to consider ways in which your programs for first-year students can be more intentionally focused on the promotion of moral reasoning and moral action in the college years and beyond.

John N. Gardner, Executive Director
The National Resource Center for the First-Year Experience
    and Students in Transition
University of South Carolina, Columbia

FROM THE PRESIDENT OF THE UNIVERSITY OF SOUTH CAROLINA

OVID'S PLEA, OUR RESPONSIBILITY[1]

About 8 A.D., having offended the Emperor Augustus,[2] the great Latin poet Ovid was banished to the furthest reaches of the kingdom, to a tiny shore town on the Black Sea. There, in this place called Tomi, Ovid wrote a series of long poems to the king, beseeching his mercy and appealing for reprieve. These entreaties fell on deaf ears, so Ovid turned his attention to Cotys, a young, Thracian client-king of the Romans. He hoped Cotys would use his influence with the emperor on his behalf. Ovid knew Cotys was a leader with an advanced education. He also knew that Cotys wanted to appear ferocious and militant to his subjects, civil and sophisticated to his Roman masters. In one passage in his *Letters from the Black Sea*, Ovid shrewdly appeals to all these attributes, writing:

> "sed quam Marte ferox et uinci nescius armis,
> tam numquam, facta pace, cruoris amans.
> adde quod ingenuas didicisse fideliter artes
> emollit mores nec sinit esse feros."

That is,

> "But just as you are fierce in war and do not know how to lose at arms
> So too are you never fond of blood once peace has been made.
> Add to this the fact that faithfully to have learned the liberal arts
> humanizes the character and does not permit it to be cruel."[3]

Upon our University's founding in 1801, the final lines of this passage became our Latin motto, which we translate, "Learning humanizes character and does not permit it to be cruel." With these words, Ovid sought to remind a well-educated

[1] My thanks to co-writer, Pete Mackey, Ph.D., director of presidential communications and research, University of South Carolina.

[2] Historians do not know precisely how Ovid committed this offense. Hermann Fränkel's *Ovid: A Poet between Two Worlds* (Berkeley: University of California Press, 1956) notes that while the reasons for Ovid's exile have always been obscure, it seems to have involved public immorality (perhaps composition of *The Art of Love*) and some form of political indiscretion.

[3] We are grateful to Dr. Brian Roots (formerly of USC's Department of French and Classics) for assisting with this translation and for providing the succinct summary of Cotys' reign.

person who held profound responsibility for others that learning should lead to moral action. Someone, we might imagine, taking certain liberties, who was not unlike our own students.

A familiar assumption in higher education arises from Ovid's argument to the young leader. We often assume that through their liberal learning, college students will expand their moral action, their grasp of what this volume calls the "uses to which acquired knowledge is put." We also frequently assume that this learning will inspire the student to act upon his or her "responsibility and obligation for other people." Ovid's predicament before Cotys anticipates a modern question: Can colleges and universities motivate students to grow not simply as learned minds but also as moral agents? That is, since an implicit assumption is that students will grow morally and ethically, can we make this goal explicit? More than that, doing so, can we measure the result of these efforts?

At our university, as throughout higher education, such matters heavily influence curricula and co-curricular activities. In 1971, USC began a program now emulated around the world and known today as the University 101 program. The National Resource Center for the Freshman Year Experience and Students in Transition, founded and led by USC's John Gardner, guides University 101 in helping new students adapt to college while also challenging them to think about their moral duties as members of a college community.

In 1990, we also established our "Carolinian Creed." Developed by students, faculty, administrators, and staff, it expresses the "code of civilized behavior" each member of our University shares with one another. For example, it declares, "I will practice personal and academic integrity," and "I will respect the rights and property of others." Like these two statements, each of the five postulates in the creed affirms the moral actions consistent with the "personal and academic excellence" toward which the University strives collectively and toward which we as individuals aim.

We also recently established a residential college at USC. Here, a faculty couple lives in the same residence hall as the students, faculty members eat with the residence's students, and upperclassmen and graduate students serve as mentors to the residence's undergraduates. The goal is to increase opportunities for reflection and discussion so that students build a holistic awareness of themselves as individuals growing not simply intellectually but also socially, physically, and ethically. Indeed, at Carolina, we hope that our emphasis during the last few years on USC's ideals has enhanced our students' awareness of how character depends upon consistency between principle and behavior.

As we know, students can learn as much about themselves outside classrooms as inside them. Such efforts as those mentioned above and pursued throughout higher education accept and build upon this situation. They provide additional living rooms of interaction so that the student's non-academic experiences become as educationally rich as possible. Institutions attuned to their ethical and moral influence on students thereby work in specific ways to encourage students to act responsibly as members of the community-at-large.

This volume makes clear that such programs, like university life itself, shape students' moral beliefs. Do such programs also change student actions? Here, this volume's answers are less definitive. But the authors rightly argue that the university must continue striving to fulfill outright its implicit role in affecting students' moral actions. As Ovid's plea to Cotys implies, the link between learning and moral action cuts to the heart of higher learning's enterprise.

It could well be argued, in fact, that the special place of colleges and universities in our society depends as much on their moral influence on students as on their objective search for truth. Institutions, like people, assume moral authority from their performance, not their motives. After all, our students don't simply learn from us, they also learn by watching us. This includes the ethics of our personnel in searching for truth, working with students, and cooperating with community agencies, for example. But if higher learning affects moral belief, as this volume concludes, we are obligated as well to more than performing our academic and administrative work ethically. We also must strive to create environments in which students can reflect on their learning, discern its moral implications, and explore how that should affect the way they think *and* act.

Exiled to Tomi, Ovid wrote from the furthest reaches of the Roman empire, water all about. He pled to a well-educated leader for empathy, underscoring the bond between learning, ethics, and action. He was, in a way, living and articulating a version of John Donne's famous observation, "No man is an island." As we consider the place of the university in our students' lives, surely we want them to realize this truth. Surely, we also want them to act upon the ties between human beings, not simply in the classroom, not simply on the campus, but also in the post-collegiate world beyond our doors. This volume compels we who hold open these doors to consider our own moral obligations to our students. In so doing, it performs a vital service to each of us and, thereby, to those we serve.

John M. Palms, Ph.D.
President
University of South Carolina, Columbia

F O R E W O R D

SIERRANS REVISITED
RESEARCH: A RATIONALE

Ralph L. Mosher

Why Character Education in College?

In the middle 1970s, Professor John Whiteley and colleagues at the University of California, Irvine, began research on the character education of freshman college students. Whiteley and his associates believed it to be a crucial task of the university intentionally to influence the moral thinking of the next generation of society's leaders and in the direction of a more just society. For me, the view that colleges should take seriously their own commencement rhetoric and consciously educate for character is the most challenging of the *raisons d'etre* Whiteley put forward: "An experience in higher education should provide an opportunity to reflect on the purposes of learning, on the uses to which acquired knowledge is put, and on the ethical dilemmas which confront citizens individually and as members of society collectively" (Loxley & Whiteley, 1986, p. *xxxviii*).

In the middle 1970s, Professor John Whiteley and colleagues at the University of California, Irvine, began research on the character education of freshman college students.

Whiteley's further reasons for doing character education included benefits *now* for those students affected (e.g., greater ethical awareness, concern for fairness and the welfare of others, "accomplishments which are ultimately self-rewarding"). A very interesting extension of the "benefits now" argument was made. It was the carefully documented thesis that personal growth and psychological maturity in one's youth are closely related to many dimensions of accomplishment in adulthood (Loxley & Whiteley, 1986, see Chapter 5). In the vernacular, "them that has now, gits later." Further, college students will become parents and leaders. Thus, there is the broader societal benefit of a "citizenry whose lives are characterized by principled thinking and moral maturity" (Loxley & Whiteley, 1986, p. *xxxix*). This seems close to John Dewey's view that "the cause of education . . . is one of development, focusing indeed on the growth of students, but to be conceived even in this connection as part of the larger development of society" (Dewey, 1897/1968, p. 89).

Related objectives of the Sierra Project were to add to prior studies of the impact of the college experience on young people, the psychological development *per se* of college students, and the broader transition from adolescence to young adulthood. Several personal reflections on character development as an aim of higher education are pertinent. As a parent, a teacher of graduate students and an educator, I am in profound agreement with the rationale of the Sierra Project. If I could choose but two competencies for my own children, rationality and character would be in a dead heat. Trying to know and to do what is right or good is, I believe, at the heart of integrity. Further, having taught for 35 years in elitist institutions of higher education, I recognize that they *do* affect students, and powerfully so. But it is the tacit and "religiously" secular nature of the institutional norms and values which worry me: A pervasive idolatry of intellect, the pressures for academic and professional achievement at virtually any cost, the relative impact of studies in science, technology, and management as compared to the humanities or normative philosophy, the "for sale" sign to corporate, foundation, or government funding sources of many of our ablest professional minds and research centers, are but a few of the institutional values which characterize the universities I have known.

The unshakable arrogance of "the best and brightest" as to what is right for America and its ablest youth would be wonderfully ironic and diverting if it were not taken so seriously (as Vietnam made abundantly clear). Are not the academy's epistemologies, our technologies, our co-option by American corporations, funding agencies, and governments to be critically examined for their worth to the individual and his or her society and lives, if not our own? In this latter connection, are we as faculty and parents numb or desensitized to our socio-moral compromises, paralyzed or uncertain in the face of the great moral issues of our time (nuclear arms, economic and social injustice in the society, sexism, racism, hunger, homelessness, and so on), or do we fear an enlightened younger generation which rejects us as compromised?

Perhaps the flaccidity of formal character education in colleges is the result of the character unraveling of faculty or administration. Clearly, however, adolescence and young adulthood are "prime times" for the building of a personal epistemology by students: the values and priorities by which the young will live and order their personal and social lives. Maturation impels them to form their norms aided or unaided (i.e., in response to many random and inimical forces). Faculty, in my view, have the wisdom and the "position" to help by listening to young people's pain and confusion, by mentoring, by example, by advice.

Willie Sutton robbed banks because "that was where the money was." Universities are where the best and brightest of America's youth spend four to eight or more formative years. That universities "teach" or model a hierarchy of values seems irrefutable. That all of us internalize the values of the important social structures (families, schools, corporations, etc.) around us is equally apparent. Intellectual honesty (*veritas*) requires that these values be acknowledged and actively examined against the same canons of critical analysis that we require students to apply and hone *vis à vis* the formal academic curriculum. To reiterate an earlier point, our young people seek to know the right, the good, the beautiful as well as the true, and they search in the worst of times: times in which two-thirds of the world's children are hungry, and Chinese students petitioning their elders for democracy and an end to official corruption are machine-gunned in Tiananmen Square. Against such profound moral dilemmas, an education which seeks truth but smuggles the right and the good is either corrupt or deformed. A higher education which pursues the true, the right and the good wherever they lead is false neither to its students nor itself.

Character Defined

The Sierra Project defined "character" generally as the college student's moral reasoning and his or her self-knowledge. The definition actually spread to more than this. Understanding what is the right, fair, or good thing to do and then doing these things, acting consistently, were seen as the moral component of character. "Ego," the young person's understanding of him/herself and his/her social world was seen as a second broad component of character. Why ego was included in the definition was not entirely clear. Basically, it seems it was included because Loevinger has applied Piagetian concepts of stage and sequence to the study of ego development. "Our discussion of ego development includes some topics previously discussed under moral development: socialization, character structure, and even cognitive development." (Loevinger, 1976, p. *ix*). Whiteley relied heavily on Loevinger's "central claim . . . that many diverse aspects of thought, interpersonal relations, impulse control and character grow at once, in some more or less coherent way" (Loevinger, 1976, p. *ix*). By considering moral actions and personal maturity, Whiteley and his colleagues went well beyond an equation of character as the emergence of more comprehensive moral reasoning. The reach was for a more holistic conception. The "character" of freshmen in the Sierra Project was made up in about equal parts of the complexity of their moral reasoning, whether their later actions were consonant, how they defined themselves as persons, and what their concepts of society were.

Against such profound moral dilemmas, an education which seeks truth but smuggles the right and the good is either corrupt or deformed.

This is a definition governed in large measure by common sense, ordering concepts from cognitive developmental psychology and, in particular, what could be measured. One cannot help but be reminded of the statement that "intelligence is what psychologists measure as intelligence." At another practical level, character in those young people was sought after, and promoted educationally, in their *thinking* about right and wrong, in the degree that they articulated a sense of social connection to their fellow students, in the amount of empathy and justice they evidenced, and in the extent to which they could assert personal rights without infringing on the rights of peers. Clearly the Sierra Project was much influenced by Kohlberg's (1981) view that morality is rooted in one's *thinking* about right and wrong, one's *understanding* of justice in individual and social relations.

It is important to recognize that Whiteley and his colleagues struggled with the thorny task of defining character. Their governing constructs are set out unpretentiously. Whiteley made no claim to have cut the Gordian knot of character's definition. Similarly, the project was not paralyzed by the philosophical, psychological and empirical crevasses that radiate everywhere on the face of "character" as a concept. Actual analysis of whether Sierra students acted as they said they should was deferred to follow-up study of their lives after graduation. Thus the "Sierrans Revisited" research which is reported in this volume was undertaken.

It is one thing to define character in college students. That act, *per se*, probably leaves most normative philosophers demanding equal time. To translate such definitions of character into commensurately complex educational practices is an act of greater temerity. To further the development of character in the busy secular, scientific and technological marketplace of a major university adds to the burden (and the reality). Further, that early educational practices may only partially represent a fuller vision of character education should surprise no one.

In the beginning, approximately 100 volunteer freshmen per year participated from 1975 to 1980. The project was named for the residence hall, "Sierra," in which the students lived. Character, as noted, was operationally defined as moral maturity based on the Moral Judgment Interview (Colby, Gibbs, Kohlberg, Speicher-Dubin, & Candee, 1979), principled thinking as measured by the Defining Issues Test (Rest, 1979), and ego development as assessed by the Washington University Sentence Completion Test (Loevinger, 1966, 1976; Loevinger & Wessler, 1970). Note that these tests measure moral reasoning and the person's understanding of himself/herself and his/her social world. They do not directly measure pro-social or moral *behavior*. Nonetheless, an extensive database exists for these students because of repeated testing of moral reasoning/attitudes during their under-graduate years. These data are described in Whiteley and Associates (1982), Loxley and Whiteley (1986), and summarized in Chapter 3 of this volume.

The character education curriculum which the Sierra students experienced is presented in detail in Loxley and Whiteley (1986). It included the experience of living in Sierra Hall, where issues of policy making for the residents, residence governance, the quality of student life and discipline were the responsibility of the students to resolve. The formal curriculum consisted of a twice weekly course attended by all residents which focused on issues such as racism, minority and women's rights and assertion training; there were community retreats; voluntary internships in the community at large; and so on. Only moderate gains in moral reasoning and ego development were found to ensue among the Sierra students in comparison to control subjects, a result probably of an imaginative but flawed curriculum. A detailed critique of this curriculum in character education is to be found in the "Foreword" to the Loxley and Whiteley (1986) book, and reprinted in Chapter 2 of this book. The first phase of the original Sierra Project, now concluded, has received four well-deserved national research awards and considerable international attention, including the translation of two volumes into Chinese.

Only moderate gains in moral reasoning and ego development were found to ensue among the Sierra students in comparison to control subjects, a result probably of an imaginative but flawed curriculum.

Sierrans Revisited

It is now easier to understand why Larry Kohlberg spent 30 years studying the growth of moral reasoning. It is a part vital to moral action, yet probably a small part (I recall correlations in the low .20s or .30s) of a much more complex psychological riddle: why people sometimes do and often don't do as they know or say they should. Put more formally, there is a very complex relationship between moral judgment and moral action (recognizing that one faces a moral dilemma, deciding why and how to act and then doing so).

Why pursue this extraordinarily complicated phenomenon? Especially as some reputable psychologists have said that there is no reason to expect a correlation at all between knowing what is right and actually doing it. The inconsistency in studies of moral judgment and action have led some theorists to say we are dealing with two essentially different systems: one a system of moral thought and the other a system of moral behavior. "There is neither paradox nor even surprise in someone talking on the high road and acting on the low road." (Brown & Herrnstein, 1975, p. 289) But that is an unsatisfactory resolution for either a moral philosopher or educator.

The answers to the prior question of why focus on moral *behavior*, and the general *raison d'etre* for the study in this book, are in several parts:

1. After devoting 15 years to moral education, and trying to promote children's and adolescents' moral reasoning, has that effort really been wrongheaded, partial or poorly conceived? Perhaps more important, what might we learn about the relationship between moral thinking and moral action that could inform new initiatives in moral education? Again, speaking personally, the writer has no interest in moral or character education which does not incorporate an integral emphasis on developing pro-social behaviors. Further, I felt a considerable boredom with what was perceived to be the inertia or redundancy in second generation Kohlberg-inspired programs of moral education.

2. The relationship between moral judgment and action is really the cutting edge research issue in the field of the psychology of moral development. It is where the brass ring for research in this field will be won. From our study we hoped to learn more about the extent to which people who know the right or the good, act to do them, and why or why not. Moreover, we anticipated learning about the influence of moral reasoning, choice and action among a sample of young adults when their first adult life structure (Levinson, 1978) was well established. Probably this is too soon in life for a mature morality but it is not too soon for major moral crises to have occurred which will have required action, or clear lack thereof.

A closely related aim was to study moral acts or behavior and their roots. The move would be from reasoning about hypothetical dilemmas (i.e., reasoning abstracted from the reality of direct implementation or action: "Should Heinz steal the drug?" (Rest, 1979) to the study of thinking and action in the context of "real" moral dilemmas. An overview of the pertinent literature (see Chapter 5) will offer a number of theoretical models (Kohlberg/Candee, Gilligan, Rest, Haan, Blasi) to explain moral action, but empirical study is in its early stages of what prompts people who know the right or good act to do to actually act on that knowledge.

Rest (1979) and colleagues have begun to study his four-component model (see Chapter 5) in the controlled context of the dilemmas facing dentists and doctors. Similarly, Gilligan for some time had been collecting narrative data about actual moral choices: First, in her well-known study of women's decisions on abortion (1982) and, more recently, in interviews with junior high school students' stories of the moral issues in their lives (1988). The methodology we chose followed Gilligan's lead, that is, a formative, qualitative investigation of naturalistic, real-life moral dilemmas, choice, and action. We deliberately chose not to be constrained by any particular *a priori* theories, although we were to draw significantly on the five cited models for the origins of moral action. The data of what our subjects told us equally would drive our findings.

3. With regard to data, we were offered a fortuitous opportunity to study moral thinking and action among the Sierrans-an ideal population for longitudinal examination. They were a decade out of college and in their late 20s and early 30s. And there was an extensive data base for each subject because of their frequent testing as participants in the original Sierra Project.

4. The implicit intellectual challenge was attractive. Perhaps as educators we were ready to rush in where a more cautious, pure developmentalist would be afraid to tread. But Kohlberg's untimely death seemed to mean that all scholars had an obligation to take up some of the slack, to push the research agenda forward. And the proposed study of the Sierrans was tailor-made for a small research team composed of faculty and advanced doctoral students. The first author was tired, as noted, of advising conceptually isolated, *ad hominum*, idiosyncratic doctoral research.

Thus, Professor John Whiteley's generous invitation to join in a first, longitudinal study of Sierran volunteers was one with great appeal. The aim was not to do a "10 years later" assessment of the impact of the original character education effort. It had, at best, demonstrated nominal initial effect in terms of the Sierrans' moral development. Rather, the study chose to focus more centrally and heuristically on the gap between knowing and doing the right or good act. The implicit intellectual and research questions embedded in the gap between knowledge, reasoning, and action were complex and demanding ones. Moreover, their importance to psychology and to education (to say nothing of society) was obvious.

Moral Reasoning and Moral Action

Something about the history of recent study of the relationship of moral reasoning and moral action is pertinent here by way of introduction. Virtually every reader is aware of the "Do as I say, not as I do" admonitions of parents and other moral educators. The most charitable interpretation of this homily is that it recognizes the possible glibness of moral knowledge or the deontic choice as contrasted to the non-linear, non-rational, stubborn and multiple determined character of moral action.

Moral behavior (however defined) does not go in a straight line from cognition to action (i.e., knowing the good or right action has been before us for a long time). From 1928-30, Hartshorne & May (1928; Hartshorne, May, & Maller, 1929; Hartshorne, May, & Shuttleworth, 1930) conducted classic studies of the relationship of moral knowledge in tests of children's honesty, service, and self-control. They particularly focused on cheating by school children. Diogenes searched Greece with a lamp seeking an honest man. He found none. "As the twig is bent, so the branch inclines." Hartshorne and May tested 10,000 children in New Jersey and found essentially none who did not cheat at times. The relationship of moral knowledge (knowing right from wrong) to moral action (defined as conformity to a social norm of honesty-not cheating) was found to be very modest, indeed low ($r = .22$). Moral knowledge explained less than five percent of the variation in cheating, which was distributed in a normal curve around a mean of moderate cheating.

Kohlberg concluded that we cannot define and study moral action within a purely behavioral approach. "An alternative explanation, which we favor, is that moral actions involved an internal component-a moral cognition or moral judgment, and second, a moral emotion component" (Kohlberg, 1984, p. 500). And, as noted, Kohlberg stayed with the study of moral reasoning for some 30 years. He goes on: After reviewing the evidence on the latter factor "we also feel that *emotional arousal* does not seem to be an internal determinant necessary to define moral behavior" (Kohlberg, 1984). So much for moral emotion! (Dupont ,1994, by contrast, argues that emotions are critical to moral understanding and in particular, action). We will return to the role of emotions in moral action in the conclusions section.

And if the Hartshorne and May (1928; Hartshorne, et al., 1929, 1930) studies are valid, so much for moral knowledge (awareness of conventional rules, moral opinions, and social attitudes). Kohlberg (1984) reaches back to an early study by Weber (1929) in which women at the University of Texas rank ordered 25 human vices (e.g., gossiping, lying, stealing). They considered "sexual irregularity" as the worst vice of all. Similarly, women prisoners at the Texas penitentiary were given the same test. Their rankings were exactly the same. No differences were found in what the two groups *"know to be right."* Their moral behavior at least in relationship to the law, however, differed dramatically. But what about *moral attitudes* (for example, guilt, self-blame, and denial of wrongdoing)? There too, studies showed low, even negative correlations with behavior.

These inconsistencies led some researchers, as noted previously, to say we are dealing with two essentially different systems: one a system of moral thought, the other a system of moral behavior. Kohlberg (1984) argues that moral development is a single track process, a unitary development process. In this model we essentially think ourselves into new ways of moral behavior and behave ourselves into new ways of thinking.

Kohlberg (1984) puts forward two philosophical issues in defining morally commendable action. First, whose standard of rightness do we use in defining an action as moral: the individual's, the society's, a "universal standard" or principle? Second, is the morality of an action determined by (a) the behavior itself as it conforms to a norm; (b) the intention, judgment or principle guiding the act; or (c) the welfare consequences of the act?

Kohlberg (1984) and Kant (1781/1969) largely come down on the side of (b) but with a proviso: Rational moral judgment is *necessary but not sufficient* for moral conduct. Kohlberg says that we have to begin by examining the necessary moral judgment component and move on to identify other factors in moral action and character. Thus, a successful research program must start by identifying some *regularities in action* (for example to constantly act to oppose racism, to consistently act to put the welfare of others first), which can reasonably be called moral. For the authors of *this* book the intention or principle guiding the act and its

Hartshorne and May tested 10,000 children in New Jersey and found essentially none who did not cheat at times.

MORAL DILEMMA

Moral Judgement	Deontic Choice: A Judgment of What is Right	Responsible to Act or Not

MORAL ACTION

To Act Consistently with One's Judgment?	OR	To Act in Reference to a Universal Standard?

welfare consequences are crucial. The authors will examine gaps between moral judgment and action. Kohlberg's model, elaborated in Chapter 5, can be schematized as follows:

Further, Kohlberg argues that there is a monotonic increase in making a judgment of responsibility consistent with the deontic choice as we move from stage to stage (i.e., an increase in the proportion of subjects acting morally).

The Kohlberg (1984) model for the steps between moral judgment and behavior is introduced here because it stresses the *importance* of moral knowledge and in particular, moral reasoning in the gestation of moral action. This is frequently presented as the "common sense" view of what individuals need to be moral. They need to know at least the moral conventions of their time and societal place, the explicit "right" and "good" things to do; and they need to be able to think through conflicts of values (the value of human life versus the right to profit from private property which underlies the Heinz dilemma), rights (the right of a fetus to life versus the right of the woman to control her own body), and obligations (the obligation of a parent to advise but not ultimately decide for a minor child her choice of undergraduate college and academic major or husband).

Most moral or character education programs probably make similar assumptions about what one needs to know and think in order to act morally. There is a neat cognitive progression laid out here-too neat and logical in all probability. Yet there is the cachet of rationality. (How could an educator advocate a non-rational approach to moral education . . . especially if one is to avoid indoctrination in a particular code?) And more intellectually and morally complex thinking is hypothesized to result in a greater likelihood of the person acting morally.

The Sierrans Revisited Project

It is now nearly 20 years since the original Sierra Project ended. Former "Sierrans" are young adults. It seemed logical, indeed fortuitous, to locate as many of these students as possible in an attempt to assess the further development (hopefully) of their character in young adulthood.

Do they evidence maturation in moral reasoning and their understanding of themselves and their social world?

Can life experiences be identified which correlate with moral growth?

In this study the central focus of examination is the relationships between the Sierrans' moral reasoning and the "real" moral decisions they make in their personal relationships and their work life. Such knowledge gathering was pure developmental research. Yet the potential applications to character education were numerous. Many writers in the field have been calling for such studies as the next logical step in the effort to understand why people act morally.

Summary

The connection between knowing the right or good thing to do and then actually doing it has long been a puzzle. "Watch what we do, not what we say" goes beyond the revealing admission of a former Attorney General of the United States to the broader reality of human behavior. Parents, teachers, employers, religious educators, and society at large have a deep vested interest in understanding the relationship between, and in knowing how better to educate for, consistency in moral knowledge and behavior. The past twenty-five years have seen much productive research on the development of moral reasoning. The other half of the loaf, doing the right or good act, now needs comparable study. The unique contribution of this book is its exploratory study of the connection between moral thinking and action. Research on this linkage is in its relative infancy. A key aim is to begin to throw light on what factors intervene between a person's moral judgment and subsequent action. Valuable, if untested, theoretical models have been put forward concerning this interaction. They will be used to guide the initial development of questions, but not to the exclusion of focusing on the unique insights provided by the young adults as to the *process* and *problems* of living one's "life-morality."

References

Brown, R., & Herrnstein, R. (Eds.). (1975). *Psychology*. Boston, MA: Little, Brown and Company.

Colby, A., Gibbs, J. C., Kohlberg, L., Speicher-Dubin, B., & Candee, D. (1979). *Standard form scoring manual* (Parts 1-4). Cambridge, MA: Harvard University Center for Moral Education.

Dewey, J. (1897/1968). *Problems of men*. New York: Greenwood Press.

Dupont, H. (1994). *Emotional development: A neo-Piagetian perspective*. Westport, CT: Praeger Publishers.

Gilligan, C. (1982). *In a different voice: Psychological theory and women's development*. Cambridge, MA: Harvard University Press.

Gilligan, C. (Ed.). (1988). *Mapping the moral domain: A contribution of women's thinking to psychological theory and education*. Cambridge, MA: Harvard University Press.

Hartshorne, H., & May, M. A. (1928). *Studies in the nature of character: Vol. 1. Studies in deceit.* New York: Macmillan.

Hartshorne, H., May, M. A., & Maller, J. B. (1929). *Studies in the nature of character: Vol. II. Studies in self-control.* New York: Macmillan.

Hartshorne, H., May, M. A., & Shuttleworth, F. K. (1930). *Studies in the nature of character: Vol. III. Studies in the organization of character.* New York: Macmillan.

Kant, I. (1781 / 1969). *Critique of pure reason.* New York: Saint Martin's Press.

Kohlberg, L. (1981). *The philosophy of moral development: Moral stages and the idea of justice,* Vol. I. *The philosophy of moral development: Moral stages and the idea of justice.* Essays on moral development series. San Francisco: Harper and Row.

Kohlberg, L. (1984). *The psychology of moral development: Essays on moral development.* Vol II. San Francisco: Harper & Row.

Levinson, D. J. (1978). *The seasons of a man's life.* New York: Knopf.

Loevinger, J. (1966). The meaning and measurement of ego development, *American Psychologist, 21,* 195-206.

Loevinger, J. (1976). *Ego development.* San Francisco, CA: Jossey Bass.

Loevinger, J., & Wessler, R. (1970). *Measuring ego development, Vol. I: Construction and use of a sentence completion test.* San Francisco: Jossey-Bass.

Loxley, J. C., & Whiteley, J. M. (1986). *Character development in college students, Vol. II: The curriculum and longitudinal results.* Schenectady, NY: Character Research Press.

Rest, J. (1979). *Development in judging moral issues.* Minneapolis, MN: University Press.

Weber, C. N. (1929). Moral judgment in female delinquents. *Journal of Applied Psychology,* 89-91.

Whiteley, J. M., & Associates. (1982). *Character development in college students, Vol. I: The freshman year.* Schenectady, NY: Character Research Press.

INTRODUCTION

FROM CHARACTER IN COLLEGE TO MORAL ACTION IN YOUNG ADULTHOOD

John M. Whiteley

This book, which addresses moral action in young adulthood, is an extension of the Sierra Project which began at the University of California, Irvine (UCI) in the middle 1970s. Taking its name from Sierra Hall in the UCI undergraduate housing program, the original Sierra Project was both a curricula development initiative for college freshmen and a longitudinal study of growth and development of character over four years of undergraduate study.

Planning for the Sierra Project commenced in 1973, with the first class of freshmen entering in the fall of 1975. There have been succeeding classes of freshmen every year which have participated in the year-long educational experience (Loxley & Whiteley, 1986). A systematic research program on character development in the college years focused only on the freshmen who entered UCI in the successive fall quarters of 1975, 1976, 1977, and 1978 (Whiteley & Associates, 1982; Whiteley & Yokota, 1988).

At the start of their freshman year, Sierrans were administered a battery of tests which measured moral maturity, principled thinking, ego development, and aspects of the college experience. The battery was repeated at the end of the freshman year, and at the end of the senior year. The basic finding was that the college years constitute a period of very significant development in the capacity for principled thinking and of more moderate progress in moral maturity (Whiteley & Yokota, 1988). This research is summarized in Chapter 3.

> The basic finding was that the college years constitute a period of very significant development in the capacity for principled thinking and of more moderate progress in moral maturity.

Twenty-five years have passed since the Sierra Project was initiated, and nearly 25 years have passed since the first class of entering freshmen participated in the initial testing of the components of character. Now well into young adulthood, the Sierra Project sample has confronted the personal and professional moral challenges of life in modern American society. Still living predominantly in Southern California, only very small numbers of Sierrans have spread across the western United States. There is a strong regional cast, therefore, to the dimensions of life experience.

Research Questions of the Sierrans Revisited Project

The Sierrans Revisited Project reported in this volume broadens the scope of the original Sierra Project from the study of the growth of moral *reasoning* and character development in the college years to chronicling aspects of moral dilemmas in the decade after college, with specific focus on understanding the nature and meaning of moral action which is in response to those moral dilemmas.

The Sierrans Revisited Project explores the following six research questions:

1. Will young adults talk about intimate moral issues in their lives?

2. What actual dilemmas do young adults identify as characteristic of their work and personal lives?

3. What factors do subjects identify as influencing their action in response to moral dilemmas?

4. Does the stage of moral reasoning relate to moral action?

5. Are there young people with exceptional characteristics whose moral behavior is exemplary? If yes, what can be learned about how they got that way?

6. Is it possible to identify a composite of factors/influences which correlates with outstanding strength of character and powerful moral agency?

One study is not going to resolve the entire puzzle of judgment and action, and it is beyond the scope of this exploratory project to investigate whether the elements in that process differ from age to age, by sex, race, education, social class, cultural group, and so on. In one exploratory study, however, it is possible to refine a personal narrative interview methodology and ways of analyzing the subjects' moral action and to learn more about the antecedents of that moral action. Findings based on this initial undertaking will guide further research with other and more diverse populations of subjects.

The next generation of research toward an overarching theory of moral action and its antecedents will be based on this and many other studies.

This Sierrans Revisited Project is intended to contribute to a greater understanding of the anatomy of moral action at least in the individual case with young adults by addressing the six questions listed above. The next generation of research toward an overarching theory of moral action and its antecedents will be based on this and many other studies. And it is important to repeat that an ultimate aim is to understand more fully the origins of moral action so that educational experiences which increase the likelihood of moral action may be intentionally designed and implemented. The roots of the Sierrans Revisited research are, after all, in a character education project.

Development of the Project

This volume developed out of two ongoing seminars on the Sierrans Revisited Project which met regularly for nearly three years in both Boston and Irvine. These seminars involved all of the authors of this book in at least one location, and all but two participated at one time or another in both seminars.

Starting in the Summer of 1987, and continuing through the Summer of 1990, the bicoastal team of researchers tested and interviewed 45 former Sierra students. Each subject was administered the Moral Judgment Interview, the Washington University Sentence Completion Test, the Defining Issues Test, and an extensive interview protocol composed collaboratively by the project researchers. As the project evolved, one planned personal narrative interview protocol became three separate ones.

Overview of the Book

While there was a principal drafter or drafters for each of the separate chapters, there was much collegial dialogue and rewriting. Also, Dorothy Fidler, Betsy Barefoot, and Corinna McLeod from the University of South Carolina played a very valuable "outsiders role" as technical editors for the manuscript when it was completed in draft form. They proved to be especially helpful in identifying where we needed to explain what we meant more fully and completely.

The book grew out of the 35-year collaboration of Professors Mosher and Whiteley. The order of authorship between them is alphabetical. The odyssey Professor Mosher traveled to explore the relationship of moral reasoning to moral action is recounted in the Foreword. He also served as chair of the doctoral dissertations at Boston University for three of the collaborators: Dr. David Connor, Dr. Katherine Kalliel, and Dr. Mark Porter. Professor James Day, now of the Université Catholique de Louvain in Belgium, focused on the part of the study examining whether there were young adults with exceptional characteristics whose moral behavior is exemplary. Ms. Norma Yokota, a researcher on the Sierra Project since 1976, served as the principal data analyst. Ms. Molly Patterson of the Department of Politics and Society at the University of California, Irvine joined the Sierrans Revisited Project in its final year to contribute the scholarship for Chapter 6. Bracketed by Professors Mosher and Whiteley, the other collaborators are listed alphabetically as well, reflecting the distinctive contribution each of them made to the conceptualization of the project, to its successful implementation, and to the completion of the book.

Organization of the Book

Section I: Origins and Results of the Original Sierra Project

Section I is composed of three chapters which appeared earlier in the development and reporting of the original Sierra Project. Nevitt Sanford wrote the Foreword to *Character Development in College Students, Volume I* (Whiteley & Associates), the first book-length report of the Sierra Project which appeared in 1982. Professor Sanford captured the commitment to nurturing a sense of community which was such a fundamental characteristic of Richmond College in Virginia where he was an undergraduate in the 1920s. Professor Sanford's distinguished career in higher education spanned over half a century of tumult and fundamental structural change in American universities. A concern throughout his long career was the role of the college years as a crucible for critical examination of moral values.

The founders of the Sierra Project were extraordinarily honored when Professor Sanford chose to write the Foreword to the first volume. His timeless message deserves the broadest possible audience. Making it available here through the auspices of the National Resource Center for The Freshman Year Experience is highly appropriate as the Center embodies the value orientation Professor Sanford so cherished. Professor Sanford's Foreword to Volume I is reprinted here as Chapter I, "Nevitt Sanford on Community and Concern with Moral Values in Higher Education."

> As John Dewey remarked in 1897, "It is commonplace to say that this development of character is the ultimate end of all school work. The difficulty lies in the execution of this idea."

Ralph L. Mosher wrote the Foreword to *Character Development in College Students, Volume II* (Loxley & Whiteley, 1986), the second book-length report of the Sierra Project. Professor Mosher addressed two emphases in the approach of the American public schools to moral education in the 1970s. The first emphasis was primarily classroom discussion of moral dilemmas embedded in the academic curriculum. American history, literature, and current events are replete with moral issues from slavery and the Nüremberg trials to the "Letter from the Birmingham Jail," "dioxin," and "acid rain." The second emphasis was the use of the school as a natural laboratory for political, social, and moral education. The subject matter in this second emphasis was the discussion by students of everyday or "real" moral issues occurring in the life of the classroom or the school. In this model of moral education, students and faculty participated in the governance of the school as well.

Drawing on lessons derived from these two quite different emphases, Professor Mosher critiqued the educational philosophy and practical approaches to creating an instructional environment employed by the Sierra Project. For college educators reconsidering their own approaches to moral education, the searching analysis of basic assumptions is illuminating. Professor Mosher's Foreword to Volume II is reprinted here as Chapter 2, "Ralph L. Mosher on The Aims of the Sierra Curriculum."

John M. Whiteley and Norma Yokota wrote the inaugural monograph for the monograph series of the National Resource Center for The Freshman Year Experience. It was originally published by the Center in 1988. They explored the venerable tradition in America of developing values and ethics by presenting eight obstacles which have been historic barriers to higher education's ability or willingness to meet its responsibility for character development. The failure to resolve the cause of each of those obstacles contributed to the general problem of not determining sooner *how* to go about developing character through higher education programs. As John Dewey remarked in 1897, "It is commonplace to say that this development of character is the ultimate end of all school work. The difficulty lies in the execution of this idea" (Dewey, 1897/1968, p. 28). The balance of the 1988 monograph describes how the Sierra Project addressed each of the historical obstacles, provides a six-part rationale for promoting character development in the college years, and outlines the curriculum intervention and principal research findings. The monograph is reprinted here as Chapter 3, "Character Development in the Freshman Year and over Four Years of Undergraduate Study."

Section II: Theoretical Underpinnings of the Sierrans Revisited Research

The challenge in drafting this section was to determine the theoretical parameters that would inform the Sierrans Revisited Project research team in constructing the research design, creating the interview protocols, and interpreting the results. These were three fundamental tasks, and each was approached differently.

First, it was necessary to increase the theoretical understanding of the research team about (a) the developmental issues associated with young adulthood and (b) the context in which young adults make personal and professional decisions about moral dilemmas. While it may be too strong a statement to claim that young adulthood is the orphan child of developmental research literature, it is absolutely accurate to state that childhood, adolescence, the college years, and adulthood have been the object of far more empirical research and theory development than has young adulthood. Together, we determined the broad content of an initial reading list which would encompass relevant developmental literature on the growth tasks of young adulthood, and then after scrutiny of that list, narrowed the focus to authors whose writings would inform the construction of the interview protocols. In reviewing the existing literature on young adults, two problems became immediately apparent: Authors defined the chronological ages associated with young adulthood differently, and intellectual themes, while appearing in numerous sources in the literature, are seldom given in-depth treatment.

With these goals in mind for the literature review, a determination was made to focus on specific authors and individual books rather than specific intellectual themes. This is the reason that the review of literature is organized around authors (Freud, Erikson, and Levinson, etc.) rather than notions of growth tasks or psychological constructs (intimacy, self, career, etc.). Since the design work for the Sierrans Revisited Project research was occurring in ongoing seminars in two geographically distant locations, the decision to review by author and individual book did facilitate communication between the Boston and Irvine researchers. The initial draft of the literature review chapter (Chapter 4) was prepared by David Connor.

Another challenge in constructing the second section of the book was to familiarize ourselves with the insights concerning moral action which could be gained by returning to the general theoretical framework which so influenced the initial formulations of character and character development in the Sierra Project—the cognitive developmental approach. In his excellent history of the study of moral action inquiry, Augusto Blasi (1980) maintains that there have been three major theoretical shifts this century in conceptualization of moral reasoning/moral action and in the empirical research which follows from that conceptualization. The first wave of researchers, exemplified by Hartshorne and May (1928), focused on moral traits in the belief that traits, either singly or in combination, were involved in moral action. The second wave of researchers concentrated on the work of Lawrence Kohlberg and his insight into how a subject formed decisions about what is moral and what is morally correct (Kohlberg, 1958). Studies of moral reasoning and moral judgment dominated the next 20 years of inquiry. The third wave of research followed Blasi's (1980) argument that investigating moral choice necessarily should be done in ways that examine the relationship of moral judgment to the actual decisions people make.

Five authors and their associates who were influential in initial formulations concerning the Sierrans Revisited Project were chosen for extensive review in Chapter 5: Augusto Blasi, Carol Gilligan, Norma Haan, Lawrence Kohlberg, and James Rest. Katherine Kalliel and David Connor were the significant contributors to the initial draft of this review. The theories of moral action sketched in this chapter are in fundamental disagreement about the structure of the morality by which people judge moral circumstances, about the decision-making processes involved prior to behavior characterized as moral, and about the forms of action which can be called moral. They disagree about the role, existence, and nature of deontic choices. The role of the self also varies from model to model.

> The theories of moral action sketched in this chapter are in fundamental disagreement about the structure of the morality by which people judge moral circumstances, about the decision-making processes involved prior to behavior characterized as moral, and about the forms of action which can be called moral.

The original Sierra Project did not address either moral action/moral choice, or the relationship between moral reasoning and moral action because when the Sierra Project was conceptualized in 1973, the most immediate research challenges were learning more about moral judgment in the college years and the character education necessary to enhance it. Also, there were numerous problems of curriculum development (Loxley & Whiteley, 1986), as well as uncharted territory in understanding the development of moral reasoning over four years of the undergraduate experience.

By the time that the Sierrans Revisited Project data collection had been completed and results were available, two intersecting insights compelled the expansion of the moral action theories being considered beyond the work of the five theorists who are the focus of Chapter 5. The first insight was understanding the depth and extent of their fundamental disagreement. The second insight was recognizing the proliferation of potentially relevant writing about moral choice and its antecedents, including the work of many authors who go well beyond the usual cognitive development paradigm.

These two insights caused us to expand the paradigms which we would draw upon in recommending directions for future research and in conceptualizing the meaning of the results. Included in this general expansion were such general questions as:

🌀 Do we need to incorporate insights from moral philosophy, and why?

🌀 Do we need to incorporate other insights from moral psychology, and why?

The real problem was the practical necessity of expanding our thinking, as comprehensively as possible, about the meaning of what young adults had been telling us.

Chapter 6 is comprised of several interesting perspectives that appeared in the 1990s after the Sierrans Revisited Project data had been collected. These perspectives broadened the theoretical net to include, for example, social cognitive theory (Bandura, 1991), the implications of moral identity for moral functioning (Blasi, 1993), the uniting of self and morality in the development of extraordinary moral commitment (Colby & Damon, 1993), the relationship between morality and personal autonomy (Nucci & Lee, 1993), and the wellsprings of altruism (Monroe, 1996).

This latter work by Monroe (1996) represents a sharp contrast to the Sierrans Revisited Project research, although both drew upon a common methodology: the personal narrative. Whereas the Sierrans Revisited researchers had interviewed young adults confronting the moral choices of everyday life, Kristen Monroe investigated extraordinary moral behavior and self-interest in extreme contexts: rescuers of Jews in Nazi-occupied Europe, Carnegie Hero Fund rescuers, and philanthropists and entrepreneurs in challenging moments. The initial draft of Chapter 6 was prepared by Molly Patterson of the Department of Politics and Society at the University of California, Irvine.

Section III: Narrative Insights into Moral Action in Young Adulthood

The common purpose of the three chapters in Section III is to contribute to a greater understanding of the anatomy of moral action in the individual case. The principal methodological approach is the personal narrative interview in three variations.

Individual members of the research team developed the three different approaches. For the data presented in Chapter 7 and for her doctoral dissertation, Katherine Kalliel (1989) constructed the Moral Action Interview (Appendix A). She selected a series of open-ended and closed-ended questions with accompanying probes about the subjects' personal moral dilemmas and the issues of rights, responsibilities, and feelings evoked by these moral dilemmas. She included questions designed to examine moral decision-making from the perspectives of Gilligan (1977, 1982), Blasi (1983, 1984), Kohlberg (Kohlberg & Candee, 1984), and Rest (1986). In her doctoral dissertation, Kalliel reiterates that the role of the five theories reviewed in Chapter 5 was to inform choices in the construction of the Moral Action Interview. The intent was never to construct the Moral Action Interview as a tool for evaluating the theories themselves, rather to be informed by them. She particularly wanted to explore issues of moral judgment as a trigger to moral action (Rest and Kohlberg), the self as it affects others as the starting point for moral action (Gilligan), and notions extrapolated from Blasi concerning the self as a mediator, but with moral action starting with a moral judgment. Kalliel sought from subjects information that was not specifically related to any of the theories which informed the Sierrans Revisited Project. This additional information pertained to a number of factors which were thought by the research team to be possible sources of influence on moral action such as parents, religious beliefs, and the role of significant others. Kalliel's doctoral dissertation describes the approach she took to data analysis based upon the Moral Action Interview. She was particularly interested in gender differences, as well as in problems of analysis of naturalistic data. The interested reader is directed to her dissertation for a fuller account.

For the data presented in Chapters 8 and 9 and for his doctoral dissertation, David Connor (1989) constructed the Moral Behavior Interview (Appendix B). As a point of departure which proved valuable in retrospect, Connor conducted eight extended interviews with non-Sierrans as a pilot project to field-test the Moral Behavior Interview. The purpose of the pilot interviews was straightforward: to test a number of different questions to see which would be likely to produce information on relevant areas of moral behavior. Connor's approach in the actual Sierrans Revisited interviewing is reported in Appendix B. In his analysis of the Moral Behavior Interviews, he focused on morality in personal life (reported in Chapter 8) and on morality in the workplace (reported in Chapter 9). Connor also related his interviews to the five models of moral action (Kohlberg, Haan, Rest, Blasi, Gilligan) which informed the Sierrans Revisited research. Any researcher contemplating the use of some variation of the personal narrative approach of open-ended and closed-ended questions with probes will find the methodology sections of both Kalliel's (1989) and Connor's (1989) dissertations relevant.

Connor (1989) advanced the notion of "moral economy" as an insight into the thinking of some interviewees in the Sierrans Revisited sample whose descriptions of their moral actions and the thinking behind them did not fit the five models which informed this project. "Moral economy" refers to whether individual moral decisions happen independently of other previous or subsequent choices. Except for aspects of Norma Haan's theory of interactive morality in which sometimes solutions are fluid or alterable, the other models seem to suggest that a particular moral dilemma may be addressed and analyzed without particular reference to other decisions the person has made or will make. Connor's basic notion is that at least some of the respondents appeared to make moral choice decisions in order to achieve what is to them an "acceptable balance of goodness in their moral self-concept" (Connor, 1989, p. 225).

Taken together, Chapters 7, 8, and 9 provide the evidence to answer the first two of the organizing questions for the Sierrans Revisited Project research: Will young adults talk about intimate moral issues, and what actual dilemmas will they identify as characteristic of their work and personal lives? Chapter 10, "Exemplary Sierrans: Moral Influences," reports evidence directly relevant to the third and fifth organizing questions: What are the factors which the subjects identify as influencing their action in response to moral dilemmas? Are there young people with exceptional characteristics whose moral behavior is exemplary and if yes, what can be learned about how they got that way?

The three subjects whose interviews are reported in Chapter 10 were drawn from the larger pool of subjects based on a consensus by the research team that they met four criteria which included (a) being especially lucid in articulating moral thought and action, (b) compelling in describing poignant dilemmas, (c) exhibiting consistency between principles and action, and (d) acting when there was risk to themselves. Professor James Day served as interviewer for this chapter, and created the Moral Influence Interview (Appendix C) to guide his interviewing.

There are three components to the Moral Influence Interview. The first component provided an opportunity to learn who had been a source of influence on the subject's formation of moral perceptions, ideas of right and wrong, learning of moral decision making, and of taking moral action. The second component guided the exploration of the relationship between moral principles and moral conduct, as well as serving as a vehicle for understanding the subjects' perceptions of the roots of their moral strength. The third and final component explored the relationship of moral meaning-making to larger meanings in the lives of the young adults.

Professor Day introduced the concept of "core moral audience" to describe something that each of his three subjects discussed when they rejected the suggestion that "moral independence" was a notion which could be applied to them. Rather, they said that their moral actions were always in relationship to others, and consistency in their action was really a function of consistency in their "moral audience." This was the group of subjects who talked the most about their experiences in Sierra Hall as freshmen and who identified exactly what it had been that was stimulating to their conceptions of moral growth.

Section IV: Conclusions and Directions for Future Research

At the start, the Sierrans Revisited Project had focused on a goal of understanding the psychological meaning of moral action in its social context as a necessary first step toward being able to educate for its promotion. There had been no expectation at the project's inception that any one study would be able to address satisfactorily the inherent complexity of the puzzle of why some people respond to a moral dilemma with a moral action and others do not.

The principal methodology employed in this research was gathering a series of individual case studies based upon personal narratives from the subjects. The focus of the inquiry and analysis in Chapter 11 became understanding the internal dynamics and anatomy of moral actions. Addressing the first four of the framing questions for the Sierrans Revisited Project was the organizational framework for Chapter 11, "Moral Dilemmas of Everyday Life: Voices of the Sierrans."

It fell to Chapter 12, "Exceptional Moral Behavior," to explore the complexities of Question 5: Are there people with exceptional moral behavior in everyday situations? This chapter explores different conceptions of individual strengths which are important to positive moral action. Of particular relevance is prior research on commitment by Anne Colby and William Damon (1993), and on altruism by Kristen Monroe (1996).

Chapter 13, "Strength of Character and Moral Agency," addresses Question 6: What factors/influences correlate with outstanding strength of character and powerful moral agency? With respect to "outstanding strength of character," by definition the term applies to a relatively small group of people. In the case of this Sierrans Revisited Project research, there were five young adults (out of just less than 50) who were identified by the research team as having "outstanding strength of character" in relation to how they approached everyday moral dilemmas. The notion of "powerful moral agency" was not a concept which had been empirically defined at the inception of the Sierrans Revisited Project. Nor was it a concept which had been an empirical part of the five theories of moral action which had been the theoretical framework for this project.

In the case of this Sierrans Revisited Project research, there were five young adults (out of just less than 50) who were identified by the research team as having "outstanding strength of character" in relation to how they approached everyday moral dilemmas.

It is in this area that the theories reported in Chapter 6 have been of special value. A number of these newer concepts for thinking about the genesis of moral action have utility for framing the next generation of research. Therefore, one of two emphases of the concluding chapter was to share what was learned from the Sierrans Revisited empirical inquiry in relationship to insights from the newer theories which gained expression after the project began.

The emphasis of the concluding chapter, Chapter 14, "Toward Promoting Moral Action in Young Adulthood," was on the implications of the Sierrans Revisited Project research for education for moral action. This extrapolation begins with a consideration of the implications of the curriculum of the original Sierra Project. It also considers the lessons from Nevitt Sanford's reminder of the importance of a sense of community and moral values in higher education (Chapter 1), and Ralph L. Mosher's analysis of the aims (and misses) of the Sierra curriculum (Chapter 2). A key purpose of the project as a whole has been to contribute, ultimately, to better understanding of education for the promotion of moral action.

References

Bandura, A. (1991). Social cognitive theory of moral thought and action. In W. K. Kurtines and J. L. Gewirtz (Eds.) *Handbook of moral behavior and development* (Vol. 1, pp. 45-103). Hillsdale, NJ: Lawrence Erlbaum Associates.

Blasi, A. (1980). Bridging moral cognition and moral action: A critical review of the literature. *Psychological Bulletin, 88*, 1-45.

Blasi, A. (1983). Moral cognition and moral action: A theoretical perspective. *Developmental Review*, pp. 178-210.

Blasi, A. (1984). Moral identity: Its role in moral functioning. In W. M. Kurtines & J. L. Gewirtz (Eds.), *Morality, moral behavior and moral development*. New York: John Wiley and Sons.

Blasi, A. (1993). The development of identity: Some implications for moral functioning. In G. C. Noam & T. E. Wren (Eds.), *The moral self* (pp. 99-122). Cambridge, MA: MIT Press.

Colby, A., & Damon, W. (1993). The uniting of self and morality in the development of extraordinary moral commitment. In G. C. Noam & T. E. Wren (Eds.), *The moral self* (pp. 149-174). Cambridge, MA: MIT Press.

Connor, D. (1989). *The moral behavior of young adults*. Unpublished doctoral dissertation, Boston University.

Dewey, J. (1897/1968). *Problems of men*. New York: Greenwood Press.

Gilligan, C. (1977). In a different voice: Women's conceptions of self and of morality. *Harvard Educational Review*, 481-517.

Gilligan, C. (1982). *In a different voice: Psychological theory and women's development*. Cambridge, MA: Harvard University Press.

Hartshorne, H., & May, M. (1928). *Studies in the nature of character: Vol I. Studies in deceit*. New York: Macmillan.

Kalliel, K. M. (1989). *Moral decisions and actions of young adults in actual dilemmas*. Unpublished doctoral dissertation, Boston University.

Kohlberg, L. (1958). *The development of modes of moral thinking and choice in the years ten to sixteen*. Unpublished doctoral dissertation, University of Chicago.

Kohlberg, L., & Candee, D. (1984). The relationship of moral judgment to moral action. In L. Kohlberg (Ed.), *Essays on moral development: Vol. II. The psychology of moral development*. San Francisco: Harper and Row.

Loxley, J. C., & Whiteley, J. (1986). *Character development in college students, Volume II*. Schenectady, NY: Character Research Press.

Monroe, K. (1996). *The heart of altruism: Perceptions of a common humanity.* Princeton, NJ: Princeton University Press.

Nucci, L., & Lee, J. (1993). Morality and personal autonomy. In G. C. Noam & T. E. Wren (Eds.), *The moral self* (pp. 123-140). Cambridge, MA: MIT Press.

Rest, J. (1986). *Moral development: Advances in research and theory.* New York: Praeger.

Whiteley, J., & Associates. (1982). *Character development in college students, Volume I.* Schenectady, NY: Character Research Press.

Whiteley, J., & Yokota, N. (1988). *Character development in the freshman year and over four years of undergraduate study.* (Monograph No. 1). Columbia, SC: National Resource Center for The Freshman Year Experience, University of South Carolina.

S E C T I O N 1

ORIGINS AND RESULTS OF THE
ORIGINAL SIERRA PROJECT

Section I is intended to introduce the scope and purposes of the Sierra Project for readers who have not previously had access to the first two books about the project, *Character Development in College Students: Volume I* (Whiteley & Associates, 1982) and *Character Development in College Students: Volume II* (Loxley & Whiteley, 1986).

Chapter 1 by Nevitt Sanford originally appeared as the Foreword to *Character Development in College Students: Volume I*. It is reprinted here under the title "Nevitt Sanford on Community and Concern with Moral Values in Higher Education." Professor Sanford had a distinguished academic career as a scholar and researcher. Throughout his professional lifetime he held teaching positions at some of America's most influential research universities and private colleges. In the late 1920s, Sanford was an undergraduate at the University of Richmond in Virginia and deeply immersed himself in the values imbued by the sense of community he found there. After college he reports that: "Most of us gave little thought to what we would do after college. All we were clear about was that we would stay as close as possible to the city of Richmond and maintain close ties with family and friends. They would find jobs for us, and if we got into trouble they would take care of us." The defining summary of what he and his fellow students found at the University of Richmond was *community*: "every opportunity for intimacy, values that were clearly defined and exemplified by professors, ways of defining ourselves that did not depend on achievement or vocational aspiration, and plenty of ways to satisfy our need for 'homonomy.'"

The balance of his chapter chronicles the decline of a sense of community in higher education after World War II and the negative consequences of that decline. Since a central component of the Sierra curriculum for college freshmen was fostering a sense of community, Professor Sanford's writing presents an important context for introducing the goals of the Sierra Project.

Chapter 2 by Ralph L. Mosher originally appeared, in modified form, as the Foreword to *Character Development in College Students: Volume II*. Whereas Nevitt Sanford focuses on a sense of community and its context in higher education, Professor Mosher addresses the general problem of how to encourage children and young adults "to think more deeply and ethically about the issues of right and wrong, good and bad, and the rights and obligations so raised." The bulk of Professor Mosher's chapter provides specific critiques of the fundamental purposes of the Sierra Project curriculum and how its organizers went about achieving its goals. He also juxtaposes the Sierra approach with other attempts to raise the level of moral reasoning, particularly those from the cognitive developmental perspective. The curriculum of the Sierra Project is reported in detail in *Character Development in College Students: Volume II*, Chapters 5, 6, and 7.

Chapter 3, "Character Development Over Four Years of Undergraduate Study," originally appeared as Monograph #1 from The National Resource Center for The Freshman Year Experience at the University of South Carolina. The purpose of the original monograph was to summarize the essential rationale for the Sierra Project and to present the results from various empirical studies. This monograph reviews the impact of the freshman year and four years of undergraduate study on a central dimension of personal development—the formation of character and its progression from late adolescence to young adulthood.

Chapter 3 also presents the following:

- The obstacles in the way of higher education's meeting its responsibility for character development;

- The six-part rationale for the Sierra Project, and for promoting the character of college students, including definitions of principal conceptual terms;

- A brief synopsis of the curriculum.

- Empirical findings on the growth of character during the freshman year;

- Empirical findings on the growth of character over four years of undergraduate study;

- Report on differential effects of a character education curriculum over the course of the freshman year; and

- Central implications of the Sierra Project for the freshman year and undergraduate education.

Readers who have already read about the original Sierra project may wish to proceed to Section II which includes theoretical underpinnings of what is being called the "Sierrans Revisited" research.

References

Loxley, J. C., & Whiteley, J. M. (1986). *Character development in college students, Vol. II: The curriculum and longitudinal results.* Schenectady, NY: Character Research Press.

Whiteley, J. M., & Associates. (1982). *Character development in college students, Vol. I: The freshman year.* Schenectady, NY: Character Research Press.

C H A P T E R

NEVITT SANFORD ON COMMUNITY
AND CONCERN WITH MORAL VALUES
IN HIGHER EDUCATION

Nevitt Sanford

American universities have been expanding and becoming differentiated at a rate far beyond their capacity to achieve the integration which is necessary to any living system. Particularly in the years since World War II we have seen a fantastic proliferation of departments, specialties within departments, institutes, centers, and programs, each of which, in the major universities, has behaved as an independent principality, bent on its own aggrandizement, relating less to other substructures in the same institution than to outside constituents, markets, and sources of funds. This has been going on long enough so that this model of a university is widely regarded as just a phenomenon of nature, something that the good Lord intended.

Enormous interest is vested in these present structures. It seems that only a few of us old-timers remember the humane and humanizing universities of the 1920s and 1930s, some of which surely achieved greatness—and this without huge inputs of funds from Washington or elsewhere. Their greatness depended on a clear vision of goals and a willingness to organize effort in their pursuit.

In my more despairing moments it seems to me that the modern university has succeeded in separating almost everything that belongs together. Not only have fields of inquiry been subdivided until they have become almost meaningless, but research has been separated from teaching, teaching and research from action, and, worst of all, thought from humane feeling.

In my more despairing moments it seems to me that the modern university has succeeded in separating almost everything that belongs together.

The effects of these changes on students, especially undergraduates, have been devastating. It is fair to say that in most of our universities—and in many of our elite liberal arts colleges—a majority of the students suffer from a lack of a sense of community, confusion about values, a lack of intimate friends, a very tenuous sense of self (including serious doubt about their personal worth), and the absence of a great cause, movement, service, religion, belief system, or anything else that they might see as larger than themselves and in which they could become deeply involved. I conclude from this that those of us who care about the nation's youth and their education must now work to construct conditions and promote values that we once took for granted.

Much of value was taken for granted at the University of Richmond (a small college with a law school) when I was there in the 1920s. I am sure it never occurred to anyone to suggest that we ought to build community. Indeed, to have talked about community at that time and place would have been like talking to a fish about water. It was not only that students and faculty alike generally shared the same values, but we all could upon occasion display our genuine school spirit. I belonged to a fraternity and to several athletic teams and was best friends with a young man who shared my interest in academic work. I never doubted that these young men cared for me and over the years I have always known that when I went back to Richmond we would take up our friendships just where we left off. My older fraternity brothers and teammates took pains to instruct me how to act in various social situations. At the same time I was sometimes able to help some fellow athletes with their homework; they took pride in the fact that one of them could "understand this stuff." I was usually able to hold my own in the innumerable "bull sessions" we had.

I was never close to my professors, being too shy to take questions or problems to any of them. I can, however, call up vivid images of at least a dozen of these men. This, I think, is not so much because they were unusually individualistic, but because they expressed themselves more freely than do professors today. They were teachers above all else; they felt safe in saying what they pleased and, most important, we could "get them off the subject." We wanted to know what they really felt and thought about issues and people, not just about Shakespeare or Bismarck but about H. L. Mencken, the Scopes trial, and the Soviet Union; in sum, about what interested us. Thus, they exposed themselves as whole persons and bearers of value.

One value that was universally espoused was that of liberal education. In "bull sessions" we debated whether the purpose of education was to learn "how to live" or "how to make a living" and came down overwhelmingly on the side of the former. Even those students who were bound for medicine, law, or the ministry thought the way to get started was to "get a liberal education."

Most of us gave little thought to what we would do after college. All we were clear about was that we would stay as close as possible to the city of Richmond and maintain close ties with family and friends. They would find jobs for us, and if we got into trouble they would take care of us. We were under no pressure to establish our "vocational identities." The selves we felt ourselves to be depended instead on such factors as family, locale, region, religion, ethnicity, school, and group memberships; also on interest, activities, and personal characteristics that were confirmed by others. The confirming—or disconfirming—of notions we had about ourselves was fairly easy in an environment where friends and relations cared enough to "straighten each other out."

I, in company with many of my fellows, I believe, had a hard time finding out what I could and could not do, suffering more than a few painful blows to self-esteem in the process; but I never doubted that in some fundamental way I was, or would be, all right. This was not only because I knew I was loved by family and friends but because our professors somehow conveyed the idea that, despite our obvious shortcomings, great things were expected of us; the reason they berated us so often was because they believed that, some day, affairs of great moment could be left safely in our hands.

In sum, we had *community*, every opportunity for intimacy, values that were clearly defined and exemplified by professors, ways of defining ourselves that did not depend on achievement or vocational aspiration, and plenty of ways to satisfy our need for "homonomy." This last is Andras Angyal's term. He wrote that every individual needs not only autonomy but homonomy, "to become an organic part of something he conceives as greater than himself—to be in harmony with super individual units, the social world, nature, God, ethical world order, or whatever the individual's formulation of it may be" (Angyal, 1941, p. 172). There were plenty of things around that people could throw themselves into: the Christian religion, the Baptist Church, Southern culture, the Democratic party, Sigma Phi Epsilon, football—to mention a few.

Richmond was not unique. In fact, it was very much like other small colleges of the time—not only in the South but nationwide. More than that, much of the culture and spirit I have tried to describe prevailed in the universities. To get along at Harvard, where I became a graduate student in 1930, all one had to do was to have some intellectual interests, to respect those of others, and to be civil in argument. The faculty displayed these values; they showed their concern for students and convinced us that they could be trusted. We students, knowing that we were in a system that really worked, felt no need to compete with each other. Instead, mutual help and cooperation were the order of the day and many enduring friendships were formed.

The University of California at Berkeley, in the early 1940s, was even more a community than Harvard, even though there were 20,000 students around. It *felt* like a community. When Provost Monroe Deutsch spoke on formal occasions everybody felt that he spoke for us all. Professors in one department fraternized easily with professors in various others. Graduate students were happy and secure, for they knew that as long as they were serious and willing to work some professor would see them through to their degree. Assistant professors, such as I, were also secure, for we knew that having been brought into a departmental family we would be looked after and promoted in our turn. The psychology department at Berkeley was already famous in the 1930s; yet it was not until 1947 that any assistant professor ever hired by that department was out instead of up.

When I went to work at Vassar College in 1952 I soon felt very much at home. The place was a lot like Richmond. Of course, the academic standards were higher, everybody was more serious about what they were doing, and there was greater liberalism in politics, but there was much of the sort of community I had grown used to. There was universal belief in liberal education and a generally agreed upon set of values, organized around something vaguely defined as "quality." This embodied some intellectual snobbery, but there was much more to it than that. The faculty cared about students and worked hard at their teaching. Although there was some social stratification in the student body there was much sisterliness and open display of loyalty to the school. It was generally agreed that Vassar was a place where "you made your lifelong friends."

...the reason they berated us so often was because they believed that, some day, affairs of great moment could be left safely in our hands.

But Vassar, like almost all other colleges and universities in the country, was to change. Shortly after World War II the federal government began pouring money into the universities to support research and graduate training. Soon the universities were putting more and more emphasis on research, less and less on teaching undergraduates. For example in the late 1940s my colleagues and I in the psychology department at Berkeley set out to make ours the strongest department in the university and the strongest psychology department in the nation. We competed fiercely with other departments around the country in our effort to get the best young researchers. We did not ask if they could teach; to sweeten our offers, we made the proposed teaching load as light as possible and promised our new recruits that they could teach their specialties. The curriculum proliferated wildly. At one time, unbeknownst to anybody in the department, the same text was being used in five courses, each with a different name. When our most senior professor retired there was no one around to worry about the integration of our curriculum. All that mattered was research and publication, and the training of graduate students in various specialties. In these circumstances nobody had time for undergraduates. They would have been dismissed altogether, I believe, were it not for the fact that the budget for psychology depended on how many undergraduate students we had.

What was happening in psychology, as I later learned, was happening in most other departments of the university, and what was happening at Berkeley was happening at universities all over the country. And after 1957, when Sputnik was launched, things took a turn for the worse. Now there was an increased accent on science and technology as a road to "national strength." The kind of science that soon got the upper hand was that modelled after 19th century physics. Understanding was to be achieved by the analysis of phenomena into finer and finer bits. Knowledge of how things fit together could wait. The required rate of publication could not be sustained if professors addressed themselves to large or complicated issues. The research that was to save us from the Russians became more and more trivial. In psychology, issues of great moment were turned into methodological problems.

In the humanities as well as in the sciences the Western techno-scientific approach to knowledge became increasingly dominant. In the excitement following Sputnik there was general acceptance of the notion that American education was mediocre. Professors now felt that they had permission to do, and to do more rigorously, what they wanted to do anyway, that is, concentrate on their scholarly specialties in their teaching as well as in their research. Professors of literature, for example, instead of focusing on the task of making great works available to undergraduates, insisted on close reading, detailed analysis, an interpretation according to their preferred conceptual schemes. In philosophy, professors who wanted to reduce their discipline to arguments about what philosophy is, or to the analysis of linguistic minutiae, took a new lease on life.

Where in the curriculum, then, were students to find anything to nurture the spirit? How were they to attain broad understanding, to find out what it means to be human, to experience wonder, to acquire a sense of values?

The liberal arts colleges, particularly the elitist ones, followed the example of the universities. The departments evaluated themselves primarily on the basis of how many of their students gained admission to good graduate schools. The safest course was to teach these undergraduates what the professors knew would be taught again in graduate school.

By 1964, as it turned out, the situation had become explosive. The student protests that began at Berkeley in September, 1964 were in the beginning protests against the "irrelevance" of the curriculum and the "impersonality" of campus life. Although the students' insistence on educational reform was soon forced into the background by protests against the Vietnam War, it persisted and became a national movement. Great energy went into this movement, but it suffered from a lack of educational leadership. Many institutions just gave the students what they said they wanted, with small attention to what they needed. Nevertheless many constructive things were done. Whole new institutions were started within and without existing colleges and universities; for example, the experimental colleges within the University of California, Berkeley, and New College in San Francisco. Unfortunately this was almost always done with soft money and very few of the innovations have persisted.

Today the excitement of the sixties and early seventies seems remote. With the end of the Vietnam War in sight the student movement ran out of steam, as movements do, and inevitably some reaction set in. Up until quite recently, and still, institutions have been busy putting back into place things that were "dislocated" in response to student activism. Neither students nor university officers are thinking about educational reform. They have other things on their minds. Students, for their part, having decided to work within the system, are very much taken up with getting into professional schools and will do whatever is required. Professors, with only pliable students to deal with, feel free to do what they like most and do best, that is, research and teaching their specialties—preferably to graduate students.

Concern with moral values seems to have disappeared from the scene. If the university has any noble purposes, or any purposes beyond preparing students for vocations, keeping the wheels turning, and maintaining the standard of living, there does not seem to be anyone around to say what these purposes are. Even with the emphasis on ethics that followed Watergate, instruction in this area has been focused almost exclusively on how to analyze ethical issues, critique ethical positions, and avoid "moral indoctrination" (Bennett, 1980). Nobody is telling students that they ought to do better or be better persons, or suggesting what *is* better; nor do students have much opportunity to learn from the example of their elders. On every university campus there are, to be sure, professors who have the self-discipline that it takes to discover and to tell the truth. But there are more who present examples of competitiveness and acquisitiveness, absorption in narrow specialties, virtuosity untempered by humane feeling. For better or worse, however, students rarely get to know their professors well enough to consider them as models. "Getting them off the subject" went out of fashion some time ago.

What is even more to be regretted, professors do not know their undergraduate students. Last year I had a letter from a former Stanford student who was in prison for murder. He is a Vietnam veteran who had become mentally disturbed and deeply involved with drugs. The prosecutor had tagged him a sociopath, and he needed the testimony of someone who knew him when he was a student. He had taken a lecture course from me and, for one quarter in 1963, a course in guided reading and research. We met six or eight times and he submitted a paper. He told enough in his letter about what he had said and what I had said so that, remarkably enough, I remembered him. I believe I was able to be of some help to him. But (and this is the point of the story) I was the only professional person at Stanford who had

If the university has any noble purposes, or any purposes beyond preparing students for vocations, keeping the wheels turning, and maintaining the standard of living, there does not seem to be anyone around to say what these purposes are.

7

known him personally and who, as he thought, might conceivably remember him. And he was there for four years. A university can be a very cold place; I have no doubt that it is as cold today as it was in 1963.

One might think that students who are alienated from their professors—and probably from most other adults—would turn to one another for intimacy and support. But not so. Colleagues and graduate students at the Wright Institute, who have been studying student life at Berkeley, tell me that these young people do not know how to make friends or behave on dates—that there is a distressing amount of loneliness on campus. I had observed the same phenomena at Stanford in the early 1960s. Apparently there is so much competition for grades and status, so much uncertainty about who one is and what one can do, that students cannot expose themselves enough to make intimate relationships possible. Most of them, most of the time, are putting on some kind of act.

Equally distressing is the fact that they cannot talk over such problems among themselves. My Wright Institute informants interviewed, in considerable depth, 15 young men who lived in a nearby fraternity house. The plan was to use the major themes that came up in the interview as a basis for group discussion. As expected, the fraternity men enjoyed the interviews; they were open, sincere, willing to talk about serious problems. But when the three interviewers arrived at the fraternity house to hold the discussion the music was turned on, the beer had been distributed, and young women soon arrived. Of course there was no discussion. It was as if each individual personality had been dissolved in the group.

Many students have told me that they and their acquaintances could not organize discussions of serious questions. Not only were they too wary of one another, but there was the ubiquitous TV and record player. This is in contrast not only with the "good old days" but with the recent past when students were involved in efforts at educational or political change. There was plenty of communication among them then, and some of it was the sort that calls for self-revelation and leads to intimacy. What they had primarily was homonomy. And this raises the question of what is there today that students can lose themselves in. For many, no doubt, preparation for their chosen vocation is enough to capture their imaginations and use up their energies. Beyond that the scene appears bleak. There seems to be very little action on the political left. The women's movement, demonstrations against nuclear weapons or in favor of environmental protection are still out there, but much of the life seems to have been drained from them. Clearly we need some new movements and, this time around, something that adults as well as students can throw themselves into. The fact that they long for homonomy is, I believe, one reason why students join cults or new religious groups.

In thinking of the pre-World War II university as a source of ideas about how we might improve the quality of campus life and better assist students in their self-development, we must remember that the culture which prevailed then had its dark side. At Richmond there was universal and completely thoughtless racism. There were *no* black students there, or at any college I knew of. Blacks were so submerged that we never saw them except in menial roles; and this state of affairs was regarded as natural. Certainly it was never discussed. I was more aware of anti-Catholicism, and may have participated in it; but the ethnocentrism that I experienced most vividly and expressed with the most enthusiasm was in connection with a traditional football rivalry. On our campus it was generally believed that William and Mary College imported "ringers," (i.e., professional athletes, with strange ethnic backgrounds) who came from places like Jersey City, New Jersey. When we went into a game with this outfit it was virtually "holy war." Some months after graduating from college I was approached on the New York subway by a smiling young man who happily identified himself as someone who had played against me in the last Richmond-William and Mary game. I was struck dumb. Did he not realize that we were enemies, and that I would not be ready to make peace? He must have thought me a fool.

I might say in my own defense that people matured more slowly in those days than they do now, that it is probably better to display one's ethnocentrism on the playing fields than to do so in the streets. More than that, I was still an adolescent when I graduated from college, and adolescents are entitled to some measure of ethnocentrism. Their big problem is what to do about the emotional impulses they regard as low, destructive, and dangerous. The conventional strategy for adolescents, and for people stuck at that stage of development, is to cling to a group or to groups that are seen as good like themselves and to see the "bad" as existing in other people, who are then put beyond the pale.

Can we, then, have community without ethnocentrism? I believe that we can. We may hope that, as they grow older, adolescents will come to see that their impulses need not be projected onto other people or stamped out completely: that they may, instead, be modified or controlled. This kind of development can be brought about through education at the college level. It is partly a matter of learning to think well, and partly a matter of character development. What we desire for our college graduates is a capacity for group loyalty *and* tolerance of other groups, identity *and* intimacy, homonomy *and* autonomy. This requires that their personalities become sufficiently expanded, differentiated, and integrated so that opposite tendencies can be held in consciousness long enough for synergistic resolutions to be found.

I have argued for more than a few years (Sanford, 1956, 1962a, 1962b, and 1980) that the development of such personalities is the overarching aim of education and that all the resources of our educational institutions should be put in its service. As various theorists have insisted, personality functions as a unit; its diverse features develop an interaction one with the other (Allport, 1937; Murray, 1938; Angyal, 1941). Intelligence, feeling, emotion, and action can be separated conceptually but no one of them functions independently of the others. I wrote in 1962:

> Just as nothing is truly learned until it has been integrated with the purposes of the individual, so no facts and principles that have been learned can serve any worthy human purpose unless they are restrained and guided by character. Intellect without humane feeling can be monstrous, while feeling without intelligence is childish; intelligence and feeling are at their highest and in the best relation one to another where there is a taste for art and beauty as well as an appreciation of logic and knowledge (Sanford, 1962b).

What we desire for our college graduates is a capacity for group loyalty *and* tolerance of other groups, identity *and* intimacy, homonomy *and* autonomy.

I believe the authors of the present volume will agree with this statement, for their work is in the same spirit. Although they focus on character, it is clear that in creating a new educational environment—which they did as part of their

9

Sierra Project—they have been guided by a conception of, and concern with, the whole person. That environment, which is fully described here, deserves our best attention and careful study. It embodies in some degree all those things whose lack I have bemoaned in the above paragraphs. (In going on so long about the poor quality of student life generally, and about what we know, on the basis of the past, might be possible, my object has been to provide a background against which the significance of the Sierra Project may be highlighted.)

In this residential learning program we find a concern about values, opportunities to serve the larger community, close relations among faculty, staff and students, intensive small group discussions, special curricular experiences designed on the basis of developmental theory—in general a humanitarian and therefore humanizing environment. And all of this at the University of California, Irvine, an institution that prides itself on how rapidly it is becoming a great research university.

There are other projects and programs around the country that are based in theory and directed to the development of the student as a person. For example, at the University of Nebraska-Lincoln and at Azusa Pacific College students are provided with mentors and keep records of their activities and achievements. I know of no program, however, that is as comprehensive and far-reaching in its implications as the one being considered here.

The question is: What are the effects of the living-learning program on the students' development—with special reference to character? Attempts to answer this question for freshmen who spent one year in the project are fully described in this book. Experimental evaluation with the use of tests and control groups was carried out with the rigor one would expect of U.C. Irvine. More to my liking, there was a great deal of interviewing and some case studies.

Finally, I should say that the Sierra Project is not only a set of actions whose effects are then evaluated; it is also pure research on character development. *Character Development in College Students: Volume I* (Whiteley & Associates, 1982) contains a thorough review of the literature on this subject but reports only part of the research results that are or will be available. Later reports will deal with the lasting effects of being in the program for freshmen and with the question of which educational procedures or experiences had what kinds of effects on which students. I can hardly wait.

References

Allport, G. W. (1937). *Personality: A psychological interpretation*. New York: Holt.

Angyal, A. (1941). *Foundations for a science of personality*. New York: Commonwealth Fund.

Bennett, W. J. (1980). Getting ethics. *Commentary, 70*(6), 62-65.

Murray, H. A. (1938). *Explorations in personality*. New York: Oxford.

Sanford, N. (1956). Personality development during the college years. *Personnel and Guidance Journal, 35,* 74-80.

Sanford, N. (1962a). Higher education as a social problem. In N. Sanford (Ed.), *The American college.* New York: Wiley.

Sanford, N. (1962b). Ends and means in higher education. In K. Smith (Ed.), *Current issues in higher education.* Washington, DC: National Education Association.

Sanford, N. (1980). *Learning after college.* Orinda, CA: Montaigne.

Whiteley, J. M., & Associates. (1982). *Character Development in College Students Vol. I: The Freshman Year.* Schenectady, NY: Character Research Press.

C H A P T E R

THE AIMS OF THE SIERRA CURRICULUM: "ON LEAPING TALL BUILDINGS IN A SINGLE BOUND"

TWO

Ralph L. Mosher

Moral education in American public schools during the 1970s was done primarily by the classroom discussion of moral dilemmas embedded in the academic curriculum. American history, literature, biology, health, and so on are subject matters replete with moral issues: Slavery, the Nuremberg trials, the massacre at Kent State, *Andersonville*, "Letter From the Birmingham Jail," dioxin, and "acid rain" are but a few of the examples. Teachers in many public schools were taught how to highlight such issues within their discipline and to conduct formal classroom discussions of them. The objective was to encourage children and young adults to think more deeply and ethically about the issues of right and wrong, good and bad, and the rights and obligations so raised. The results were encouraging: The moral thinking of many students became more mature from such instruction.

A second emphasis in public school moral education in the 1970s was the discussion by students of everyday or "real" moral issues occurring in the life of the classroom or the school. Here the effort was to have students and faculty participate in the actual governance and adjudication of "their" special institution. Again, the use of the school as a natural laboratory for political, social, and moral education yielded some encouraging evidence as to its effects in promoting students' character development.

Although broadly influenced by this parallel movement in the public schools, the Sierra Project did not, by and large, include the systematic formal discussion of either abstract moral dilemmas nor those naturally occurring in the residence. This happened for several reasons. There was no psychologist associated with the project who had made moral development his/her principal theoretical focus. (That would be true in most colleges, incidentally). Nor was there a normative philosopher or ethicist aboard. Almost all the Sierra students were at a very similar stage in their moral reasoning, and therefore, it was difficult for them to "bootstrap" themselves. The student staff was reluctant to identify the moral issues which arose naturally. The project leadership saw the necessity for sequenced moral discussions but felt such to be beyond the scope of the project. Hindsight might suggest that was an opportunity lost.

Moreover, the Sierra Project had multiple and very ambitious goals for its students, the problem of leaping tall buildings in a single bound. These included: to help the freshmen make the transition to young adulthood, to become more responsible for themselves, to take a more active role in their education, and to become aware of cultural and social issues. They were concerned also with moral, ego, and character development and with fostering a sense of community (adapted from Loxley & Whiteley, 1986, p. 51-56). One may question (as Whiteley does whimsically) whether goals this broad make any sense. Conversely one may ask whether an education which does not respond comprehensively to the life demands of freshmen can add meaning to the difficult psychological and social transformations being experienced. One wonders whether the Sierra team, in retrospect, would pursue more singular, developmental goals; whether in developmental education we need to learn to walk before we run.

The immediate point is that the Sierra curriculum went much beyond the promotion of moral reasoning. Yet one of the principal educational means to promote character, as the project *operationally* defined it, was not used. Here I refer to the formal discussion of ethical issues in the academic disciplines of the undergraduate curriculum. That omission, understandable as it was, put added burdens on the formal Sierra course and on the residence life to carry the day for character. It is also important to note a related bind. Whether Sierra was successful in promoting character was to be measured by an instrument very responsive to the formal, structural properties of moral reasoning and their exercise.

The Sierra staff tried to enhance the moral atmosphere of the residence through efforts at community building, and at bringing moral/conflict issues before the group rather than covering them up. Examples of the latter were stealing, racial conflicts, and roommate conflicts. Also the live-in student staff tried to highlight issues as they occurred and to aid students in resolving them. It is not easy for the reader to ascertain how systematically this was done. Two impressions: First, it was done less than Whiteley believes; second, that the hidden moral curriculum, everyday life in Sierra Hall, and the "peer culture," largely worked their will (as probably they always do in significant degree). A case study in *Portraits in Character* (Lee & Whiteley, in preparation), for example, very courageously reports how several students, caught smoking "dope," blackmailed the staff by threatening to withdraw from the research project and take other Sierrans with them. A further possibility is that many of the Sierra Project's effects on the freshmen were as attributable to this hidden curriculum as to the Sierra course proper.

In a project with as many objectives and activities as this one, identifying cause and effects is a most complex matter. But a 24-hour residential community in which all subjects break bread together and live together was a curriculum designer's dream nonetheless. With such an extraordinary complex interaction of people and experiences to manage and understand, missed opportunities and so on may be the obverse side of all this. Yet as we learn from initiatives such as Sierra, such 24-hour communities may yield a rich harvest of human growth.

Taking the Measure of the Man and the Woman

It is hard to be critical of a project so honest about its gaffes. It is not hard to learn from it, however, and that is the great contribution of the Sierra Project. Sierra underscores that a first premise of education for character development is to know how mature, morally, one's students are. Here the writer bears a direct responsibility. At the inception of the project, I had suggested to Whiteley that Sierra would be the first character education project in a position to promote the transition to what Kohlberg had termed post conventional moral thinking. Along with other so-called "experts" in the field, I assumed that late adolescence/early adulthood was the time when the conventional thinking to post conventional thinking transition would be happening normally. Thus Sierra aimed its initial curricula at a moral Stage 4 (the last stage of conventional thinking) to Stage 5 transition (the first stage of post conventional thinking). Much to my embarrassment, the Sierra Project staff found themselves confronted with a population of very conventional, Stage 3 moral thinkers (the first stage of conventional thinking). They were still prototypical high schoolers.

While Sierra did not test for the freshmen's cognitive development, in Piagetian terms, it is likely that less than half of American high school graduates are capable of fully abstract thought.

To the degree that the Sierra curriculum incorporated, or presumed thinking about intellectual or ideological themes relatively abstract to 18 year old freshmen (for example, Module 2: democratic decision making; Module 3: conflict resolution in society), to that extent a meeting of the minds would be difficult. Again and again in the discussion of the Sierra curriculum, it is reported how the thinking of the freshmen was to prove a stumbling block to the aspirations of the investigators. The authors report that ease with the concrete and difficulty with the abstract or theoretical was to reoccur in every module. Again and again when asked a question requiring an abstract answer—"How were decisions made in your Region?'—they would reply with concrete details—"We decided to get money and travel passes for everyone" (Loxley & Whiteley, 1986, p. 114). When confronted with the notion that there is "no one right answer" to moral dilemmas or most conflict situations, the authors reported that students experienced genuine dissonance: "When conflict arose during SIMSOC, poor listening followed by an aggressive reaction often led to an unpleasant scene" (p. 114). And so on.

While Sierra did not test for the freshmen's cognitive development, in Piagetian terms, it is likely that less than half of American high school graduates are capable of fully abstract thought. The author's repeated references to the concretism of the Sierra students raises again the question of how many of these students were ready for the intellectual demands: for abstraction, hypothetical-deduction thinking; for many of the basic instructional concepts such as "conflict resolution," "just" or "democratic community" central to the course. But in theory we would want to expose students to thinking and behaving just beyond their present understanding, in what Vygotskii calls their "zone of next development" (Vygotskii, 1978). To do that with the range of objectives of the Sierra Project would be an extraordinarily sophisticated task. But knowing where freshmen are in their present thinking and behavior is a *sine qua non*.

The Sierra Curriculum in Practice

The formal Sierra curriculum consisted of 10 modules taught in the fall, winter, and spring quarters, the journal which each student kept, and the community service opportunity for those who chose to participate. The overall rationale for the particular modules/experiences is not explicitly stated in terms of current developmental theories. For example, Erikson (1967) contends that Sierra freshmen are preoccupied with identity or epistemological issues: Who am I? What will I be when I grow up? By what values will I live? The forming of intimate, caring relationships with others might be a further preoccupation. Levinson believes Sierrans face two psychosocial tasks: to terminate adolescence and begin early adulthood. Further they are in the earliest phase of that transition: "A young man needs about 15 years to emerge from adolescence, find his place in adult society and commit himself to a more stable life" (Levinson, 1978, p. 71). Separating from one's family and "breaking up that old gang of mine" are but two of the painful changes facing the Sierra cohort. My point is that a closely reasoned linkage between one or more developmental theories of late adolescence and the curriculum is not included. Perhaps it may appear in later volumes or as a retrospective; certainly it would be an invaluable contribution to those building subsequent character education curricula in college.

Much collective time and thought was given by the Sierra staff to the development of the several modules. That is as it should be in education for development. As Dewey said,

Much collective time and thought was given by the Sierra staff to the development of the several modules. That is as it should be in education for development.

> Withdrawal from the hard and fast and narrow contents of the old curriculum is only the negative side of the matter. If we do not go on and go far in the positive direction of providing a body of subject matter much richer, more varied and flexible and also in truth more definitive, judged in terms of the experience of those being educated, than traditional education supplied, we shall tend to leave an educational vacuum in which anything may happen (Dewey, 1897/1968).

For the reader, *Character Development in College Students: Volume II* (Loxley & Whiteley, 1986) defines Sierra's aims in character education and describes a plethora of means for their realization. My purpose is not to review all ten modules; that is a task for others. But the rich tapestry of character education practices reported in *Character Development in College Students: Volume II* merits some general commentary. Following the author's lead, let me review the curriculum of the first quarter. My purpose is to draw out some, by no means all, of the curricular insights into curriculum development for anyone wishing to emulate Whiteley and Associates' pioneering work (Whiteley & Associates, 1982; Loxley & Whiteley, 1986).

The aim of the first module is perfectly clear. Sierra was full of freshmen anxious about their academic success. The focus on learning and study skills (how to "survive" in your native university) was a natural one. "Adjustment" has long been a preoccupation of counselors. The academic anxiety associated with the transition to college somewhat allayed, the project turned to "Community Building," through democratic decision making and students planned classes, and to "Conflict Resolution in Society."

The project, with its usual commendable honesty, reports that the students initially did not know how to act in class: "For some, the informal atmosphere seemed a signal to relax totally, and especially to stop thinking. For others, it seemed the perfect opportunity to socialize, to see their friends and to chat with them" (Loxley & Whiteley, 1986, p. 65). With the great advantage of hindsight, it is probable that is exactly what one should expect Stage 3 adolescents to do—i.e., to stop thinking about what adults wanted them to consider academically and to think about one another, to build social community as they understand it.

Another objective of the staff was to get freshmen to take a more active role in their own education and lives. Loxley shares two very telling anecdotes. One is the comment from a freshman: "If I hear the staff mention the 60s once more, I think I'll throw up" (Loxley & Whiteley, 1986, p. 67). A second reports an exchange. Staff member: "This is your class. You can decide what happens here. Here is your chance to have control over your education" (p. 67). One of the many topics under consideration was attendance policy. After a brief discussion, one student said, "We're wasting time with all this arguing. You decide about attendance. You're the teacher, and that is what you are paid for, isn't it?" (p. 67). The authors report that the opinion received almost unanimous support. And why wouldn't it? The Sierra freshmen were solidly conformist, very *other* directed, still very dependent on influential others for the rules of the game: parents, friends, Irvine professors who lectured, gave notes, tested rigorously and so on. The autonomy espoused by the project must seem, as yet, alien, even frightening, a developmental gain won by the staff, inch by inch or year by year. Whether the freshman could be "given" autonomous choosing by this, or any curriculum, is moot. However, it may be that the Sierra approach provides the next feasible step toward autonomy.

The power of the students' prior academic and competitive socialization to confound the character aims of the project was brought home in other ways as well. The faculty decision was to grade the formal Sierra class on a Pass/No Pass basis. The freshmen, in turn, were displeased. They wanted the opportunity to earn better grades and the chance to get an 'A'. The moral issues seem to have been overlooked, the academic and personal competition, win-lose, being number one, and meritocracy explicit in this trivial, every-day dilemma.

The last module of the fall quarter was "Teaching Empathy and Social Perspective Taking." The aim was to help the Sierra students listen, understand and respond to one another. The theoretical reason for the module was that "an increase in capacity for empathy has been found to have a positive association with an increase in level of moral reasoning (Loxley & Whiteley, 1986, p. 116). Understanding people whose views and values are different can create dissonance, challenge and, thereby, pace growth in one's own thinking. The Sierra Project also valued better communication and understanding as practical ends in themselves with friends and family. Whiteley argued their special relevance for college freshmen, who are frequently self-absorbed and egocentric. Nor was it possible to imagine a Sierra "community" without the presence of such capabilities. Yet Sierra devoted six formal classes only to the development of these capacities. That is somewhat puzzling.

A very systematic, "micro-counseling" way of teaching empathy and communication "skills" was adopted. It included a sophisticated combination of modeling by the principal classroom instructor (herself a clinical psychologist), direct instruction and practice, the use of audio and video tapes in coaching students and so on. The findings of this module are interesting. Sierra students uniformly were unempathetic to one another in their first attempts, yet thought they were doing fine. Such courses have often found the phenomena of advice giving, interrupting, not listening, moralizing, and projecting one's own solutions or difficulties onto the other person. In the staff's view, few students did anything resembling empathy or social perspective taking (at first) although most wanted to be helpful and supportive. In a nutshell, Sierrans (and probably most young people) communicate like ships that pass in the night.

By the end of the module, 90% of the students said their listening skills had improved. What the empirical data are on this point have not yet been presented. But there is evidence from analogous, if longer, courses with high school students that such skills can be taught (Mosher & Sprinthall, 1978). The staff felt less success in persuading the students of Albert Ellis' view that how we think about painful, difficult, or confusing events determines our actual feelings, that we can control, rationally or stoically, our feeling (Ellis, 1977). Obviously, cognition cannot always control or modulate emotion, especially when abstract thinking is still very new or tenuous, experience is limited, and the emotions are very strong, as is often the case in adolescence.

Having been associated with some of the first attempts to teach counseling to adolescents, one or two reflections may be pertinent. The objectives of doing so have changed very little. Counseling psychologists are teaching, "giving away" as part of the general social education of young people, what they as a profession have learned about the subtleties of communicating with people who are confused or in pain. The link between enhancing empathy and moral reasoning is now much clearer. The method of teaching has become far more direct, systematic, indeed behavioral than was the case in the earlier high school peer counseling programs. I think some opportunities to make personal meaning may have been sacrificed to efficiency in teaching skills. Further, whether counseling is a generalizable model of "ideal" human communication merits careful re-examination.

The Sierra students, as quoted by Loxley and Whiteley (1986) in *Character Development in College Students: Volume II*, sound like they desperately need these skills. ("Parent Effectiveness," "Teacher Effectiveness," "Executive Effectiveness" programs, all of which incorporate similar curricula, suggest that adolescent miscommunication foreshadows much adult "deafness" and "dumbness.") Yet many of the Sierra students did not understand or take to the experience. The developmental status of those students who especially benefited as compared to those who did not is worth examining. There is some suggestion that empathy/listening skills training may be especially pertinent for adolescents who are moving from pre-conventional moral reasoning to Stage 3 conventional thinking, but not so for students already there.

Nonetheless empathy, being heard and understood, is a rare and, I believe, precious experience in life. Knowing how and when to offer it (and not to do so) is a human capacity with great power for the general good. Part of wisdom (is that part of character?) is to know what is good and valuable between people and to act accordingly. Eighteen year olds have more excuses than most of us if they do not understand the power and potential of such competencies.

The Benefits of Hindsight

Several general observations about the formal Sierra curriculum may be pertinent to those considering replication efforts. First, the curriculum was developed and taught by a team: a clinical psychologist who served as professor, a counseling psychologist, a resident assistant in Sierra, six sophomore student staff members who lived in the residence hall, and assorted others. In my own experience, a curriculum planned by a committee becomes, to some degree, a conceptual bouillabaisse. But there are countervailing benefits. The Sierra team, for example, underscored a powerful point about character education made by Erikson:

> There is also an age specific ethical capacity in older youth that we should learn to foster. That we, instead, consistently neglect this ethical potential and, in fact, deny it with the moralistic reaction that we traditionally employ toward and against youth (*anti-institutional, hedonistic, desacrilizing*) is probably resented much more by young people than our dutiful attempts to keep them in order by prohibition (Erikson, 1967, p. 870).

Sierra, to its credit, gave slightly older college students a major responsibility in the character education of freshmen. Student staff and the Resident Assistants were front line teachers; living in the residence hall, they interacted as more than peers and less than formal instructors. Had there been a significant number of seniors living as staff in Sierra, this mentoring effect probably would have been even greater. Yet the powerful influence these older students, as people presumably at the next stage of experience, and possibly development, had on the freshmen seems clear. Further is the stimulus to their own character development which being front line teachers may have yielded.

It is also interesting to note what kind of curriculum and teaching emerges when psychologists turn to education to realize their aims. Whiteley acknowledges that teaching character and building a sense of community are not the province of psychology any more than other disciplines. Further, Sierra would have been different if planned and implemented from another disciplinary perspective. That the two principal authors of the Sierra curriculum were counseling/ clinical psychologists, therefore, must be figured in any assessment. Loxley and Whiteley, as professional psychologists, came to their task with less subject matter preoccupation than had they been in ethics, moral philosophy, or the law. Rather, their experience with students' pain and confusion in the adjustment to college probably caused them to see the person as the critical or "hard" factor in higher education, with academic discipline the "soft" factor. (In virtually every other class attended by the Sierrans these priorities most assuredly would be reversed.)

Clearly the authors came to the Sierra Project with values: character, community, the Dewey view that students and their all-around development come first; that an academic response to the non-academic aspects of coming of age to the person becoming the physicist, is as important, or more so, than his/her knowledge of physics. The authors also drew on very diverse forms of "psychological education." A long disquisition on psychological education is not warranted here. Suffice it to say that the reference is to systematic education, including curriculum, teaching and active experiences disjoined to promote broad human competencies: cognition, moral reasoning, personal development, and so on (Mosher & Sprinthall, 1971).

Sierra … gave slightly older college students a major responsibility in the character education of freshmen. "Six members of the student staff and the Resident Assistant were our front line teachers; living in the residence hall, they interacted as more than peers and less than formal instructors."

The Sierra curriculum is the first organized to further character development in college freshmen. The point is that there are first and second generation, initial and more comprehensive curricula. The great value of any generation of curriculum is what may be learned about promoting human competencies more effectively. That is the spirit in which the Foreword to *Character Development in College Students: Volume II*, and this chapter, are written. In the most literal sense, the authors are explorers in an area, the definition and education of character, for which, apart from the teaching of ethics, the preaching of the Bible or the Talmud, the modeling of Mr. Chips, the Peace Corps, or the Marine Corps ROTC, colleges are without answers.

A further reflection comes with the professional territory of the authors and the locale of the college. I might be tempted to make too much of the fact that the project, and its students, had their roots in southern California, with its traditions of encounter groups and a rainbow-like proliferation and popularization of psychologies applied to the human condition. Behavioral psychology (Jacobsonian deep muscle relaxation, Jacobson, 1938); desensitization to test anxiety; non-verbal behavior ("inane topic exercises"); elaborate role-playing (SIMSOC, Gamson 1978a; Gamson, 1978b) all figure prominently in the curriculum.

Sierra used a mind boggling variety of psychological experiences with its students. Yet woven throughout what might uncharitably seem like a Woody Allen satire of "life adjustment at UCI" lies a much older, more conservative concern: by what norms youths will live their personal and social lives, and the concern of the elders for the moral character of the young.

> Sierra used a mind boggling variety of psychological experiences with its students. Yet woven throughout ... lies a much older, more conservative concern: by what norms youths will live their personal and social lives, and the concern of the elders for the moral character of the young.

On Doing What We Say

At the risk of sounding like a broken record, I want to illustrate again how attentive one must be to the opportunities presented by the hidden curriculum in such efforts at character education. Let me cite several examples. Early in the fall quarter, the Sierra students and staff went on a retreat to a conference center in the California mountains. The formal curriculum was to be Module 3: "Conflict Resolution in Society." The aim was to promote understanding of conflict resolution and of society building in general. The unanticipated learnings were potentially rich ones. A first was that several men ducked clean-up and cooking duties. "One student said proudly that his mother had always done everything for him, and that no one had ever expected him to do any kitchen or clean-up work. At this point in the year freshmen chose not to confront each other about issues like this" (Loxley & Whiteley, 1986, p. 108). A second issue was the unfamiliarity and fear that a camping experience provoked in some Sierrans who had never been outside of an urban environment before. "For some, the trees, insects, darkness, cold and somewhat primitive conditions. . .ranged from unpleasant to frightening" (Loxley & Whiteley, 1986, p. 109). These students suggested that, in future, we describe the conditions in detail before the trip. Many of the other students thought this attitude was "stupid."

A third opportunity was the failure of the student staff members to confront Sierrans observed stealing T-shirts and other items from the camp storehouse. The staff members as a group were divided on how to handle this real moral dilemma. The student staff had been afraid to confront freshmen directly because it was the beginning of the school year, they did not yet know them well, they were still unsure of their real roles, and they had concerns that confrontation would bring more conflict than they could handle:

> . . .informing the instructor and asking her to confront the students would be like calling in a parent or "ratting" on the students. As result they did nothing at the time and brought up the issue at the next staff meeting. The instructor believed each individual who had stolen should be confronted directly, asked to discuss the theft and to return the items. Most of the (student) staff disagreed and were unwilling to tell the instructor *who* the students were. (Loxley & Whiteley, 1986, p. 113)

The compromise was a class to present the issue of stealing. And the class was imaginatively done. But the opportunity for the Sierra community to confront a real moral issue in its own life was missed.

As a final illustration of how the hidden curriculum of Sierra worked its will on the formal curriculum, there is the authors' acknowledgment that "most of the community building aspects came from going on a retreat with the group, not from playing a game" (Loxley & Whiteley, 1986, p. 95-96). My point is not that such contradictions between what curriculum planners say and do can be avoided. Rather, they come with the territory. The craft of curriculum development and teaching is increasingly to recognize and capitalize on such contradictions and serendipities. The character of character education is forged in how consistently they are acknowledged and resolved.

A Summary

It should be palpably clear that *Character Development in College Students: Volume II* is a very detailed book about the *practices* of character education in college. The volume is richly replete with curricular and teaching details. Everything the reader might want to know about how character education was conducted at the University of California, Irvine is here. Clearly my attention has been much distracted by the curriculum and really only one-third of the educational practices described. For readers aspiring to replication studies, Loxley and Whiteley (1986) is incredibly valuable, I believe, precisely for the richness of practice which it describes (warts and all).

Levinson (1978), in his *Seasons of a Man's Life*, dismisses the first 18 years as "only a prelude" to adult life. One might add: some prelude! Similarly Levinson looks at the "early adult transition" (the developmental period of Sierra freshmen) through the lens of the whole adult life. He sees the principal tasks facing the young adult man as separating from his family of origin and forging an initial adult life structure, albeit a very tentative one. Levinson, who talked to men in their 40s does not ascribe great importance to this young adult transition. In the long view he implies: Why bother very much about what is happening? It is all to be shaken up, undone, and reconstituted several times over before 40 or 50 anyway. And success is ultimately elusive for us all.

But with Whiteley and his collaborators, I believe there are compelling reasons to act educationally on behalf of character in the college years. Life itself requires major commitments/decisions from young people: academic or other achievement, choice of a "major," vocation, job relationships long before they have had the experience to acquire the wisdom or the moral insight to make such choices sagely. Time and event wait for no man or woman. Nor do the problems Sierra youth face get any easier.

The "Cindy and "Cody" case studies to appear as part of *Portraits in Character* (Lee & Whiteley, in preparation) vividly document the mind warping, existential moral choices facing young people at Irvine. Nor is there any reason to believe these are peculiar to fast lane living in the land of the lotus eaters, southern California. And the protagonists' bewilderment, pain, and inability to bootstrap themselves, to live with integrity either by the old or the newest norms comes through powerfully in these case studies. To remain impassive, relativistic, or unavailable in the face of such anguished young people is itself a failure of character at both the personal and institutional level. That is something, I am sure, which Whiteley and his colleagues were responding to in the Sierra Project.

Conversely, as we have already observed, the souls of these young people are actively sought by many secular gods in the modern university. The idolatry of intellect is but one. The promise of ineluctable individual and human progress for young people if they will only follow science, technology, medicine and so on is another. So, too, corporations outside the university actively solicit brains and "management" skills on behalf of individual financial gain and stockholder profit. ROTC programs openly buy youth for country and war with tax-payers' dollars. Against this secular, ostensibly "value-relative" college environment (which, in my view, is hustling all kinds of character priorities) are arrayed very few voices for deliberation, moral principle, an examination of what is right, just and good. And the voices that are raised are often pitted one against another rather than on behalf of the young (philosophers who won't deign to talk to psychologists or educators; psychologists who insist on unconditional positive regard for every person, no matter how fascistic, racist, or authoritarian their view may be; women developmentalists who argue that women's special moral voice has been denied, and who boycott the forum, and so on).

In a university world, then, in which intellect seems so dominant, so sure; where the personal and social mores seem so fractured and up for grabs; where young people experience so much adult cant, moralizing, hypocrisy, and flat-out seduction; where anguishing moral dilemmas are answered only by secularism, Sierra burns like a beacon in the darkness.

References

Dewey, J. (1897/1968). *Problems of men*. New York: Greenwood Press.

Ellis, A. (1977). Rational-emotive therapy: Research data that support the clinical and personality hypotheses of RET and other models of cognitive-behavior therapy. *The Counseling Psychologist*, 7(1), 2-42.

Erikson, E. (1967). Memorandum on youth. *Daedulus, 96*, 860-870.

Gamson, W. A. (1978a). *SIMSOC simulated society: Instructor's manual*. New York: Free Press.

Gamson, W. A. (1978b). *SIMSOC simulated society: Participants' manual*. New York: Free Press.

Jacobson, E. (1938). *Progressive relaxation.* Chicago: University of Chicago Press.

Lee, L., & Whiteley, J. M. (In preparation). *Portraits in character.*

Levinson, D. J. (1978). *The seasons of a man's life.* New York: Alfred A. Knopf.

Loxley, J. C., & Whiteley, J. M. (1986). *Character development in college students, Volume II: The curriculum and longitudinal results.* Schenectady, NY: Character Research Press.

Mosher, R. L., & Sprinthall, N. A. (1971). Psychological education: A means to promote personal development during adolescence. *The Counseling Psychologist,* 2(4), 3-28.

Vygotskii, L. (1978). *Mind in society.* Cambridge, MA: Harvard University Press.

Whiteley, J. M., & Associates. (1982). *Character development in college students, Vol. I: The freshman year.* Schenectady, NY: Character Research Press.

CHAPTER

CHARACTER DEVELOPMENT OVER FOUR YEARS OF UNDERGRADUATE STUDY

THREE

John M. Whiteley and Norma Yokota

The development of values and ethics during the college years has a venerable tradition in America. From the statements of purpose of the earliest colleges founded in colonial times to the role assigned by society to the multiversities of the 20th Century, there has been an expectation that components of the experiences which students have during the college years would contribute to their personal as well as to their professional development.

From their origins in the 17th Century, American colleges and universities have included in their mission the development of the capacity to think clearly about moral issues and to act accordingly. In the early 1800s ethics and values were part of the core curriculum of those liberal arts colleges with religious traditions (McBee, 1980). This emphasis on morals and ethics occurred in the context of a broader concern for fostering social development—what Rudolph (1962) referred to as an "impressive arsenal of weapons for making men out of boys" (p. 140). During the formative years of U. S. higher education, "the academic curriculum and the entire campus environment clearly viewed the formation of student character as a central mission of the collegiate experience" (Nucci & Pascarella, 1987). This chapter will review the impact of the freshman year and four years of undergraduate study on a central dimension of personal development: the formation of character and its progression from late adolescence to young adulthood.

> From their origins in the 17th century, American colleges and universities have included in their mission the development of the capacity to think clearly about moral issues and to act accordingly.

Historically there have been a number of obstacles in the way of higher education's meeting its responsibility for character development. These have included:

- the lack of definition of higher education's role in meeting this responsibility;

- the lack of attention by institutions of higher education to establishing effective character education programs;

- the lack of agreement on what constitutes character, character development, and character education;

- the absence of controlled studies of long-term psychological interventions designed to promote character;

- the lack of knowledge concerning which experiences have the greatest impact on promoting individual growth in moral reasoning; and

- the relative absence of longitudinal studies of character development in college students.

Each of those obstacles contributed to the general problem of determining *how* to go about developing character through higher education programs. As John Dewey remarked in 1897, "It is commonplace to say that this development of character is the ultimate end of all school work. The difficulty lies in the execution of this idea" (p. 28).

The Sierra Project and the Obstacles to Character Development

A significant portion of the empirical data reported in this chapter is a product of the Sierra Project, a curriculum intervention and longitudinal research study which had its origins at the University of California, Irvine in the early 1970s. The Sierra Project addressed each of the historical obstacles; the remainder of this section will report how this was done, and form the basis for much of this chapter.

The first obstacle, that the nation's colleges and universities have neglected to define their responsibility, was addressed by providing a six-part rationale. The Sierra Project presents a curriculum designed to develop in university students a greater capacity for ethical sensitivity and awareness, an increased regard for equity in human relationships, and the ability to translate this enhanced capacity and regard into a higher standard of fairness and concern for the common good in all realms of their lives. These accomplishments are viewed as ultimately self-rewarding. Their development constitutes a central rationale for the Sierra Project effort at character education. There is, however, a second rationale which is to be found in the benefit to society of citizenry whose lives are characterized by principled thinking and moral maturity. Such individuals will be more responsible citizens, leaders, participants, and parents. Society as a whole is therefore a beneficiary of character education for college students.

Personal growth and psychological maturity are closely related to many dimensions of accomplishment in adulthood. The Sierra Project's approach to character education emphasizes ego development *and* the achievement of a higher level of moral reasoning in order to produce general personal growth and psychological maturity in interpersonal relationships. Therefore, a third rationale for the Sierra Project is in the ultimate benefit to its participants throughout their adult lives in terms of greater potential for accomplishment.

The fourth rationale for the Sierra Project is the impact of moral and psychological education programs on the level of moral reasoning and ego development of junior high school, high school, and college students (Erickson & Whiteley, 1980; Mosher, 1979; Mosher & Sprinthall, 1971; Rest, 1979a; Scharf, 1978; Whiteley & Bertin, 1982).

The evidence is conclusive that properly sequenced educational and psychological experiences raise the level of moral reasoning and ego development of adolescents and young adults. This research is extraordinarily hopeful in its implications: For society, education can make a difference in the moral reasoning of the citizenry.

Inquiry into devising curricula for character education, however, is in its infancy. Research has just begun on the crucial problem of determining the optimal match between the developmental level of students and the sequencing of educational experiences. Nonetheless, the legacy of the past decade is one of documenting the extraordinary potential of our educational institutions for positively impacting the character of students.

The fifth rationale for the Sierra Project is the nature of the challenges addressed during the four years of undergraduate education. For perhaps the first time in their lives, college students are physically and psychologically autonomous from those who have previously been highly influential in their lives: parents and siblings, school-age chums, and high school teachers and friends. Since the vast majority of beginning college students reason in a highly conventional manner, their moral referents are those people immediately around them. It is to significant others and to the peer group that college students look for guidance in formulating their thinking about ethical issues. Homogeneity of influence predominated in high school. The typical college environment, however, contains the opportunity for exposure to, and intellectual confrontation with, diversity in beliefs, lifestyles, and personality types. This is especially the case where there is a coed, multicultural, and mixed socioeconomic population, as in the Sierra Project.

> The evidence is conclusive that properly sequenced educational and psychological experiences raise the level of moral reasoning and ego development of adolescents and young adults.

A further reason why the college years forcefully impact moral reasoning is the challenge of the growth tasks of late adolescence and early adulthood: securing identity, seeking intimacy, choosing enduring values, and initiating career and educational explorations of crucial significance. Each of these tasks contains the seeds of significant moral dilemmas. Their satisfactory resolution involves thoughtful moral choices. The extraordinary opportunity provided by the college years for impacting moral reasoning, therefore, is a fifth rationale for character education in the university.

A sixth rationale for the Sierra Project is a declarative statement about a central purpose of higher education, and about what should be provided as an educational challenge to the men and women of all ages who spend a vitally important segment of their lives studying and learning in colleges and universities. An experience in higher education should provide an opportunity to reflect on the purposes of learning, on the uses to which acquired knowledge is put, and on the ethical dilemmas which confront citizens individually and as members of society collectively.

This is a viewpoint which considers an essential goal of a college education to be the cultivation of a capacity for reflection about, and analysis of, issues in society both of a personal and a political nature. While consistent with purposes of a college education as preparation for life and career, and as a time for personal development, this sixth rationale stresses the importance of achieving a capability for integrating these two aspects of experience during the college years. It is a statement that the opportunity to focus on the *process* of learning, to think carefully about questions of values and valuing, is vital to a well-rounded college student. All too often such an opportunity is insufficiently a part of the usual experience at college and university.

That distinguished philosopher of higher education and the American scene, *Doonesbury*, presented a very similar rationale in one of the commencement address vignettes which Gary Trudeau has written on various occasions. In addressing the assembled graduates, the commencement speaker commented with concern upon the students' "obsessive concern for the future," an approach which has been "the salient shaping influence of your attitudes during a very critical four years. . ." He then went on to state eloquently our sixth rationale: "It could have been more than that. This college offered you a sanctuary, a place to experience PROCESS, to FEEL the present as you moved through it, to EMBRACE both the joys and sorrows of moral and intellectual maturation! It needn't have been just another way-station. . ." (Trudeau, 1972).

In summary, there is a six-part rationale for promoting the character development of college students:

1. For individuals, it is ultimately self-rewarding to have a greater capacity for ethical sensitivity and regard for equity in human relations.

2. Society benefits from citizens whose lives are characterized by principled thinking and moral maturity.

3. For individuals, the development of increased psychological maturity leads to greater accomplishment in adulthood.

4. Research has shown that educational experiences can raise the level of moral reasoning.

5. Experiences during the college years provide many opportunities for impacting moral reasoning.

6. Higher education should provide students with an opportunity for reflection on knowledge, values, and moral choices.

The second obstacle—that colleges and universities have not devoted much time and effort to actual character development activities—was approached by surveying relevant psychological literature identifying promising theoretical constructs on which to base an intervention and reviewing the literature that does exist on character development methodology and practice (Whiteley & Associates, 1982).

The third obstacle—the lack of agreement on what constitutes character, character development, and character education—was addressed by reviewing the use of these terms historically and currently, defining them conceptually, and then defining them empirically by three proximate measures of character: moral maturity, principled thinking, and ego development. The definitions selected are as follows:

Character, as we have defined it conceptually, has two parts. The first part refers to an *understanding* of what is the right, fair, or good thing to do in a given circumstance. The second part refers to the *ability* to do those things (the courage to act in accordance with one's understanding of what is right, fair, and good). Thus, *character* constitutes understanding what is right and acting on what is right.

Character Development, as we have conceptually defined it, refers to the progression of an individual's capacity for *understanding* what is right or good in increasingly complex forms, and the willingness or courage to *act* on those conceptions. Our emphasis is on understanding the internal (intrapsychic) progression within a maturing individual through his/her interaction with others and the environment.

Character Education refers to the planned and unplanned experiences which promote the development of *character* in individuals. Within the Sierra Project, the planned portions of the *character education* intervention are the classroom experiences provided by the curriculum modules. The unplanned portions of this *character education* are student interactions with the rest of the educational institution, other institutions of society, family and, particularly, friends and peers.

Principled Thinking is a measure of moral reasoning which refers to the degree to which individuals use principled moral considerations in making moral decisions. Principled thinking is measured by the Defining Issues Test (DIT), a paper-and-pencil test exploring level of moral reasoning developed by James Rest and associates (Rest, 1979a).

Moral Maturity is a measure of moral reasoning which refers to the responses which individuals give to issues raised by a series of moral problems. Moral maturity is measured by the Moral Judgment Interview (MJI), a structured individual interaction between tester and subject in which the subjects are encouraged to clarify the reasons for their particular responses (Colby, Gibbs, Kohlberg, Speicher-Dubin, & Candee, 1979).

Ego Development is a measure tapping broad dimensions of the interwoven relationship of impulse control, character, interpersonal relations, conscious preoccupations, and cognitive complexity. Ego development is measured by the Washington University Sentence Completion Test (SCT), a written measure yielding a placement of each subject at one of a series of impressionistic discrete stages of ego development (Loevinger, 1966, 1976; Loevinger & Wessler, 1970).

The fourth obstacle, the absence of controlled studies involving long-term interventions designed to promote character, was approached in two ways. The first approach was to design and implement an educational and psychological intervention extending throughout the freshman year. Participants, consisting of 44 freshmen (22 men and 22 women whose ethnicity was fairly equally divided between Asians, Anglos, Blacks, and Hispanics), lived in Sierra Hall. They enrolled in a four-unit class (a normal load is 16 units) each of the three academic quarters. The curriculum for the year was divided into 10 modules:

Module 1   *Survival Skills*: What freshmen need to know that most seniors already do: how to organize their time, how to study effectively, and how to prepare for and take examinations.

Module 2   *Community Building*: Helping students work together to create an atmosphere of openness, trust, and group support in an environment characterized by conflict resolution through democratic decision making. This is not an entirely self-contained module; often the *content* of the class fell into another module, but the *process* was designed to enhance the building of community. This module includes student-planned classes.

Module 3   *Conflict Resolution in Society*: Includes participation in SIMSOC (Gamson, 1972a; 1972b; 1978a; 1978b), a commercially available simulation game in which students are given vaguely structured roles and allowed to form their own society. In the implementation of SIMSOC in Sierra Hall, emphasis is placed on survival issues, personal goals, problems of power and authority, and what type of society provides the most good for the most people. Principles of fairness and justice as well as conflict resolution skills are involved throughout the game.

Module 4   *Empathy and Social Perspective-Taking*: Basic listening and communication skills for the development of empathy—defined as the ability to understand the point of view of another—and of the ability to communicate that understanding.

Module 5   *Socialization*: What are people like now? How did they come to be that way? Values and life styles were examined as salient factors and pressures in the socialization process.

Module 6   *Sex-Role Choices*: How socialization by gender affects current values, behaviors, and interests.

Module 7   *Race Roles*: How race relates to socialization. Examines stereotyping, racial values and attitudes, and cross-cultural relationships.

Module 8   *Assertion Training*: Enhances relationships by helping students learn to identify the personal rights involved in a conflict situation and to resolve that situation, assuring their own legitimate rights without violating those of others.

Module 9   *Life and Career Planning*: Students explore decision making. This module helps students in the decision-making process by exposing them to a variety of life and career options.

Module 10   *Community Service*: Provides the opportunity for students to work with people with real problems in a naturalistic setting, allowing them to apply the skills they have been learning in Sierra in a community setting. This module allows the students to have positive contact with agencies outside the university community while still receiving support from the campus (this module was optional and was in addition to the regular class).

The second approach to the fourth obstacle was to evaluate the character development of college freshmen using multiple sources of data with an experimental group (Sierra Hall residents) and two control groups. This approach involved studying college freshmen in the context of an intensive year-long residential program, focusing on their development of the three empirical dimensions of character: principled thinking, moral maturity, and ego development.

The fifth obstacle, the lack of knowledge concerning those collegiate experiences which best promote individual growth in moral reasoning, was approached by conducting a series of research investigations ranging from intensive interviewing during the freshman year (Resnikoff & Jennings, 1982) to collecting student retrospective reports (Bertin, Ferrant, Whiteley, & Yokota, 1985; Burris, 1982; Lee & Whiteley, in preparation).

The approach to the sixth and final obstacle, the absence of longitudinal studies concerning growth in college students on dimensions of character, was to establish and conduct such a longitudinal study. Freshmen were tested and interviewed at the start of their freshman year, at the end of their freshman year, and at the end of their sophomore, junior, and senior years.

The Growth of Character During the Freshman Year

A consideration of the growth of character during the freshman year may be made in the context of what is known about the growth of character in general. There has been extensive research on the character measures of moral reasoning: moral maturity and principled thinking. In the 20 years that extensive research has been possible methodologically on the correlates of development in moral reasoning, the strongest relationship has been years of formal education.

The two studies of this phenomena merit special attention, as they are the definitive research reports using the different instruments for assessing moral judgment. Lawrence Kohlberg and associates (Colby, Kohlberg, Gibbs, & Lieberman, 1983) reported on their longitudinal data with the Moral Judgment Inventory (MJI). They found correlates of moral judgment development with formal education to range between .53 and .60.

Rest and his associates, using the Defining Issues Test (DIT) measure of moral judgment, came to a similar conclusion with different data. In a 1979 study (Rest, 1979b), a secondary analysis of demographic correlates found that education was the strongest correlate. Rest and Deemer (1986) extended this analysis and reported a ten-year longitudinal study of DIT scores over four testings (covering the period 1972 through 1983). They grouped educational accomplishment into three groupings (as illustrated in Figure 1): a high level of education since high school, a moderate level of education since high school, and those with a low amount of post-high school education.

Those subjects with a high level of post-high school education continued to increase over time. Those subjects in the middle classification increased some as a group,

In the 20 years that extensive research has been possible methodologically on the correlates of development in moral reasoning, the strongest relationship has been years of formal education.

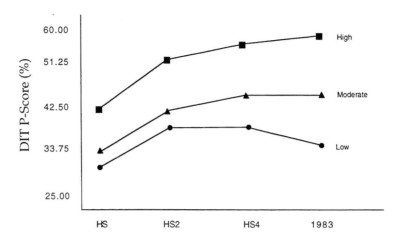

Figure 1. Longitudinal mean DIT by education (from Rest and Deemer, 1986).

then leveled off. Those subjects in the lowest grouping of post-high school education increased in level of moral reasoning for the two years immediately following high school, then actually decreased. Rest and Deemer (1986) concluded that whether an individual continues in schooling seems to determine his general course of development after high school.

Two figures adapted from research reports by Rest (1979b) further illustrate this linkage of education and increased levels of moral reasoning. Inspection of both Figures 2 and 3 reveals a direct relationship between years of formal education and increased scores on the DIT measure of principled thinking. In Figure 2, for example, junior high school students had an average score of 21.9, high school students had an average score of 31.8, college students had an average score of 42.3, and graduate students had an average score of 53.3. In Figure 3, this relationship of education and level of principled reasoning is further refined with the addition of categories within graduate study at the higher end of the spectrum, and at the lower end of the spectrum with such groups as institutionalized delinquents (18.9) and adults who did not continue their formal education beyond high school (28.2).

The legacy of two decades of research on the moral reasoning component of character is the important finding that level of moral reasoning is directly linked to education. For educators, the discovery of this linkage is of profound importance. Schools and colleges can now assert with empirical support that educational experiences can raise the level of moral reasoning. For those who value character development as a significant aim of education, there is now evidence from two different approaches to measurement of the effectiveness of education in achieving this aim.

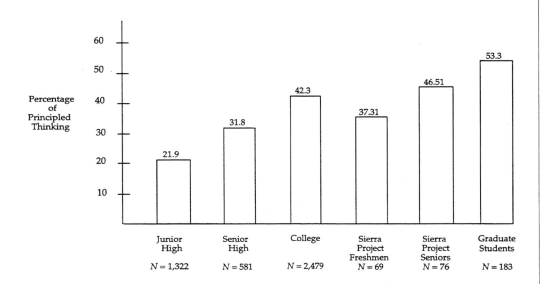

Figure 2. Comparison of Sierra Project students with national norms on principled thinking —combined groups. (Adapted from Rest, 1979a, Table 5.2)

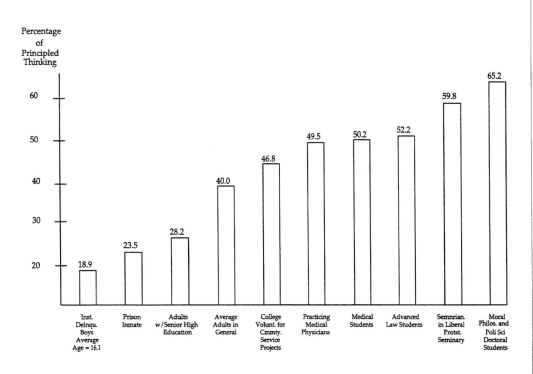

Figure 3. National norms on principled thinking for selected groups. (Adapted from Rest 1979a)

The Growth of Character During the Freshman Year: Sierra Project Results

The research design of the Sierra Project addressed the following question for the character measure of principled thinking: *Are there changes during the freshman year which are common to all of the groups sampled?*

Analysis of variance is the statistical method utilized to distinguish differences among groups of scores when there is more than one factor involved (i.e., sex, class, group); it estimates the amount of variance attributable to each of these factors and their interaction, including a built-in error variance factor. The Repeated Measures Analysis of Variance (RMAV), as described by Jenrich and Sampson (1979), was performed in order to determine the effects of time (pre versus posttesting), sex, cohort group, and treatment condition—as well as to identify any interactions among these factors. A RMAV further examines the differences in scores from multiple testings (e.g., pretest and posttest). Statistical tests indicated that our data met requirements of the RMAV to appropriately apply and interpret its methods.

We chose the following basic categories to use in analysis:

Class: Differences among the classes of 1980, 1981, and 1982, (i. e., cohort differences).

Sex: Differences between scores for male and female subjects.

Change over time: Changes occurring during the freshman year as assessed by the interval between pretest and posttest.

Group: Differences among the three populations of our project: Sierra (Experimental Group), Control Group I (Lago), and Control Group II (Random Control).

Notions such as Class x Sex or Change over time x Sex refer to the interaction between those categories. The findings from administering the Defining Issues Test measure of principled thinking to freshmen in the classes of 1980, 1981, and 1982 are reported in Table 1. Inspection of Table 1 reveals that freshman students as a group made a large and statistically significant gain ($p<.0001$) in moral reasoning over the course of their first year of college study when the measure focused on their percentage of principled thinking. This gain was characteristic of all three classes studied. Sex of students did not influence the degree of change over the freshman year, even in the case of women in the Class of 1981, who entered the university scoring at a comparatively very high level. There were significant differences among the cohort groups in the percentage of their responses which were based on principled moral reasoning, with men and women in the Class of 1981 both entering and leaving at a level higher than that of the other two classes ($p <.0003$).

The Growth in Character Which Occurred Over Four Years of Undergraduate Study: The Sierra Project Results

A similar pattern of change over four years of undergraduate study was found when freshmen were followed over all four years and retested at the end of their senior year. The longitudinal data on character which is available to address the question of changes in character development over four years of undergraduate study,

Table 1

Mean Test Scores and Repeated Measures Analysis of Variance Results for The Defining Issues Test Measure Of Moral Reasoning for Freshmen in the Classes of 1980, 1981, and 1982.

	n^1	Mean Pretest Scores	Mean Posttest Scores
Class of 1980			
all males[2]	34	34.43	41.56
all females	35	30.97	38.82
Class of 1981			
all males	11	46.18	50.73
all females	34	45.29	45.21
Class of 1982			
all males	33	34.95	39.30
all females	40	41.83	43.21
All Groups X	187	38.12	42.20

Repeated Measures Analysis of Variance

	Degrees of Freedom	F Value	Significance
Class	2	8.39	.0003
Sex	1	.02	ns[3]
Class x Sex	2	2.66	.0728
Change over Time	1	15.88	.0001
Change over Time x Class	2	2.87	.0592(ns)
Change over Time x Sex	1	1.19	ns
Change over Time x Class x Sex	2	.59	ns

[1]n's are smaller than reported elsewhere because the repeated measures analysis of variance requires that complete data (all testing times) be available for all subjects used; hence, subjects on whom we have incomplete data are not used in this analysis.
[2]For this analysis, males and females from all groups are combined.
[3]ns=not significant at the .05 level of confidence.

consists of two measures on the Sierra Experimental Group only (moral maturity and ego development), and one measure (principled thinking) on the entire population (the Sierra Experimental Group and two control groups).

Change in Moral Maturity of the Sierra Experimental Group Occurring during the Four Years of Undergraduate Study (No Control Group)

Table 2 reports the mean test scores and the repeated measures analysis of variance results for the Moral Judgment Interview (measure of moral maturity) for the Sierra Hall Classes of 1980, 1981, and 1982 comparing their mean freshman year pretest with their mean senior year posttest scores. Inspection of Table 2 reveals that there were no significant class (cohorts of 1980, 1981, and 1982) or gender differences.

Table 2
Mean Test Scores and Repeated Measures Analysis of Variance Results for the Moral Judgement Interview Measure of Moral Reasoning for the Sierra Hall Classes of 1980, 1981, and 1982 Comparing Their Mean Freshman Pretest With Their Mean Senior Posttest Scores. (No Controls)

	n	Sierra Mean Freshman Pretest Scores	Sierra Mean Senior Posttest Scores
Sierra Class of 1980			
males	12	313.25	347.67
females	11	264.91	315.00
Sierra Class of 1981			
males	11	244.09	348.45
females	17	285.24	307.82
Sierra Class of 1982			
males	10	292.30	337.85
females	14	296.71	320.86
All Sierra Males	33	282.85	344.85
All Sierra Females	42	283.74	314.05
Both Sex Combined	75	283.79	327.60

Repeated Measures Analysis of Variance

	Degrees of Freedom	F Value	Significance
Year	2	1.40	ns
Sex	1	3.32	.07(ns)
Year x Sex	2	2.20	ns
Change over Time	1	65.89	.00
Change over Time x Year	2	2.34	ns
Change over Time x Sex	1	6.35	.01
Change over Time x Year x Sex	2	6.27	003

There were statistically significant ($p<.001$) changes for Sierra participants as a group. The freshman pretest sample had a combined mean of 283.79 and the senior posttest sample had a combined mean of 327.60. While this was a statistically significant finding, it is of only modest theoretical importance: A change of only 40% of a stage over four years of undergraduate study is not very large. Further, the sample as a whole was finishing the transition from Stage 2 to Stage 3 at the start of their freshman year. At the end of their senior year, they were still solidly rooted in the initial portion of Stage 3: basic conventionality.

Change in Ego Development of the Sierra Experimental Group Occurring during the Four Years of Undergraduate Study (No Control Groups)

The mean test scores on ego development from the fall of the freshman year and the spring of the senior year, along with a repeated measures analysis of variance for Sierra residents, combined for all three years, is reported in Table 3.

Table 3
Mean Test Scores and Repeated Measures Analysis of Variance Results for the Washington University Sentence Completion Test for Measuring Ego Development for the Sierra Classes of 1980, 1981, and 1982 Comparing Their Mean Freshman Pretest Scores With Their Mean Senior Posttest Scores. (No Controls)

	n	Sierra Mean Freshman Pretest Score	Sierra Mean Senior Posttest Scores
Sierra Class of 1980			
males	12	4.67	4.92
females	12	4.67	5.00
Sierra Class of 1981			
males	9	3.89	4.67
females	18	5.33	5.39
Sierra Class of 1982			
males	9	4.33	4.89
females	12	4.25	4.92
All Sierra Males	30	4.33	4.84
All Sierra Females	42	4.83	5.14
Both Sex Combines	72	4.62	5.01

Repeated Measures Analysis of Variance

	Degrees of Freedom	F Value	Significance
Year	2	.47	ns
Sex	1	3.13	.081(ns)
Year x Sex	2	3.09	.05
Change over Time	1	9.64	.002
Change over Time x Year	2	.42	ns
Change over Time x Sex	1	.39	ns
Change over Time x Year x Sex	2	.96	ns

Key to Loevinger Scores:
1 = I-2	3 = Δ-3	5 = I=3/4	7 =I-4/5	9 = I=5/6
2 = Δ	4 =I -3	6 = I-4	8 = I-5	10 = I-6

Inspection of Table 3 reveals that there were no significant class (cohorts of 1980, 1981, and 1982) or gender differences overall. There were some gender differences which reach statistical significance in some years.

There was a statistically significant change ($p<.002$) when the three cohorts were combined. The freshman pretest sample had a combined mean of 4.62 (4.0 is the I-3 Conformist Stage and 5.0 is the I-3/4 transitional Conscientious/Conformist, Self-aware Stage). The senior year posttest score was a combined mean of 5.01 (I-3/4). While statistically significant, this was not a very important area of psychological growth over a four-year span. Based on this data, reflecting change in a relatively homogeneous sample of highly conventional college students who as freshmen had participated in a freshman year curriculum, the college years do not appear to be a time of fundamental progression in ego development.

Change in Principled Thinking which Occurred During the Four Years of Undergraduate Study

The mean test scores on principled thinking from the fall of the freshman year and the spring of the senior year, along with a repeated measure analysis of variance for Sierra residents and Control Group I, combined for all three years, is reported in Table 4. Inspection of Table 4 reveals that there were no significant class (cohorts of 1980, 1981, 1982) or gender (sex) differences in the growth of principled thinking over four years of undergraduate study. However, there were statistically highly significant ($p<.00001$) changes for the entire sample (both sexes combined for all classes). The freshman pretest sample had a combined mean of 36.94 in comparison with the senior posttest sample which had a combined mean of 48.14.

In addition to being a difference of major statistical significance, a change of 12 points on percentage of principled thinking is a finding of major theoretical and practical importance. It is a finding of theoretical importance because of the magnitude of the change during the college years. The college years have been determined to be a period of major growth in moral reasoning when moral reasoning is empirically defined as principled thinking. It is a finding of practical importance to college educators: They are working with a portion of the general population which is making major changes on a significant dimension of the human condition—namely, growth on a dimension of character.

Differential Effects of a Character Education Curriculum Over The Freshman Year: The Sierra Project Results

The research design of the Sierra Project allowed the assessment of the differential effects of the curriculum on the character dimension of principled thinking by the contrast of the differential change between the Sierra Experimental Group and the two control groups. It also allowed the reporting of the pre- and posttest scores for the Sierra Experimental Group on the character dimensions of moral maturity and ego development.

In analyzing group differences between pretest scores and posttest scores, we chose to adjust for initial differences among the groups. We chose this statistical technique because our goal was to understand differences among the three groups in *patterns of change* evidenced over the course of the freshman year, not to assess their *initial* differences or the final result. If we simply examined the

Table 4
Mean Test Scores and Repeated Measures Analysis of Variance Results for the Defining Issues Test Measure of Moral Reasoning for Sierra And Control Group I for the Classes of 1980, 1981, and 1982 Comparing Their Combined Freshman Pretest Scores with Their Senior Posttest Scores.

	n	Mean Freshman Pretest Scores	Mean Senior Posttest Scores
Class of 1980			
all males	16	34.59	42.09
all females	21	34.03	49.51
Class of 1981			
all males	10	34.40	51.70
all females	20	44.25	53.50
Class of 1982			
all males	14	34.52	42.34
all females	14	37.57	48.58
All Groups	95	36.94	48.14

Repeated Measures Analysis of Variance

	Degrees of Freedom	*F* Value	Significance
Class	2	1.68	ns
Sex	1	2.18	.097(ns)
Class x Sex	2	.07	ns
Change over Time	1	46.79	.0000
Change over Time x Class	2	.46	ns
Change over Time x Sex	1	.08	ns
Change over Time x Class x Sex	2	2.06	ns

Note: The mean scores for the collateral control group (Control group II) are as follows:

	n	Mean Freshman Pretest Scores	*n*	Mean Senior Posttest Scores
Class of 1980				
males	20	32.90	11	44.81
females	13	44.39	15	42.45
Class of 1981				
males	11	38.09	8	36.66
females	15	48.13	8	47.91

difference between pretest and posttest scores, our analysis would be affected by regression towards the mean. If we examined only the posttest scores of the three groups, our analysis would not be responsive to initial differences among the groups.

In order to examine differences in change from pre- to posttesting related to treatment condition, we employed the analysis of covariance, using the pre- to posttest gain score as the dependent variable and the pretest score as the covariate (Hendrix, Carter, and Hintze, 1973, p. 101). This method of analysis allows us to examine differences in degree of change among the three treatment groups while controlling for initial differences among groups. We need this technique to compare three groups at two test administrations so as to distinguish the variance accounted for by variations in treatment.

Principled Thinking

With respect to group differences in moral reasoning (as reflected by percentage of principled thinking), Table 5 reveals that Sierra residents in the Class of 1980 experienced a major increase in moral reasoning (a mean adjusted gain score of 11.9224). This is in contrast to increases of 3.0458 for Control Group I (Lago) and 4.9085 for Control Group II (Random Control). When the analysis of covariance was performed, the differences among adjusted gain scores approached significance ($p<.0596$). For the Class of 1981, the differences among the three groups on moral reasoning were more pronounced, reaching statistical significance ($p<.0009$) largely because Control Group II scores declined sharply, with a loss of 6.4511. In the case of the Class of 1982, scores for all three groups increased, with no significant differences among them.

Table 5
Analysis of Covariance Using Adjusted Gain Scores for Each Year on Moral Reasoning for Freshmen in the Classes of 1980, 1981, and 1982 Comparing Sierra, Control Group I, and Control Group II.

	Moral Reasoning (DIT)	Experimental Group (Sierra)	Control Group I (Lago)	Control Group II F Value	Significance
Class of 1980	11.9224	3.0458	4.9085	2.9456	ns(.0596)
Class of 1981	2.8989	6.8531	-6.4511	8.3459	.0009
Class of 1982	2.9597	1.8065	3.7244	.1852	ns

Since the analysis of covariance for the adjusted gain scores showed a significant difference for the Class of 1981 ($p<.0009$), it was permissible to employ a post hoc analysis to identify the location of that difference. The results of this analysis are presented in Table 6.

The post hoc analysis revealed that both Sierra and Control Group I scores differed from those of Control Group II for the Class of 1981 ($p<.01$ for each). Control Group II declined in percentage of principled thinking, registering an adjusted gain score of -6.4511, while Sierra and Control Group I (Lago) increased, registering adjusted gain scores of +2.8989 for Sierra and +6.8531 for Control Group I.

Table 6

Differences in Moral Reasoning Using Covariance Analysis of Adjusted Gain Scores, and Planned Contrast and Post Hoc Analysis for the Defining Issues Test Measure of Moral Reasoning for Freshmen in the Classes of 1980, 1981, and 1982 Comparing the Sierra, Lago (Control Group I), and Control Group II.

Adjusted Gain Scores

Class	Sierra	(Lago)	Control Group II	F Value	Significance
1980	11.9224	3.0458	4.9085	2.9456	.0596 (ns)
1981[1]	2.8989	6.8531	-6.4511	8.3459	.0009*
1982	2.9597	1.8065	3.7244	.1852	ns

Planned Contrasts *t*-test

Class	Contrast	t value	t probability
1980	Sierra vs. Lago & Control II	2.3634	.0211
	Lago vs. Control II	.4129	ns
1981	Sierra vs. Lago & Control II	1.0399	ns
	Lago vs. Control II	3.8984	.0004
1982	Sierra vs. Lago & Control II	.0805	ns
	Lago vs. Control II	.5669	ns

*Post Hoc Analysis (For Class of 1981)

Contrasted Groups	Degrees of Freedom	F Value	Significance
Sierra vs. Lago	59	1.0329	ns
Sierra vs. Control II	59	6.4657	.01
Lago vs. Control II	59	12.7259	.01

[1]The Class of 1981 met the requirements for post hoc analysis; no other group met the requirements.

Another way to explore the differential changes in principled thinking among Sierra and the control groups is to compare the amount of growth in moral reasoning for all years combined. This analysis is presented in Table 7.

A review of Table 7 reveals that there were differences in the amount of change among the groups. Combining all Sierra classes, we find an adjusted gain score of change of +6.2662 in percent of principled thinking. The corresponding increases in principled thinking were +3.1606 for Control Group I and +1.2887 for Control Group II. This difference was statistically significant ($p<.05$). The planned comparison of the Sierra group to the combined control groups revealed that the group which received the experimental treatment (Sierra) was found to differ significantly from the aggregated control treatments ($p<.0188$).

In terms of our overall evaluation of the psychological intervention provided through the Sierra Project, this is an extremely important finding. Principled thinking was the only measure of character (the others being moral maturity and ego

Table 7
Adjusted Gain Score Analysis of Covariance of Percent of Principled Thinking from the Defining Issues Test Comparing All Sierra Classes of 1980, 1981, and 1982 with all Control Group I (Lago) Subjects from 1980, 1981, and 1982 with all Control Group II (Random Control) Subjects from the Classes of 1980, 1981, and 1982 Followed by Planned Comparison t-Test Contrasts of Sierra (Experimental Group) Versus All Control Groups (Control Group I and Control Group II) and Control Group I Versus Control Group II

	Principled Thinking Adjusted Gain Score Analysis of Covariance		
	Sierra (all classes combined) $n = 83$	Control Group I (all classes combined) $n = 58$	Control Group II (all classes combined) $n = 46$
Adjusted Gain Score F value -3.0080 Degrees of freedom = 2 $p < .05$	+6.2662	+3.1606	+1.2887

Planned Comparison Contrast *t*-Test		
Sierra versus all Control Groups	$t = 2.3720$	$p = <.0188$
Control Group I (Lago) versus Control Group II (Random Control)	$t = .8236$	$p = ns$

development) which we were able to collect on the entire sample: the two control groups as well as the Sierra group. On this measure, Sierra residents exhibited greater change toward a higher level of moral reasoning than students in both control groups. The differences were moderate in size, one class (the Class of 1980) accounting for a large proportion of the positive change in Sierra scores. The conclusion we draw, however, is that the Sierra curriculum can make a moderate contribution toward furthering character development in college freshmen during a year in their lives which would normally include a small but persistent gain in level of moral reasoning.

Ego Development

Except with the Class of 1981, it was not possible for us to measure the ego development of the control groups. Table 8 provides the analysis of the data collected on the Class of 1981, comparing Sierra and Control Group II. Examining Table 8 we see that the initial level of ego development was significantly lower in the Sierra group than in Control Group II for the Class of 1981 (p<.05). However, the Sierra group had greater growth between fall and spring testing (p<.0019). Sex and the interaction of sex and group were also found to exert effects on student change (p<.0141 and p<.0026 respectively). Sierra men from the Class of 1981 increased in ego level (from I-3 to I-3/4) while Sierra women and students of both sexes in Control Group II declined slightly.

Table 8

Mean Test Scores and Repeated Measures Analysis of Variance for the Washington University Sentence Completion Test for Measuring Ego Development for the Classes of 1981 Comparing Sierra and Control Group II.

	n^1	Mean Pretest Scores	Mean Posttest Scores
Class of 1981			
Sierra Males	16	4.19^2	5.13
Control Males	13	5.31	5.00
Sierra Females	18	5.06	4.89
Control Females	16	5.38	5.19

Repeated Measures Analysis of Variance

	Degrees of Freedom	F Value	Significance
Group	1	4.23	.0442
Sex	1	1.28	ns^3
Group x Sex	1	.23	ns
Change over Time	1	.50	ns
Change over Time x Group	1	10.60	.0019
Change over Time x Sex	1	6.40	.0141
Change over Time x Group x Sex	1	9.92	.0026

[1]n's are smaller than reported elsewhere because the repeated-measures analysis of variance requires that complete data (all testing times) be available for all subjects used; hence, subjects on whom we have incomplete data are not used in this analysis.

[2]Key to Loevinger Scores:

1 = I-2	3 = Δ-3	5 = I-3/4	7 =I-4/5	9 = I-5/6
2 = Δ	4 =I -3	6 = I-4	8 = I-5	10 = I-6

[3]ns=not significant at the .05 level of confidence

Central Implications of the Sierra Project for the Freshman Year and Undergraduate Education

The freshman year has been found to be a period of moderate growth in the level of the principled thinking dimension of character. This growth occurred in freshmen who had a high expectation for the sense of community which they would experience at college. Uniformly, this high level of expectation was met with a lessened perceived reality of community. The reasons they stated for this situation were clear and unambiguous:

- The intense competition from peers

- The psychological distance from faculty and staff

- The perceived low level of community which existed on the UCI campus

Residents of Sierra Hall reported *less* of a gap between what they expected and what they actually received. Given the emphasis the Sierra staff placed on developing a high level of community, the gap students reported between the myth of community in higher education and the perceived reality of lack of community is noteworthy.

Of the three sources of disappointment students reported on the community issue, one was especially specific to Irvine at the time of intervention. There was no University Center (Student Union), the average commuter student traveled 11 miles each way to the university, and only 30% of the student body was housed on campus. Students with similar interests and enthusiasms had a hard time getting together. (This situation has been improved subsequently with the opening of the University Center with its many and diverse gathering places, activities and programs.) The other two sources of disappointment, however, are not at all specific to the Irvine campus of the University of California: intense competition from peers, and psychological distance from faculty and staff.

The residents of Sierra Hall reported they had experienced a higher level of community than did their peers in other living arrangements without the curriculum. For theoretical reasons previously reviewed in Whiteley and Associates (1982), the creation of a sense of community was viewed as a vital contributor to raising the level of moral reasoning. The basic notion is that it is possible to challenge students much more intensely when that challenge occurs within the context of an environment which is personally supportive and which is characterized by a psychological sense of community. The lineage of such a notion is Nevitt Sanford's (1956, 1962) pioneering work on student development in higher education.

The Sierra research design did not permit differential attribution of effects by components of the curriculum. Our impressions, however, substantiated by student retrospective reports, are that the psychological sense of community was an important contributor to the most significant empirical finding to emerge from the freshman year curriculum intervention; namely, that the Sierra experimental group which experienced the curriculum increased on principled thinking twice as much as did the two control groups. This moderate differential change attributable to the curriculum occurred in the context of freshmen as a group making small but persistent positive change in their scores on the principled thinking measure of moral reasoning.

Finally, as reported in the student retrospective (Bertin, Ferrant, Whiteley, & Yokota, 1985), the freshman year *itself* turned out to be a positive catalyst for change. The psychological distance from previous support groups including parents and high school chums, the opportunity for making important decisions, the consequences of increased personal autonomy from all authority, and the immersion in a new multicultural, coed educational culture all combined to create a catalyst for personal change in the crucible of the freshman year.

Undergraduate Education. The college years have been found to be a period of significant growth in the principled thinking dimension of character development. This growth was found to be both statistically significant and psychologically important: 12 points of change on principled thinking from 36% to 48% is major by any yardstick.

There is perhaps no period in young people's lives when they are more open to new experiences *and* alternative ways of thinking about those experiences. In retrospective interviews, in detailed case studies, and in the context of regular interviewing throughout an academic year, students were nearly unanimous in reporting that they would not be who they had become if it were not for the college experience, especially on dimensions of thinking about moral issues. They did make one important qualifier: They had not *changed* as much as they had *developed*.

As we struggled to understand their meaning in using development in contrast to change, it seemed to us that they were expressing that the core of who they were had remained the same. It was their appreciation of the world of moral choices and their stance in relation to those choices which had become more acute and sensitive, and this was appropriately considered by them to be development.

Irrespective of the meaning attributed to their characterization of the subjective experience of change during four years of college, and the context in which they understand that change to have occurred, the empirical measures confirm the magnitude of what occurred, at least on the principled thinking dimension of character.

It proved possible in the Sierra Project to stimulate the personal psychological development of college students *within* a framework of rigorous academic accomplishment. The elective course structure of a publicly assisted research university allowed Sierra students to earn four units of graduation credit (in contrast to departmental credit toward an academic major) each of the three quarters of their freshman year.

> It proved possible in the Sierra Project to stimulate the personal psychological development of college students *within* a framework of rigorous academic accomplishment.

The four year graduation rate for Sierra Hall students was 60% in contrast to the campus average of 44%. This we attribute to two factors: the sense of community, and the closeness of relationships with significant faculty and staff during the freshman year. The sense of community contributed to a level of support which we view as highly significant. Students made enduring friendships during the first year which were nurtured in an environment of shared experiences and trust.

The chief effect which close relationships formed with faculty and staff in the freshman year had on retention was that students could and did make "connections" with the support structures of the university: the formal and informal academic advising structure, personalized advice on how to make the "system" work, and personal introductions to counseling, career planning, health, and faculty personnel. While such introductions and advice may be an integral part of life on a liberal arts college campus, it is not in a research multiversity.

Implications for Higher Education of Rethinking the Context for Promoting Personal Development in The Freshman Year

The concluding section of this chapter on the potential for promoting the development of character during the freshman year will center on three different perspectives. The first perspective is provided by summarizing what is possible to accomplish with college freshmen that could not be done three decades ago as a consequence of accumulated theoretical advances, instrument development, and empirical research.

Three decades ago, reflecting the general status of psychological and educational theory and measurement, promising constructs for understanding the course of college student development had not yet become embedded in general theory, and the development of instrumentation relevant to the transition from late adolescence to early adulthood was in its infancy.

At this point in time, however, it is now possible to accomplish a number of tasks central to promoting value and ethical development which have heretofore not been within the capacity of teachers and researchers. The power of the impact of the educational experience on college students can be enhanced by the following:

1. Assessing accurately the psychological and educational status of students on a host of significant developmental dimensions

2. Charting change in students over time using the initial assessment as a base

3. Identifying developmentally relevant curricula which will produce desired change

4. Sequencing educational experiences within that curricula in such a manner as to optimize their impact

5. Determining the portion of student development which is attributable to maturation and that which is attributable differentially to the effects of the curricula

The second perspective is provided by recounting a perhaps apocryphal story told by Nevitt Sanford about the encounter between the parent of a Brown University student and a college dean:

> There is a story about the mother whose son went to Brown University. In reading the catalogue, she found it said that they were going to teach him how to think for himself, be sensitive to the needs of other people, etc., etc. And the mother, a little bit skeptical, said to the Dean, "Are you really going to do all these things?" And he said, "Ma'am, we guarantee results, else we'll return the boy!" (Whiteley, 1984)

Perhaps those with fiduciary responsibility for higher education cannot fully endorse the guarantee to produce results or return the child, but we have entered a new era of the possible, and that new era is extraordinarily hopeful.

The third perspective is gained from a consideration of the central implications of the Sierra Project, which centered on the freshman year experience, for higher education. The central implications for higher education, beyond those covered in the perspectives on the freshman year and undergraduate education, are four: level of student interest, hospitality of the campus, generalizability of the curriculum, and the overall impact of higher education on character development.

First, students chose to participate in all levels of the Sierra Project with a willingness and enthusiasm far beyond our expectations. Whether it was the willingness of the control groups to subject themselves to recurrent testing, the sophomore staff to dedicate a vast amount of time to the success of the project, or the freshmen to pass along to prospective students that the Sierra experience was well worth a year of their involvement, the professional staff each year had a host of vitally interested freshmen students and student staff colleagues.

Second, the university itself proved to be far more hospitable to the Sierra Project intervention than we had imagined. The faculty communities responsible for granting instructional improvement funds, approving academic courses, and authorizing research on human subjects acted positively in support of our endeavors. The Chancellor of UCI at the time of the intervention, Daniel G. Aldrich, Jr., made a number of public statements about the significance of a university engaging in character education. Finally, the staff of the Housing Office involved themselves in the program, assisted with myriad details involved in administering a living-learning program and continued the program intact after the initial primary classroom instructor (Janet Clark Loxley) and principal research investigator (John M. Whiteley) had gone on to other tasks.

Third, the Sierra curriculum as it was implemented and reported (Loxley & Whiteley, 1986) provides a week-to-week road map of what we did, problems we encountered, and feedback we received. It is a curriculum, however, tied in important respects to the freshman year of students in a research university who were highly conventional in terms of the theories of moral reasoning and ego development. Therefore, while the general presentation of character issues and the sequencing of educational experiences constitute a model we have found valid for our population, the actual presentation of classes needs to be adapted by subsequent researchers and teachers to the developmental level of student participants and to the particular characteristics of the educational institution in which the character intervention takes place.

In adapting the curriculum to the requirements of different colleges and universities, it may be useful to keep in mind that in our assessment the key components of the Sierra Project curriculum are as follows:

- The psychological sense of community

- The presence of more mature role models in the residence halls

- The assertion training model which developed students' skills in identifying the rights of oneself and others and learning to resolve conflicts fairly

- The empathy training module which increased students' perceptions of how other people experience situations

- The greater responsibility for their educational experiences which was demanded of students

- The structured exercises which required students to rethink a number of previously unexamined beliefs

The consideration of sex roles and race roles which stimulated more complex thinking about ways of relating to other people

In our assessment, the provision of both moral and psychological educational experiences is essential.

Fourth, and most significantly, the Sierra Project demonstrated once again that education can make a difference in promoting what John Dewey (1897) called the development of a "free and powerful character." Consistent with an emerging number of research studies on different populations in diverse settings, the effect of formal education as a catalyst to significant moral growth was again demonstrated, this time in the context of the freshman year at college, and subsequently affirmed over four years of undergraduate study.

References

Bertin, B. D., Ferrant, B. A., Whiteley, J. M., & Yokota, N. (1985). Influences on character development during the college years: The retrospective view of recent undergraduates. In J. Dalton (Ed.), *Promoting values education in student development.* NASPA Monograph Series, No. 4.

Burris, M. P. (1982). *Influences of college experiences on moral reasoning.* Unpublished master's thesis, Program in Social Ecology, University of California, Irvine.

Colby, A., Gibbs, J. C., Kohlberg, L., Speicher-Dubin, B., & Candee, D. (1979). *Standard form scoring manual* (Parts 1-4). Cambridge, MA: Harvard University Center for Moral Education.

Colby, A., Kohlberg, L., Gibbs, J. C., & Lieberman, M. (1983). A longitudinal study of moral judgment. *Society for Research on Child Development Monograph, 48,* (1-2, Serial No. 200).

Dewey, J. (1897). *Ethical principles underlying education.* Third Yearbook of the National Herbart Society. Chicago, IL: The Society.

Erickson, V. L., & Whiteley, J. M., (Eds.). (1980). *Developmental counseling and teaching.* Monterey, CA: Brooks/Cole.

Gamson, W. A. (1972a). *SIMSOC simulated society: Instructor's manual.* New York: Free Press.

Gamson, W. A. (1972b). *SIMSOC simulated society: Participants' manual.* New York: Free Press.

Gamson, W. A. (1978a). *SIMSOC simulated society: Instructor's manual.* New York: Free Press.

Gamson, W. A. (1978b). *SIMSOC simulated society: Participants' manual.* New York: Free Press.

Hendrix, L. J., Carter, M. W., & Hintze, J. L. (1973). A comparison of five statistical methods for analyzing pretest-posttest designs. *Journal of Experimental Education, 47*(2), 96-102.

Jenrich, R., & Sampson, P. (1979). Analysis of variance and covariance including repeated measures. In W. J. Dixon & M. B. Brown (Eds.), *BMDP-79: Biomedical computer programs, p-series* (pp. 540-580). Berkeley, CA: University of California Press.

Kohlberg, L. (1973). Continuities in childhood and adult moral development revisited. In P. R. Baltes & K. W. Schaie (Eds.), *Life-span developmental psychology: Personality and socialization.* New York: Academic Press.

Lee, L., & Whiteley, J. M. (In preparation). *Portraits in character.*

Loevinger, J. (1966). The meaning and measurement of ego development. *American Psychologist, 21,* 195-206.

Loevinger, J. (1976). *Ego development: Conceptions and theories.* San Francisco: Jossey-Bass.

Loevinger, J., & Wessler, R. (1970). *Measuring ego development, Volume I: Construction and use of a sentence completion test.* San Francisco: Jossey-Bass.

Loxley, J. C., & Whiteley, J. M. (1986). *Character development in college students, Volume II: The curriculum and longitudinal results.* Schenectady, NY: Character Research Press.

McBee, M. (1980). The values development dilemma. In M. McBee (Ed.), *Rethinking college responsibilities for values.* San Francisco: Jossey-Bass.

Mosher, R. L. (1979). *Adolescents' development and education: A janus knot.* Berkeley, CA: McCutchan.

Mosher, R. L., & Sprinthall, N. A. (1971). Psychological education: A means to promote personal development during adolescence. *The Counseling Psychologist, 2*(4), 3-82.

Nucci, L., & Pascarella, E. T. (1987). The influence of college on moral development. In J. Smart (Ed.), *Higher education: Handbook of theory and research, Volume III.* New York: Agathon.

Resnikoff, A., & Jennings, J. S. (1982). The view from within: Perspective from the intensive case study. In J. M. Whiteley & Associates, *Character development in college students, Volume I: The freshman year.* Schenectady, NY: Character Research Press.

Rest, J. R. (1979a). *Development in judging moral issues.* Minneapolis: University of Minnesota Press.

Rest, J. R. (1979b). *The impact of higher education on moral development.* (Technical Report No. 5), Minneapolis: Minnesota Research Projects.

Rest, J. R., & Deemer, D. (1986). Life experiences and developmental pathways. In J. R. Rest (Ed.), *Moral development: Advances in research and theory.* New York: Praeger Publishers.

Rudolph, F. (1962). *The American college and university.* New York: Vintage Books.

Sanford, N. (1956). Personality development during the college years. *Personnel and Guidance Journal, 35,* 74-80.

Sanford, N. (1962). *The American college.* New York: Wiley.

Scharf, P. (1978). *Readings in moral education.* Minneapolis, MN: Winston Press.

Trudeau, G. B. (1972). *Doonesbury.* New York: Universal Press Syndicate.

Whiteley, J. M. (Producer). (1984). *Nevitt Sanford on community during the college years,* with John M. Whiteley, (videotape). Falls Church, VA: American College Personnel Association.

Whiteley, J. M., & Associates. (1982). *Character development in college students, Volume I: The freshman year.* Schenectady, NY: Character Research Press.

Whiteley, J. M., & Bertin, B. D. (1982). Research on measuring and changing the level of moral reasoning in college students. In J. M. Whiteley & Associates, *Character development in college students, Volume I: The freshman year.* Schenectady, NY: Character Research Press.

Whiteley, J. M., & Loxley, J. C. (1980). A curriculum for the development of character and community in college students. In V. L. Erickson & J. M. Whiteley (Eds.), *Developmental counseling and teaching.* Monterey, CA: Brooks/Cole.

SECTION 2

THEORETICAL UNDERPINNINGS OF THE SIERRANS REVISITED RESEARCH

Section II was undertaken with a very specific purpose: to serve as a catalyst for discussion among the research team as its members worked on the construction of the interview protocol which would guide data collection from young adults about the moral challenges they confronted and how they acted in response to those challenges.

The researchers were attempting in an exploratory study to discern recurring patterns of moral action and the social contexts in which those patterns occurred with a goal of creating an evaluative portrait of moral action in young adulthood. The method of data collection was first and foremost to listen, but while listening, to be prepared to ask questions intended to be empathic, but also thoughtfully catalytic to promote further elaboration by the young adults sharing parts of their lives with us.

While the operative constructs guiding the research were *moral action* and *young adulthood*, we were not proceeding from any prior ideological or theoretical perspective. Nor were we trying to prove in some scientific way the validity of specific theories of moral action or to provide support for a particular viewpoint on the psychology of young adulthood.

The team of researchers were intending to ask young adults about moral action dilemmas in their lives. And as we listened to them, we wanted to be prepared to ask questions which would further illuminate for them the meaning of the moral actions they took, and the broader context for their actions in terms of the challenges they were encountering in the rest of their lives.

In a phrase of sociologist Herbert J. Gans (1992), the method of the researchers was "being with and talking to people" (p. xi). But beyond that, the researchers wished to be poised to probe the thinking and its contexts of these young persons as they told stories from their lives. Therefore, a decision was made to study major theories of both young adulthood and moral action in order to serve as a resource to guide spontaneous questioning so that it was as informed as it could be in a context of spontaneity.

David Connor prepared the initial drafts of Chapter 4 on Young Adulthood in the Life Cycle; Katherine Kalliel and David Connor were the substantial contributors to the drafting of Chapter 5 ,"Doing the Right or Good Act: Theories of Moral Action." Both chapters were written to spur collegial discussion among members of the research team, and as a resource for constructing the interview questions for the research protocol. Molly Patterson authored Chapter 6, "Further Theoretical Perspectives on Making Moral Choices." This chapter introduced some promising new approaches to thinking about moral choice which appeared after the inception of the Sierrans Revisited Project.

References

Gans, H. J. (1992). Preface. In A. Wolfe, *America at century's end.* Berkeley: University of California Press.

C H A P T E R

YOUNG ADULTHOOD IN
THE LIFE CYCLE

The period of life immediately after the college years was the focus of the Sierrans Revisited research. From a practical point of view, we wanted to construct an interview protocol which would allow young adults to talk about their lives in a psychologically meaningful manner. Therefore, one reason to examine selected professional literature was to gain an understanding from previous research of the salient issues in the lives of young adults. A second reason to examine the literature was more theoretical: to understand as fully as possible the developmental context in which young adults make personal and professional decisions about moral dilemmas.

Finally, the substantive design work of the Sierrans Revisited Project occurred in the context of ongoing seminars in Boston and Irvine, two geographically distant locations. Since a goal of both sets of seminar participants was to facilitate communication between them, a decision was made to focus on specific authors and individual books rather than specific intellectual themes as an organizational category for reviewing the literature. This is the reason that the literature is organized around authors (Freud, Erikson, and Levinson, etc.) rather than notions of growth tasks or psychological constructs (intimacy, self, career, etc.).

Despite widespread belief to the contrary, life-span developmental theory is not exclusively a concern of the 20th century.

Different authors define variously the chronological ages associated with particular stages of life. They also differ on the issues they elect to include in the specific treatment of young adulthood. Since our goal in conducting the literature review was to determine what we could learn from the perspective of constructing an interview protocol and to facilitate communication among us, the decision to organize the review by specific author and individual book proved satisfactory. The purpose of including this review herein is to alert the interested reader to existing basic directions of the literature and what we considered most salient about it.

Despite widespread belief to the contrary, life-span developmental theory is not exclusively a concern of the 20th Century (Baltes, 1983; Wertheimer, 1985). In recent decades, however, work on the young adult has flourished. In this chapter, the particular contributions of Sigmund Freud, Carl Jung, Charlotte Buhler, Erik

Erikson, Robert Havighurst, Roger Gould, George Vaillant, Daniel Levinson, Lawrence Kohlberg, Carol Gilligan, and Bernice Neugarten will be discussed. In some cases it will be necessary also to summarize a researcher's perceptions of adolescence and middle adulthood in order to highlight the characteristics particular to young adulthood.

Early Influences: Sigmund Freud and Carl Jung

Bocknek (1986) pointed out what he considered an unfortunate influence of Sigmund Freud on the history of developmental psychology—namely, a lack of detailed concern with development in adulthood. Freud (1916/1963) argued that the conflicts he saw at the core of personality development were the result of the acting out of unconscious motives and forces not generally available to adult awareness. The major influences on adulthood have their roots, according to Freud (1933/1964, 1938), in the psychosexual processes of childhood. The central core of personality and the overall organizational structure of the individual are set in the first decade of life. Adult life is the staging area for expressing the tendencies, the characteristics, and the underlying conflicts formed in childhood. Maturity is synonymous with adequate functioning in work and relationships. Change in adulthood may occur, but by implication, further development is possible only by the fundamental reworking of childhood crises which is achieved through psychoanalysis.

For our purposes, a limitation of Freud's (1933/1964, 1938) theories is that they do not provide a direct basis for understanding those qualitative changes in young adulthood which occur with age or experience. The same underlying dynamic is seen as operating throughout life. Ego defenses are brought into play at all stages. The reworking of material from the psychosocial stages of infancy and childhood can take place at any age. Beyond this, Freudian theory has little to say directly about change which is related to the aging process in adulthood.

Carl Jung, (1931/1953) Freud's one-time close disciple, assumed that development occurs over the course of the entire life span. Inherited tendencies to think and feel in certain ways are passed on from ancestor to ancestor and are represented in the memory that is the collective unconscious. Individual personality is the result of interaction between the emerging sense of self and various archetypes. Expressed in Jungian archetypes, life is a passage from morning knowledge (the *cognito matutina* of St. Augustine) to evening knowledge (*cognito vespertina*). Jung (1963a) characterized his own journey as "a story of the self-realization of the unconscious" (p. 10). The unconscious can be made manifest in the real world: The word *seibstverwirklichung* in the original (Jung, 1963b) does not have the implications of awareness inherent in the English term "self-realization." The unconscious becomes real in Jung's view and therefore is susceptible to influence.

Jung (1931/1953) divided the journey of life into four parts. In the first part, childhood, we are not conscious of any problems of our own and cause problems to others. The next two parts contain many problems caused by conflicting impulses of which there is conscious awareness. New adults must shoulder responsibilities; they must face the demands of the external world, the "also-I." The archetypal potentials—the figures they might become—must to some extent be discarded since humans cannot in one lifetime become all they have the ability to become. Between childhood and middle age, of which the onset is age 40, choices must be made and compromises worked out.

54

This central Jungian theme—that the development of a life is the result of a series of dynamic tensions, choices, and adjustments as an individual moves from narcissism to increasing awareness of the outside world and others—is appealing as a source of ideas in a research study of young adults. The elaborations of Jung's ideas of myths and symbols in this applied context are generally less useful. Jung's work did focus attention on the lifelong quality of development and on the first part of adulthood as characterized by increasingly conscious interaction between the emerging self and one's surroundings.

Developmental Transitions: Erik Erikson

Erik Erikson's (1959) theories about development owe much to psychoanalytic theory. He had a central concern with the dynamic interaction of opposing forces. Erikson also believed that personality is to some extent formed by the individual's culture. Cultures are organized to mold the individual for ends which lie in the future.

In Erikson's (1959) view, the individual faces a series of crucial choices between opposing forces: If a normative crisis is resolved in a manner which is more or less satisfactory, the individual can move on to healthy functioning at the next of the eight differentiated life stages. Each of Erikson's "ages of man" has a core emotional or social concern expressed in the polarity of two extremes. The outcome of each normative crisis (for example, identity formation) affects the individual's ability to negotiate successfully the crisis of the next stage. Outcomes can range from primarily healthy and positive to primarily negative.

In order to illustrate Erikson's (1968) conception of young adulthood, it is necessary to bracket that age by describing what precedes and what follows. For Erikson, adolescence is the period of getting ready for the tasks of adulthood. The dynamic polarity is between the formation of personal identity and role confusion: A healthy outcome is the establishment of a stable personal identity.

After the identity crisis has been resolved, the young adult next faces the dialectic of intimacy versus isolation. Whereas much of adolescent identity is formed within groups, the tasks of adulthood require that one see oneself as an individual who encounters other individuals (Erikson, 1968). Encounters with other individuals at first threaten the new-found identity. The reaction to encounter can be inner tenseness, reserve, caution, holding back from commitment. Carried towards an extreme, this reaction can lead to stereotypic relationships or to a series of dismal encounters with a hectic succession of ill-chosen partners. At worst, the encounters are "mutual narcissistic mirroring" (Erikson, 1968, p. 167). A healthy resolution of the dynamic polarity, on the other hand, leads to the virtue of love. The individual who can love is able to enter into relationships with another without being threatened; intimacy does not lead to identity fusion with the other.

A healthy adolescent is one who is looking ahead towards productive work and to a constructive role in society. The successful adolescent is conscious both of himself and of society, sees a role for himself, and sees that role as acknowledged by society. He is confident of his identity. An unsuccessful adolescent, on the other hand, is confused, either seeing no role which is assumable or attainable, or choosing a role

> A successful adolescent is conscious both of himself and of society, sees a role for himself, and sees that role as acknowledged by society.

that society views negatively (Erikson, 1959, 1968). A healthy adolescent has achieved the Eriksonian virtue of fidelity.

According to Erikson (1964), women's achievement of fidelity is essentially different from men's. He rejected Freud's concept of penis envy as central to the female's view of herself in the world and postulated an identity based not on the lack of an organ but on the possession of a distinctive feature, inner space. Observing ten to twelve year old children at play with blocks and figures, Erikson noted the girls' tendency to produce interior, enclosed scenes, involving static humans. The boys built high towers and acted out fights and automobile accidents. From these observations Erikson postulated that a woman formed her identity differently because:

> . . . her somatic design harbors an "inner space" destined to bear the offspring of chosen men and with it, a biological, psychological, and ethical commitment to take care of human infancy. Is not the disposition for this commitment (whether to be realized in actual motherhood or not) the core problem of female fidelity? (Erikson, 1964, p. 5)

These research findings have been criticized for Erikson's lack of controls and the age of the subjects (Hyde, 1985). For someone who in other contexts took account of cultural influences on behavior, Erikson's theories did not directly address the formative role of differential societal expectations of boys and girls on the children themselves and on the observing adult.

Research by Hodgson and Fischer (1979) supports the contention that Erikson explains male development better than female development. They found that college students whom they studied defined themselves in different ways—males in terms of competence and knowledge, and females in terms of relationships to others. These findings are supported by Carol Gilligan's research (1982). Prager (1983) found no significant differences between men and women in her study of 87 college students in terms of the development of committed relationships. Both men and women in committed relationships were older than those in uncommitted or superficial relationships. Her finding supports Erikson's (1964) observation that relationships combining depth and commitment are the most mature. Similar results were obtained by Orlofsky, Marcia, and Lesser (1973).

More Complex Strands: Charlotte Buhler and R. J. Havighurst

Charlotte Buhler postulated a complex interaction of several universal laws which shape both human development as a whole and individual development in particular (Buhler & Massarik, 1968). Buhler divided the life span into five stages, with Childhood extending from birth to age 14, Youth from 14 to 25, and the first stage of Adulthood lasting from 25 to 45 or 50 years of age. The dynamic of each age is an interplay of various forces including the desire to satisfy needs, self-limiting adaptation, and creative achievement.

In Youth, individuals become aware of their potential and realize for the first time that to a large extent their lives are their own: The stage is set for them to direct those lives. In Adulthood I, people are increasingly specific about their goals and how to achieve them. At this stage of life, creative achievement is the primary focus of the individual's energies.

Development for Buhler (1935) was the result of a complex interaction of influences. In Youth, physical ability is experienced as progressive growth, and the onset of reproductive ability occurs. In Adulthood I, physical ability is experienced as predominantly static. The concept of time changes also as people first become more aware of a future that expands and then realize that it is contracting. This succession of expansion and contraction is found in other aspects of human experience. The individual becomes more aware of a growing list of needs, for example, and then must make choices among them. Creative achievement involves envisioning ways of influencing the shape of the external world and then coming to terms with the limitations inherent in what is created, whether it be a child, a book, or a living room. Aiming for self-fulfillment entails also exercising self-restraint—adapting both one's goals and oneself to the constraints of others and personal circumstances.

Buhler's work added to the study of the life span the contention that development occurs along several different dimensions at the same time, but not necessarily at the same rate. She drew attention to the active role of the self in development. In particular, she outlined how personal goals change over the lifetime. Specific to each age are overall categories of the goals: The definitions and refinements are individual. Presumably Buhler's factoring in of physical maturation had an influence on how she decided when one unit of the life span ends and the next begins. The first stage of adulthood, for example, includes people who are 25 years of age and also people who are twice that age. There is relatively little physical change between 25 and 50, and therefore for Buhler those years represent a developmental whole.

R. J. Havighurst (1972) believed in a hierarchy of development, each stage building on the accomplishments of the previous stage. For each stage of development, however, Havighurst identified a specific and elaborate group of tasks. Each group of tasks has two possible outcomes: Success leads to individual contentment and the ability to work on later tasks, whereas failure leads to unhappiness, societal disapproval, and difficulties with the tasks of the next stage. As in Erikson's (1964) theory, Havighurst's tasks are influenced by society. There is room, however, for personal choice. Out of the interaction between the individual and the environment, a self is evolved that is a force in later development. The self may make choices and direct the course of further development.

According to Havighurst (1972), the self is expressed in personal motives, wishes, and values which affect such choices as which occupations one aims for and how one chooses to prepare for them. The tasks of adolescence have to do with preparation for an adult life. They involve preparing to achieve financial independence, establishing a degree of autonomy, and attaining satisfactory interpersonal relationships including setting up and maintaining new and more mature relationships with people of both sexes and achieving societally accepted masculine or feminine roles. Adolescents must accept their physiques and learn to use their bodies effectively. They must strive for emotional independence from their parents and other adults and prepare for marriage and family life. Taking appropriate steps towards an economic career is also required. Adolescents are further called upon to develop a set of values and an ethical system which will guide their behavior: To fit in with society at large, they must both desire and achieve behavior which is socially responsible.

Aiming for self-fulfillment entails also exercising self-restraint—adapting both one's goals and oneself to the constraints of others and personal circumstances

Early Adulthood (which lasts from 18 to 30 years of age) builds on the skills learned in the achievement of the tasks of adolescence. Choices are refined, and more responsibilities are assumed. The major tasks include selecting a specific mate and learning to live with that person as a marriage partner. Having started a family, Early Adults must learn the skills needed to rear children and to manage a home. They must start an occupation. Social tasks involve both finding a congenial social group and establishing a family. On a broader scale, the Early Adult must now also learn how to take on civic responsibility (Havighurst, 1972).

Havighurst (1972) provides a diagnostic checklist of more or less observable achievements which are likely, in a stable American society, to lead to a reasonable level of societal acceptance for heterosexuals and which allow the adult to move on to later productive work. It cannot be assumed, however, that all the tasks necessarily have to do directly with individual development. Development is not simply the acquisition of specific skills and techniques. It is possible to imagine an individual encumbered with a degree of pathology who is able to learn many of the growth tasks of a stage of life but is not able to achieve a healthy adaptation.

Havighurst's (1972) theory says little about those interactions between individual and environment which lead to modifications in one's view of the world. Though he postulates an observing, deliberative, and active self, Havighurst did not develop notions of the internal experience of Early Adulthood and how the world-view and self-view of that age differ from those of earlier and later stages.

What Does It Feel Like to be You at Your Age? Roger Gould

Roger Gould (1972) shares with Erikson (1959) and Buhler (1935) the general conception that one aim of human development is to own the self, to achieve the ability to affect the course of one's own life. Gould notes qualitative differences at different times in life which characterize how the world is organized. He writes of this experiencing of existence as "the out-of-focus, interior, gut-level organizing percepts of self and non-self, safety, time, size, etc. that make up the background tone of daily living and shape the attitudes and value bases from which decisions and action emanate" (Gould, 1972, p. 524). What Gould is describing here as one's "sense of the world" is a complicated phenomenon not expressible in Erikson's elegantly sparse vocabulary of abstract polarities. Gould's language is full of visual and auditory images and rich elaboration.

One thread running through Gould's (1972) description of what it feels like to exist at various ages is the individual's sense of time. Childhood is similar to living in a time capsule: Children never really believe that they will truly escape the family and its constraints. As one leaves childhood, one's perspective is more and more that the future is without end; the individual hurries towards one clear vision of where he or she wants to be. By age 30, however, one is aware of having not only an adult future but also already having an adult past. Time ahead is no longer limitless, and alternative paths from which to choose are no longer experienced as straightforward.

Ages can also be differentiated on the basis of to whom one "belongs." The first steps of adulthood are away from parents. Movement away from parents is associated with challenging false assumptions that represent unfinished business left over from childhood (Gould, 1978). The late teens and early 20s are characterized by the fear that one will always belong to one's parents and always believe in their world. The belief that they and they alone can guarantee one's safety, and that they and they alone can be one's family creates anxiety. Parents are replaced by an influential peer group, which for a time becomes a focus of interest. By 22 years of age, an individual may enter the third stage of adulthood, a period characterized by the assumption of more new roles—namely, those related to establishing a career, becoming a marriage partner, and raising children.

During this third period of adulthood, which corresponds roughly to the stage of Young Adulthood in other theories, the person feels fairly established and autonomous, separate from the family of origin, and involved in the work of being an adult. Important decisions have been already made: They are not yet scrutinized, however, as to whether they were right or wrong. People at this stage feel that the self has been well-defined, "even if they are not fully satisfied with it" (Gould, 1972, p. 525).

Individuals in the third adult period are still concerned with receiving their parents' approval by proving themselves competent. They feel less vulnerable than they were earlier to the opinions of peers and to judgments made about them from the collective perspective and values of the peer culture. Their emotions are somewhat more controlled; they avoid extremes, and try to discover and maintain an appropriate emotional tone for adult life by modulating their feelings in contrast to the wider swings of earlier stages. At age 28, the perspective shifts to more self-evaluation. Decisions already made are questioned. Life itself appears more complicated, and options seem not as readily achievable or as clear as they did before. Above all, there is a distinct emotional shift vis-à-vis living an adult life: After age 28, people are tired of trying to be what they ought to be, and instead just want to be who they are (Gould, 1972).

According to Gould, moving towards healthy adulthood involves recognizing and reworking a succession of false assumptions. Among those false assumptions to be examined in the third stage of adulthood are the following: Being strong and committed will lead to success and acclaim. Life is fair. Good deeds are rewarded, not punished. There is a right way to do anything, and only one way. Loved ones can do for one what one has been unable to do for oneself. In general, the myths avow that if one is rational, hardworking, and loyal, he or she can prevail over all obstacles (Gould, 1978).

Towards the end of the decade of the 20s, another set of assumptions needs to be confronted: Life is simple. My self is simple. I am unified inside, without contradictions—to know something intellectually is to know it emotionally. I do not resemble my parents in ways I do not want to resemble them. My perception of those close to me is in focus, clear, and unobstructed. My security is not in any real way threatened (Gould, 1978). During this period of life, people need to come to terms with the complicated nature of life. They must realize that they, like others, are complex and not easily known. Life provides no certainty, and outcomes cannot be entirely predicted. Parents, despite wishes and claims to the contrary, still have influence.

Gould's (1978) descriptions of the subjective experience of life are rich and many-dimensional. After all, when most of us wake up each morning or look back on the day, rarely do we experience ourselves as in the grip of some two-dimensional

Eriksonian polarity crisis. Our experience is likely to be multifaceted and less clear-cut. Gould's observations provide a rich summary of day-to-day living in its complex interrelationships. Also, his research method was ingenious. By monitoring the discussions of groups of people of given ages, and by controlling for both individual idiosyncratic and cross-group themes, he was able to identify concerns, concepts, and a tone which was peculiar to each age. However, the subjects he used for the initial stage of the research were all in psychiatric treatment and therefore not representative of the adult population at large. Gould subsequently carried out research, mainly through questionnaires, with 524 members of a control group—all of whom were white, middle class, and educated. Identifying themes in one population, however, and asking whether they are applicable to another may lead to the omission of themes which are characteristic of the second group. There may well be themes, thoughts, and tones which occur in the general population that are not represented in the conversations of the original psychiatric groups or Gould's subsequent control group. Neither of his research samples are representative either of North American society or of the more particular culture of Southern California which so influenced the Sierrans Revisited sample. The portraits and characterizations which emerge from Gould's work, however, are provocative.

Man's Life: George Vaillant and Daniel Levinson

The work of George Vaillant (1977) to some extent adds additional adult stages to the general Eriksonian framework. Between the ages of roughly 23 and 35, Vaillant identifies a core concern with career consolidation. He points also to what amounts to a secondary polarity between concerns for the self and concerns for the outside world: Too much personal preoccupation can lead to difficulties in career and marriage. Vaillant's findings are based on interviews with some 94 Harvard graduates. Much of the lively and interesting material he gathered is based on recollections. Vaillant's subjects were recounting, for the most part at a later stage, what they remember their experiences to have been a decade or more before. Vaillant's work is limited by the generalizations from the sample he used: His subjects were all male and all Harvard graduates.

The theories of Daniel Levinson, Charlotte Darrow, Edward Klein, Maria Levinson, and Braxton McKee (1978) follow the stage progression envisioned by Erikson (1968), and the task approach found in Havighurst (1972). Levinson et al. find adult development to be characterized primarily by the process of self-evaluation. Each individual life has its own underlying pattern or design. At the same time, there are also similarities from life to life. As well as conceptualizing adulthood in terms of comparative stability, Levinson et al. also identify themes and times of change or transition. They identify four partially overlapping eras in the young adult life cycle. After adolescence a young man enters the *Early Adult Transition*, passes through a stage labeled *Entering the Adult World*, and then moves on to the *Age Thirty Transition.*

Early Adult Transition is characteristically a time of looking at the self and making modifications in the self-image. It is a time of leaving behind former conceptualizations of the self, of the family of origin, and of their interrelated roles. Thoughts of financial independence are coupled with separation from the family. During this novice phase of adulthood, the young man emphasizes differences between himself and his family, and tries out new identities in the adult world (Levinson et al., 1978).

60

Entering the Adult World is an elaboration of tentatively chosen roles and themes. The person has made decisions about what in the self is valued: Now is the time to discover how to maintain and maximize those values in the context of adult society. Keeping options open is sensed as crucial: Strong commitments are avoided as limiting, and the opportunity to choose among a wide array of alternatives is an appealing prospect. At the same time as the young man continues to develop life goals, he must make choices that do involve commitments in both career and partner selection. This is a time to put down some roots, but not to become firmly entrenched (Levinson et al., 1978).

Early Adulthood is characterized by drama, contradiction, stress, and by optimal intellectual and physical functioning. In his 20s a man makes choices that form his preliminary adult identity: He decides (not for the last time) where to live, how to live, with whom to live, and how to earn his living. At the same time, he increasingly contributes to society. In the important arenas of adulthood—work, family, community—the young man is a Novice Adult. He strives to achieve recognition as an adult in the eyes of his parents, while at the same time learning how to be a spouse and a father (Levinson et al., 1978).

As the decade ends, another transition occurs, this time the *Age Thirty Transition*. Themes from the period of *Entering the Adult World* are now re-examined and reworked. Time is felt as pressing, and life seems a more serious undertaking than before. Cherished ambitions may seem less realizable. Disappointment and anger can result. The person may feel hemmed in, constrained, and may seek relief in drugs, rebellion, sexual adventure, or dissolution of the marriage. On the other hand, the *Age Thirty Transition* may bring more clarity about the self, more acceptance, renewed vigor and a clearer focus on the need for productive stability (Levinson et al., 1978).

Four components characterize Levinson et al.'s (1978) novice adulthood: the Dream, the Mentor, forming an occupation, and love relationships. The characteristics of each component vary from individual to individual depending on the underlying life structure. The Dream is a "vague sense of self-in-adult-world" (Levinson et al., 1978, p. 91). It is a guiding image, an inspiring and sustaining vision which generates excitement and vitality. The Mentor is someone half a generation (8 to 15 years) older, who serves as teacher and sponsor. This person welcomes the novice adult, explaining the values of the adult world in the social and the occupational realm and in many ways gives protected entry into adult communities. The Mentor helps with preliminary realization of the Dream. Mentorship is a temporary role; the need for a mentor lasts only through the apprenticeship phase of adulthood.

Forming an occupation is not the same as choosing one. Successful forming requires increasing awareness of one's interests, and tentative exploration of work options. Premature commitment will be regretted. Marriage brings about considerable changes in relationships to the outside world. If the marriage partner has a Dream which involves substantial independence and autonomy, difficult clashes will arise (Levinson et al., 1978).

The theories of Levinson et al. (1978) are based on extensive interviews with 40 men and their wives and the reading of biographies and novels. It is not clear which of the findings in Levinson's study are culture, gender-, or time-specific.

Reworking Assumptions: Bernice Neugarten

The theories discussed up to this point may all be classified to one degree or another as developmental, based on the assumption that succeeding ages of humankind can be differentiated by distinctive characteristics. They paint qualitatively different pictures of childhood, adolescence, and adulthood, and isolate various themes and concerns as the special focus of particular ages. They differ in their choice of themes and in the number of distinct periods into which they divide the life span.

Bernice Neugarten (1975a, 1975b) has taken her work in a different direction from these other theorists on many counts. According to Neugarten, chronological age can offer, at best, only a rough indication of a person's psychological development. In order to study continuity in the human personality, she directed attention to which coping styles people develop, to the ways in which they achieve satisfaction in life, and to the perseverance with which they pursue their goals (Rosen & Neugarten, 1964). The changes that occur as people progress developmentally may be observed in terms of their inner orientation versus their outer orientation, in active versus passive mastery of life tasks, and in their sense of control over life. The amount of change varies depending on the interaction of a person's stable and changing characteristics and on the dimension of time. Time, however, is not simply physical aging (Rosen & Neugarten, 1964; Neugarten & Datan, 1973).

In order to understand the effect of time, Neugarten believes it must be studied as three separate but connected phenomena: chronological time, social time, and historical time. Life time is not the same as social time; individual history, social history, and societal mores have considerable effect on development. For example, in the latter half of the 20th Century, the average husband works 15 years longer than was the case at the turn of the century. Now, both husband and wife are usually alive when the last child leaves the home: In 1900 this was not the case. For women particularly, expectations, roles, and typical life events have changed considerably. Women now marry later, are educated differently than before, and have different and expanded roles in society (Neugarten, 1975a, 1975b).

Whether studying men or women, Neugarten (1975a, 1975b) did not find the neat and tidy categories described by other developmental psychologists or theorists. She pointed out that there is more than one culture in a society, and that cultures themselves change as a result of history. She has written about the difficulty of clustering people into age brackets marked by particular conflicts: The conflicts do not stay put, and neither do the people. Choices and dilemmas do not sprout forth at ten-year intervals. Neither are major life decisions made once and for all and then left behind. The issues of intimacy and freedom, which other theorists label as particular to young adults, Neugarten found important over and over again throughout the life span. Neither did she find the assessment and reformulation of goals as the major preoccupation of any one particular age group.

Neugarten's (1975a, 1975b) collective works are a reminder that the process of development is gradual and that differences from one life decade to another may be neater in theory than in real life. What is presented as absolute may be relative: Identifying a different emphasis at one stage of life does not necessarily mean that the concerns of an earlier age have disappeared.

Morality and Self: Lawrence Kohlberg and Carol Gilligan

Because they are treated at greater length in the next chapter, what follows here is a brief summary of the theories of Kohlberg and Gilligan as they illuminate the challenges of young adulthood. Kohlberg's theory of moral development outlines the changes in people's thinking about morality (Kohlberg, 1969; Colby, Kohlberg, Gibbs, & Lieberman, 1983). He identified three levels of morality, each divided into two stages. According to Kohlberg, it is necessary to go through the stages in a set sequence. How many stages a person passes through will depend on factors other than mere chronological age. Longitudinal studies have shown that early adulthood is associated mainly with Stage Three and Stage Four reasoning (Kohlberg, 1984). That is to say, young adults tend to apply conventional morality when thinking about moral situations.

At Stage Three, which is characterized by a "good-boy/good-girl" orientation, it is important to conform to rules in order to gain the approval of others, and to avoid their disapproval. Norms are understood as expectations based on relationships. Stage Four is characterized by taking the perspective of a generalized member of society. The purpose of rules at this stage is seen as the maintenance of the formal social system (Kohlberg, 1984).

The work of Carol Gilligan (1982) is intended to correct errors from assuming that the experiences of males can be taken as representative of those of females. Disagreeing with Lawrence Kohlberg (1984) about whether the moral development of women was the same as moral development of men, Gilligan claimed that there are far-reaching differences in more than moral judgment. The contrasts arise from a basic difference in self-definition between men and women (Gilligan, 1982).

Gilligan contrasts Kohlberg's (1984) morality of justice with a morality of care and responsibility which she finds characteristic of women's approach to moral situations, to themselves, and to their roles in life. Whereas justice morality is concerned with the rights of individuals—rights which are sometimes weighed without consideration of their effect—a morality of care focuses not so much on agreements and contracts as on attachments and respect for feelings. A justice orientation is based on equality and a sense of fairness: Responsibility is based on equity, and a recognition of differences in needs. Women therefore tend to see moral dilemmas in terms of conflicting responsibilities, not of conflicting rights. A woman's concern with issues of intimacy is, in contrast to Erikson's model, a life-long concern (Gilligan, 1982).

Gilligan (1982) identifies three distinct stages in women's moral judgment, each having to do with different orientations towards themselves and others. Although Gilligan does not specifically tie these to age-related developmental stages, they all three nevertheless appear in the interviews she conducted with women (mainly late adolescents and young adults). The three stages, and two transitions, represent a developmental progression from selfishness to greater awareness of interdependence of self and others.

In the first stage, a woman's focus is on care for the self to insure survival. The transition from this stage comes with the realization that this orientation is selfish: The good is then defined as caring for others, the second stage. A woman's obligation thus becomes to exercise care and to avoid hurt; causing hurt is equated with not caring. The direction is towards a kind of social happiness: The good world is one in which nobody feels bad. Attempts to achieve such a system bring about a second transition. The conflict between responsibility to others and self-sacrifice leads to questioning how it can be right to hurt oneself. Strict categories are re-examined, and many situations are seen less clearly black and white but rather more ambiguous. In this third stage, care becomes an obligation which extends not only to others, but also to the self. There has thus been a shift from not hurting others, to helping others, to being mindful of the interdependence of self and others, and to a measure of time devoted to caring for one's own needs as an expression of personal integrity (Gilligan, 1982).

Like Neugarten (1975a, 1975b), Gilligan (1982) suggests that women's development is influenced by historical as well as intrapsychic factors. Thus the struggle to guarantee legal equality for women has had an effect on women's thoughts about themselves and others. As some of the barriers fall which previously hindered women's entry into traditionally male jobs and as women rise in the corporate hierarchy, Gilligan (1984) sees a potential work-related crisis in women's moral self-definition. On the one hand, women may be criticized for their fear of success, and for caring about their co-workers. They may become more aware of the human cost of the rules that operate in male-dominated business and of the general indifference to human relationships. At the same time they will receive external validation and will therefore perhaps be more likely to see their own claims as legitimate. The work place can therefore provide an impetus to change in their moral thinking as they include their female self in the moral domain.

Longitudinal and large-scale cross-sectional studies need to be undertaken to validate Gilligan's (1982) findings that the categories men and women use to look at the social world are different. Her theory has implications that go far beyond moral development.

Generalizations about Insights from Developmental Theory

The labels developmental theorists and psychologists have used to describe young adulthood vary, but remarkable similarity emerges in the themes they identify. Young adulthood is a period of gradual movement from dependence to independence. This independence may be expressed in economic terms, in the setting of life priorities different from one's parents', or in social behavior. The field of vision broadens from a focus on self to the inclusion of others; there is a change in emphasis from a preoccupation with personal identity to concern with issues of intimacy, though with regard to this particular aspect there may be gender-specific differences (Douvan & Adelson, 1966; Gilligan, 1982).

Developmental theorists and psychologists tend to look for universal themes. Most of the theorists discussed in this chapter identify patterns and show qualitative differences between people of different ages. They see development as sequential, with people at each age building on the structures which were put together during earlier stages.

64

This is not to say that there are no differences in the qualities theorists ascribe to young adulthood. Freud (1938) and Jung (1953) expected little fundamental age-specific change during early adulthood. Vaillant (1977), Gould (1972), and others identified young adulthood as a period of considerable change. Erikson (1968) saw culture as important in determining the concerns addressed throughout the life span, and identified a hierarchy of crises having to do with choices between polarities. Vaillant expanded Erikson's scheme to include two more stages, and Levinson et al. (1978) identify further conflicts encountered in young adulthood. Havighurst (1972) defined a range of age-specific tasks dictated by the society, indicating that the ways in which those tasks were addressed were a function of individual choice and self-definition. Most theoreticians see young adulthood not as an emergence into relative calm from the storm and stress of adolescence, but as a confrontation with new anxieties in an age at least as turbulent. There is general agreement that young adulthood is an age during which two of the primary concerns are initiating independent family relationships and initial explorations into the establishment of career.

A Caution about Conceptions of Family and Career

The psychological, sociological and cultural definition of the family in America is a changing concept (Wolfe, 1992). Some theorists may have labeled as family-focused concerns that have more to do with close relationships in general. The ideal of the nuclear family, consisting of two living, biologic parents and their children, is relatively modern. The past was not a time, as is often assumed, of a three-generational family: Few children had living grand-parents (Uhlenberg, 1980). Indeed, in the last century in North American and European societies, adolescents and young adults tended to leave home much earlier than they do today and to have only infrequent interactions with their parents. The family was more likely to include strangers than adolescent and young adult offspring (Hareven, 1983). Also, the median age at first marriage in the United States has changed considerably (Laslett, 1978). Changes are very large in the numbers of single adults, of never-married young adults, and in the divorce rate (Cargan, 1981). Such changes can be taken—and in the popular press often are—to mean the decline of the Family as it always was. On the contrary, the figures simply suggest that as a society we are generally ignorant about social history from earlier times. We tend to take as the norm whatever is current and rework perceptions of the past in terms of what is perceived to be lacking in the present.

As far as attempting to understand the role of initial employment and career exploration in a specific research sample of college students, generalizing from the meaning of employment and career in the larger population is fraught with difficulty. For example, the media and advertisements leave the impression that most young women see entering the work-force as a lifelong commitment to the pursuit of increasing responsibility. In working-class white society, however, young women's jobs may have a different function and a different meaning. According to one study, young working-class white women tend to go to work with the stated goal of buying consumer goods, not of entering a career: For them the world of work, therefore, has a very different meaning. White working-class females' commitment to the world of work has been found to occur later, generally after dissatisfaction is experienced in a marriage, or when marriage at all seems unlikely (Simon, Gagnon, & Buff, 1972).

In summary, this century has seen increasing interest in young adulthood as a qualitatively different segment of the life span. Researchers have successively added to our knowledge by pinpointing more and more factors which help differentiate young adulthood from the decades which precede and follow. Unfortunately, much of the research has excluded women, the course of whose development is now increasingly seen as different from that of men. Subjects for many studies have tended also to be articulate, college-educated, young adults from research oriented universities as is the sample studied in this Sierrans Revisited research. Elegantly simple generalizations about young adulthood are tempting. But young adults themselves seem anything but elegantly simple.

References

Baltes, P. B. (1983). Life-span developmental psychology: Observations on history and theory revisited. In R. M. Lerner (Ed.), *Developmental psychology: historical and philosophical perspectives.* Hillside, NJ: Lawrence Erlbaum.

Bocknek, G. (1986). *The young adult: Development after adolescence* (Rev. ed.). New York: Gardner Press.

Buhler, C. (1935). The curve of life as studied in biographies. *Journal of Applied Psychology, 19,* 405-408.

Buhler, C., & Massarik, F. (Eds.). (1968). *The course of human life: A study of goals in the humanistic perspective.* New York: Springer.

Cargan, L. (1981). Singles: An examination of stereotypes. *Family Relations, 30*(3), 377-385.

Colby, A., Kohlberg, L., Gibbs, J., & Lieberman, M. (1983). A longitudinal study of moral development. *Monograph of the Society for Research in Child Development, 4.*

Douvan, E., & Adelson, J. (1966). *The adolescent experience.* New York: Wiley.

Erikson, E. H. (1959). Identity and the life cycle. *Psychological Issues, 1.*

Erikson, E. H. (1964). Inner and outer space. Reflections on womanhood. In R. J. Lifton (Ed.), *The woman in America.* Boston: Beacon.

Erikson, E. H. (1968). *Identity and the life cycle: Identity, youth, and crisis.* New York: Norton.

Freud, S. (1938). *The basic writings of Sigmund Freud.* New York: Random House.

Freud, S. (1916/1963). *Introductory lectures on psychoanalysis.* Standard Edition, Vol. 15 & 16. London: Hogarth. (Original work published 1916)

Freud, S. (1933/1964). *New introductory lectures on psychoanalysis.* Standard Edition, Vol. 23. London: Hogarth. (Original work published 1933)

Gilligan, C. (1982). *In a different voice: Psychological theory and women's development.* Cambridge, MA: Harvard University Press.

Gilligan, C. (1984). Marital dialogues. In V. Rogers (Ed.), *Adult development through relationships*. New York: Praeger.

Gould, R. (1972). The phases of adult life: A study in developmental psychology. *American Journal of Psychiatry, 129*(5), 521-531.

Gould, R. (1978). *Transformations: Growth and change in adult life.* New York: Simon & Schuster.

Hareven, T. K. (1983). American families in transition. In A. S. Skolnick & J. H. Skolnick (Eds.), *Family in transition.* Boston: Little, Brown.

Havighurst, R. J. (1972). *Developmental tasks and education.* New York: D. McKay Co.

Hodgson, J. W., & Fischer, J. L. (1979). Sex differences in identity and intimacy development in college youth. *Journal of Youth and Adolescence, 8,* 27-30.

Hyde, J. S. (1985). *Half the human experience: The psychology of women.* Lexington, MA: Heath.

Jung, C. G. (1931/1953). Structure and dynamics of the psyche. In H. Read, M. Fordham, & G. Adler (Eds.), *The collected works of C. G. Jung,* Vol. 8. New York: Pantheon Books. (Original work published 1927/1931)

Jung, C. G. (1963a). *Memories, dreams, reflections* (A. J. Jaffe, Ed.), (R. & C. Winston, trans.). New York: Random House.

Jung, C. G. (1963b). *Erinnerungen traeume gedanken* (A. J. Jaffe, Ed.). Zurich: Rascher Verlag.

Kohlberg, L. (1969). Stage and sequence: The cognitive-developmental approach to socialization. In D. A. Goslin (Ed.), *Handbook of socialization theory and research.* Chicago: Rand McNally.

Kohlberg, L. (Ed.). (1984). *Essays on moral development,* Vol. 2. San Francisco: Harper and Row.

Laslett, B. (1978). Family membership, past and present. *Social Problems, 25*(5), 478-490.

Levinson, D. J., Darrow, C. N., Klein, E. B., Levinson, M. H., & McKee, B. (1978). *The seasons of a man's life.* New York, Knopf.

Neugarten, B. L. (1975a). The future and the young-old. *Gerontologist, 15,* 4-9.

Neugarten, B. L. (1975b). Adult personality: Toward a psychology of a life cycle. In W. C. Sze (Ed.), *The human life cycle.* New York: Jason Aronson.

Neugarten, B. L., & Datan, N. (1973). Sociological perspectives on the life cycle. In P. B. Baltes & K. W. Schaie (Eds.), *Life span developmental psychology.* New York: Academic Press.

Orlofsky, J. L., Marcia, J. E., Lesser, J. M. (1973). Ego identity status and the intimacy versus isolation crisis of young adulthood. *Journal of Personality and Social Psychology, 27*(2), 211-219.

Prager, K. J. (1983). Development of intimacy in young adults, a multidimensional view. *Psychological Reports, 52*(3), 571-756.

Rosen, J. L., & Neugarten, B. L. (1964). Ego functions in the middle and late years: A thematic apperception study. In B. L. Neugarten (Ed.), *Personality in middle and later life.* New York: Atherton Press.

Simon, W., Gagnon, J. H., & Buff, S. A. (1972). Son of Joe: Continuity and change among white working-class adolescents. *Journal of Youth and Adolescence, 1,* 13-34.

Uhlenberg, P. (1980). Death and the family. *Journal of Family History, 5*(3), 313-320.

Vaillant, G. E. (1977). *Adaptation to life.* Boston: Little Brown.

Wertheimer, M. (1985). The evolution of the concept of development in the history of psychology. In G. Eckart, W. G. Brigmann, & L. Sprung (Eds.), *Contributions to the history of developmental psychology.* Berlin: Mouton.

Wolfe, A. (1992). *America at century's end.* Berkeley: University of California Press.

C H A P T E R

DOING THE RIGHT OR GOOD ACT:
THEORIES OF MORAL ACTION

This selected review of literature from the developmental perspective on moral action was undertaken for two basic reasons. As with the rationale for undertaking the review of the literature on young adulthood in the life cycle (Chapter 4), the collaborators on the Sierrans Revisited Project wanted to learn about the status of this literature as a guide to constructing our Moral Action Interview. A second reason was more theoretical: to identify what was known and not known about this dimension of human experience from the perspective of developmental theorists. The developmental perspective was chosen because that was the framework which had guided the original theoretical constructs underlying the Sierra Project.

As with the literature on young adulthood, we elected to organize our review by specific author and individual book to facilitate communication between the reviewers in Boston and in Irvine. The paradigms put forward for study were by James Rest (1986), Augusto Blasi (1980), Lawrence Kohlberg (1984a, 1984b), Carol Gilligan (1982) and Norma Haan (Haan, Aerts, & Cooper, 1985).

The Historical Background

As Augusto Blasi (1980) has pointed out in his excellent history of the study of moral action, there have been three major shifts of theoretical and empirical emphasis in this century. The first wave of researchers, whose work centered in the 1920s, believed that moral traits were involved in moral action. They studied primarily either disparate moral traits or their interrelationships in some specified combination. The subject's verbal answers were used to assess one or more moral factors (e.g., conscientiousness, empathy) and their relationship to the subject's observed actions. The studies of Hartshorne and May (1928), Hartshorne, May, and Maller (1929), and Hartshorne, May, and Shuttleworth (1930) with regard to cheating are classic examples of a moral trait approach and its general assumptions.

Hartshorne et al. (1929) posited the existence of moral information or knowledge (Blasi, 1980). They set out to document their subjects' ability to recognize the moral norms of their particular place and time. They further assumed that at least some of their subjects possessed such traits as honesty and self-control. They believed that when faced with temptations to cheat, the honest person would remain steadfast and the dishonest person would fall into temptation. In fact, their extensive studies showed little consistency from one tempting situation to another: Some subjects cheated on one test but not on another. A moderate amount of cheating turned out to be the norm. What subjects had previously declared to be their conviction about the morality of cheating was not particularly helpful in predicting who would cheat or how often that cheating would occur.

Years later the work of Lawrence Kohlberg and his associates would approach the study of moral action from the perspective of moral reasoning. What the Kohlberg group provided was a way of studying both how and what the subjects thought about morality. One of Lawrence Kohlberg's many significant contributions to the field was his insight that what needed to be studied next was not so much a subject's decision about whether or not to act in a way that the researchers had previously identified as morally right or wrong, but how a subject formed decisions about what is moral and what is morally correct (Kohlberg, 1958).

Blasi set the stage for the next shift in the field by demonstrating the need to study once more what has been the original object of scrutiny before Kohlberg's work on moral judgment: moral action.

The next 22 years (1958 - 1980) were characterized by an increasing attention to Kohlberg's cognitive-developmental theories about moral judgment, by critical analyses of the validity of his findings (e.g., Kurtines & Grief, 1974; Simpson, 1974), and by studies of the educational and social implications (e.g., Kohlberg, 1966, 1971a, 1971b; Kohlberg and Turiel, 1971; Mosher, 1980; Mosher & Sprinthall, 1972).

Blasi outlined how studies of moral judgment represented a radical departure from the thinking of the past (Blasi, 1980). Blasi set the stage for the third phase in the field, beginning in 1980, by demonstrating the need to study once more what had been the original object of scrutiny before Kohlberg's work on moral judgment: moral action. According to Blasi, research about moral choices should necessarily be done in ways that examine the relationship of the newly explored concept of moral judgment to the actual decisions people make (Blasi, 1980).

Models of Moral Action: An Overview

The Rest Model

James Rest (1986) postulates four components of moral action. Each component deals with one related group of inner processes. Each involves some predominantly cognitive and some mainly affective behaviors as well as cognitive-affective inter-actions. All four components have developmental features but include non-developmental factors also. The four components are not separate one from the other. Each can be influenced by other components. Though presented in a numerical order, they are not necessarily interconnected in linear fashion.

Component I involves interpretation; included are the processes used when some-one identifies a situation as moral and then appraises and selects the factors that define the particular nature of that situation. Also part of Component I are the processes needed to imagine the initial feelings and thoughts of any other actors in the situation as well as their reactions to potential and actual solutions. Along with such mainly cognitive factors as moral judgment, affective features may come into play such as empathy, shame, satisfaction, and pride. Component I incorporates a sensitivity to others and an awareness of their thoughts and feelings. Moreover, it includes ways of perceiving those data and understanding the situation. In some circumstances, there may be comparatively little cognitive activity, in others a great deal (Rest, 1986).

Component II is identification of the action which is felt and thought to be the one right solution, the moral ideal. Values, attitudes, and stage of moral development all come into play. Ideological or religious factors can have a role also (Rest, 1986). So, presumably, can history and culture.

Component III is the selection of the action the person will actually perform. A morally ideal course of action (Component II) may conflict with other options, both moral and nonmoral. Many different motives may come into play, and a range of values may as well. Several motivating forces may be involved. In effect, Component III encompasses the processes of selecting between different affective needs and between different affective results (Rest, 1986).

Component IV encompasses the processes involved in carrying out the selected plan of action. Persistence, intelligence, and social skills may be involved. Having selected an action, the person needs both the stamina to follow through and the skills to bring about the desired ends. Will-power and social knowledge are necessary to carry out the planned action (Rest, 1986).

Though presented individually, the four components are not separate entities, and a considerable amount of interaction occurs. Nor are the components necessarily connected in linear fashion. Someone may conceivably react to a situation with the selection of a moral choice (Component II), immediately start to carry it out (Component IV), as a result learn more about the situation and reappraise it (Component I), and then have to negotiate between the motives behind the first choice, and the motives behind other possible courses of action (Component III), and so forth.

James Rest's model identifies four major elements of "behaving morally" (Rest, 1986), which for Rest means moral action in accordance with deontic choice. Doing the right thing, Rest argues, involves at a minimum thinking that the situation is one in which there is a choice and an outcome which will affect someone; knowing, thinking out, or intuiting a right solution; choosing this option over other impulses, thoughts, or values; and carrying it out. Various factors are involved in these four components, including cognitions, affect, and their interactions. The four components are not necessarily active in any particular order. Any component can have an effect on another. He acknowledges that contributions from many different branches of psychology have contributions to make. He does not rule out the possibility that in the future other components may be added.

The Kohlberg Model

Lawrence Kohlberg's model of moral action is based on the importance of moral judgment as a determinant of moral action. Two aspects of his later work need to be considered with respect to the connection between moral cognition and moral action: The elaboration of the Kohlberg moral judgment stage to include Substages

A and B (Kohlberg & Higgins, 1984; Kohlberg, Levine, & Hewer, 1983), and the paradigm for moral action laid out in the article "The Relationship of Moral Judgment to Moral Action" (Kohlberg & Candee, 1984). His introduction of the substages served to increase the relationship between moral judgment stage and moral action. The paradigm sets out a theoretical basis for defining that relationship empirically.

Substages. Kohlberg explicitly indicated that the Moral Judgment Interview he used to determine a subject's stage of moral development was not also a test of moral conduct (Kohlberg & Candee, 1984). Moral judgment does influence, however, the affective components of morality in that the ways one looks at a situation determines to some extent the way one feels (Kohlberg, 1969). The importance of moral judgment for moral action was to some extent redefined by Kohlberg's introduction of the Substages A and B (Kohlberg & Higgins, 1984; Kohlberg, Levine, & Hewer, 1983).

> "Kantian" principles, norms, or duties are experienced as having a validity external to the structure of an individual's moral judgment.

Every stage of moral development has both a Substage A and a Substage B. Each substage incorporates developmental features relating to the content of moral choice as well as to the formal, structural aspects of moral judgment. Some individuals move from Substage A to Substage B, and others go from Substage B at one stage to Substage B at the next higher stage (Kohlberg & Higgins, 1984). Substage B contains features that increase the likelihood of moral action in conformity with deontic choice (Kohlberg, Levine, & Hewer, 1983).

Kohlberg used the words "deontic choice" with respect to two somewhat different concepts. Mainly, deontic choice refers to an individual's moral knowledge of the one preferred or prescribed moral choice, the action dictated by duty. However, Kohlberg also used the words "deontic choice" to describe a consensual decision as to the appropriate action: In such cases the deontic choice is the action chosen by more than 75% of subjects at Stage V in answer to a given dilemma (Kohlberg & Candee, 1984). By reference to the consensual deontic choice, the actions of people at a *lower* stage can also be evaluated in terms of whether they choose the morally "right" action. Selecting the deontic choice picked by the majority of people at Stage V of moral development is one of the criteria for inclusion in Substage B. The reasons for the selection will differ in accord with the subject's own stage of moral judgment. Added to this criterion are specific "Kantian" and four "Piagetian" criteria.

"Kantian" was used by Kohlberg to describe criteria having to do with an autonomous orientation towards moral action. "Kantian" norms, principles and duties are prescriptive. Every person is treated not as a means but as an end *per se*. Moral choice is more than personal; by action the subject makes choices that have the quality of establishing norms for other people also (Kohlberg, Higgins, Tappan, & Schrader, 1984). "Kantian" principles, norms, or duties are experienced as having a validity external to the structure of an individual's moral judgment. They share characteristics with the transcendental categorical imperatives of Immanuel Kant (1724-1804). Categorical imperatives make their own demands, but are not experienced as alien to the experience of the actors. The language of categorical imperatives is our own, the moral tone our own moral tone, but the primacy of the imperative is experienced as transcendental (Kant, 1781/1969).

Five "Kantian" criteria were listed for inclusion in Substage B (Kohlberg, Higgins, Tappan, & Schrader, 1984). The subject must show evidence of having a hierarchy of values, with the values of life, of acting in conformity with conscience, and of respecting earned property placed above the other values in the resolution of the moral judgment dilemmas (*hierarchy*). Values must be seen as intrinsic to humanity and human personality (*intrinsicalness*). The deontic choice must be prescriptive in that it demands a given action no matter what the costs or contradictory inclinations of the actor (*prescriptivity*). The individual must decide in such a way that the choices have the quality of establishing norms for all others in a given set of circumstances (*universality*), and beyond that for actors in similar circumstances (*universalizability*).

The first "Piagetian" criterion is that the subject must make the action choice which opposes arbitrary rules and authority and aligns with human well-being, welfare, and reciprocal rights (*choice*). The subject must also show understanding of moral choice as a process by which one arrives autonomously at answers by logical means (*autonomy*). A core assumption about the interpersonal relationships between the people involved in a moral dilemma must be that they respect each other (*mutual respect*). The subject must demonstrate consideration of the points of view and concerns of other actors in the dilemma and must show mutual perspective-taking (*reversibility*). Finally, the subject must be aware that rules and roles do not exist *a priori*: There must be demonstrated awareness that institutions and rules are put together as a result of cooperation between people (*constructivism*) (Kohlberg, Higgins, Tappan, & Schrader, 1984). Substage B subjects have in common, therefore, a number of interpersonal and intellectual skills, as well as a generally questioning, potentially independent way of thinking.

Moral Action. Kohlberg's model of the relationship between moral judgment and moral action differs from Rest's in that non-cognitive-developmental factors are specifically ruled out (Kohlberg & Candee, 1984). Kohlberg did not deny the potential validity of Rest's model, and he stated that he would himself have arrived at one similar had he used the same criteria. Kohlberg's model demonstrates how the one factor of moral judgment relates to moral action. Like Rest's, his model has four parts, each a separate psychological function which also interacts with the other psychological functions.

Function I involves interpretation of the situation. The cognitive structures of Selman's (1980) perspective-taking are used to enable the subject to become aware of the point of view of all actors in the dilemma, their feelings, and their claims. The interpretation of the dilemma depends on the subject's stage and substage of moral judgment.

Function II, which depends on Function I, has to do with identifying the deontic choice. According to Kohlberg's research, subjects at a principled stage of moral judgment will tend overwhelmingly to make the same deontic choice. So also will subjects at lower stages who belong in the Substage B category. To some extent they will intuit the same answer reached by the principled thinkers.

Function III, which follows from Functions I and II, involves a judgment of personal responsibility to act in accordance with the choice made in Function II. According to Kohlberg, subjects at each higher stage, and those in Substage B, hold themselves increasingly responsible for acting in accordance with their deontic choice.

Function IV includes the "non-moral" skills necessary to follow through the moral action in accordance with the deontic choice. The three skills Kohlberg cited (Kohlberg & Candee, 1984)— intelligence, attention, and delay of gratification—are all cognitive.

Kohlberg's theory does not appear to account explicitly for those moral situations in which someone is not aware of a deontic choice. He acknowledged that such a situation could occur, but restricted his model to "actions engaging a deontic judgment of rightness or justice" (Kohlberg & Candee, 1984, p. 519). Also, recognizing a deontic choice does not necessarily lead to deciding one is responsible or obligated to follow it. Another course may be selected over the one which is deontic. Moreover, a decision to choose the deontic solution may be made for non-cognitive, or even non-moral, reasons. Kohlberg's model does not appear to account explicitly for how or why this may happen.

The Gilligan Model

Carol Gilligan's fieldwork study of moral judgment in action (1982) led her to identify in women a structure of moral judgment fundamentally different from the one outlined by Kohlberg (Kohlberg, 1958). Gilligan's theory of an ethic of care and responsibility involves a developmentally structured view of a self which is intrinsically moral, and is at the heart of a network of relationships based on a responsibility to attend to the needs of others. Moral action consists of responding to the needs of those involved in a situation.

Gilligan's theory of an ethic of care and responsibility involves a developmentally structured view of a self which is intrinsically moral, and is at the heart of a network of relationships based on a responsibility to attend to the needs of others.

In this ethic, at the conventional level—the one most likely to be found in young adults—moral judgment defines as moral the action that is caring and avoids hurt to others. Looking after one's self is seen as selfish. The inherent paradox of caring for others but not for self may then create disequilibrium, and the concept of care may as a result be expanded to include the self. Self-care thus becomes a matter of self-integrity (Gilligan, 1982).

The central concern of women in Gilligan's model is with relationships between the self and others. First in their initial response and then subsequently in appraising a situation, women are more sensitive to others' *needs*, and give more weight to them, than do men. In contrast, when men appraise a situation, they are more concerned with others' *rights*. For women, the perspective-taking inherent in moral judgment has to do more with the emotional well being of the other actors. Where men structure a moral judgment based on rights and fairness, using reciprocity and the principle of equality, women's moral judgment has more to do with needs and care and is based on connections and equity (Gilligan, 1982).

In Gilligan's (1982) model the cognitive and the affective are closely interwoven. The moral appraisal of a dilemma calls for concern, empathy, and compassionate understanding. Moral action consists of responding to the identified needs of those involved in the situation. The self is defined by its actions. Since situations are viewed in terms of relationships and caring, and the moral imperative is to take care of wants and needs, the self is therefore a moral self. The self is evaluated in terms of whether the requisite care is being expressed and how adequately it is being expressed. Because relationships are a major content and structure of moral judgment, the self is therefore also evaluated in terms of its connectedness with others. By implication, there is no moral action which does not involve the self.

In her interviews with women facing the crisis of whether or not to have an abortion, Gilligan found that for many there was no action choice that was experienced as deontic, no clear path dictated as duty (Gilligan, 1982). What emerged instead was an underlying concern with whether and how the self was acting responsibly—that is to say, how well the self was taking into consideration the needs and wants of all concerned and responding to those needs and wants. In Kohlberg's (1984a, 1984b) conception of the morality of justice, deontic choice arises mainly from the analysis of the situation. In Gilligan's ethic of care and responsibility, the equivalent of the deontic choice is inherent in the basic definition of the ethic: The path of duty, the deontic choice, is to care. Out of the structure of the ethic of care and responsibility arise both the deontic choice and the motivation to moral action. To some extent, the equivalent of Kohlberg's deontic choice is the appraisal of how well the self is carrying out its role in caring. This is essentially an assessment of the worthiness of the self's performance. Care and responsibility in this ethos characterize day-to-day living. Moral action can thus become part and parcel of everyday experience.

The Blasi Model

A major theoretical contribution of Augusto Blasi's model of moral action is his analysis of the motivational force of moral cognition. According to Blasi, moral judgment is not only the basis for appraisals, but also an impelling force behind action. A rational belief is considered true by the agent, and truth can be the reason for action (Blasi, 1983). Secondly, when someone makes a judgment of personal responsibility, one of the influencing factors may be the moral self (Blasi, 1983, 1984, 1993; Blasi & Oresick, 1986). Moral integrity is maintained by preserving self-consistency. Not all people, however, consider or see the self as moral.

Blasi did not redefine Rest's (1986) encompassing, taxonomic model. On one hand, he called attention to the losses inherent in moving away from an essentially cognitive-structuralist approach (Blasi, 1980, 1983, 1993). On the other hand, like Rest, he acknowledged the contributions made by researchers from other branches of psychology (Blasi, 1983). Blasi's model owes a great deal to Kohlberg and Candee (1984), but differs from it in several ways. Blasi does not take issue with Kohlberg directly, but does refer to Norma Haan's objections to Kohlberg's theory in a way which suggests he shares at least some of those objections (Blasi, 1983).

Blasi focuses on the role of cognition in impelling people to understand and make sense of reality, both internal and external. The cognitive structures of moral judgment both define the situation and motivate the actor towards moral action. The constant interaction between reality and cognitive structures is motivated by a need to understand as much and as well as possible, and to find the truth (Blasi, 1980, 1983, 1984). In moral situations, the truth is found in action. The normative drive of cognitive processes is to discover the truth, and the normative drive of moral cognitive structures is to put that truth into action (Blasi, 1983).

Under certain circumstances, Blasi believes, there is an intermediate step from moral judgment to moral action (Blasi, 1983, 1984; Blasi & Oresick, 1986). This step Blasi labels a judgment of moral responsibility: The person seeks an answer to the question whether the moral choice is binding on him or her. The question is decided by the moral self. The structures of the self are assumed to be developmental (see also Damon, 1984). There are also structural-developmental stages in the concept of the self-as-moral. Not all people, however, see themselves as moral (Blasi, 1984; Blasi & Oresick, 1986).

Blasi's presentation of the concept of the self-as-moral is close to Erikson's descriptions of integrity (e.g., Erikson, 1964, 1968; Blasi, 1983, 1993). The tendency to self-consistency is a cognitive motive in the direction of moral action. If a deontic choice is made, and moral action does not ensue, guilt is experienced. However, for some people under some circumstances moral action may also be consistent with a nonmoral identity, and inconsistent with moral judgment (Blasi, 1984, 1993; Blasi & Oresick, 1986). Even though the self is aware that in the hierarchy of values truth is paramount, for example, the self may in some circumstances decide against the action selected by moral judgment as representing truth (Blasi, 1983). The integrity of the self can, however, be a powerful motivating force: Integrity is experienced as being connected to the essential core of the person's existence. It demands respect for one's view of reality and has strong implications for being true to oneself in behavior (Blasi, 1983).

The Haan Model

Norma Haan's model on moral action differs fundamentally from the others reviewed here. For her, the realm of morality is interpersonal interaction, and moral action is the managing of relations between participants. Thinking about a moral situation does not mean a process of deciding upon a hierarchy of rights and of selecting an ideal answer. Rather, it is engaging in joint evaluations with the other participants, and working out a compromise, not some absolute solution (Haan, Aerts, & Cooper, 1985). She cited examples of individual actors in the same group using both interactional morality and Kohlberg's morality of rights and justice. She suggested that the moral choice may have to do with situational and personality factors (Haan, et al., 1985).

"Morality is a particular kind of social agreement that equalizes people's relations with one another" (Haan, et al., 1985, p. 11). It follows from such a definition that moral solutions are specific to a given situation, a given group of actors, and a given time. They take into account what people need and what they deserve, and this may be changed over time. The negotiation that supplies an answer today may need to be continued tomorrow. A reason to continue tomorrow could be to redress an imbalance that is having an effect on harmonic relations in the group, and cannot be allowed to continue (Haan, et al., 1985).

Haan argued that while humans develop morally, they do so by gradual movement through a sequence of five levels, not by stage progression. Four year olds and adults have the same basic moral understandings and concerns: What changes with development are their actions which are a result of social experiences and personality factors (Haan, et al., 1985; Haan, 1963, 1977).

Levels of Interactional Morality. Haan's five levels of interactional morality measure more than where a subject belongs on a continuum. Though different, the levels in the Haan system are not discrete. They gain their identity from their position on an external observer's scale, rather than from the cognitive structures of the actors (Haan et al., 1985).

Interactional morality deals with the management of inequalities in groups. The primary differentiation between levels is the way in which these inequalities are conceived. Subjects at Level I are concerned with assimilating experiences in their own interests. Their egocentricity is marked. Though they can be aware fleetingly of the interest of others, such attention is not sustained. There is no sense of the mutuality of interest. The basic orientation to the social world is of a contest or conflict between self and other. Compromises are few: Most social balances happen because of relative indifference. Major interactions involve either going along with the other or blocking the other (Haan et al., 1985).

Movement from Level I to Level II depends on several factors. The person must have enough skills not to need the protection of a (quasi-) parental figure and must become aware of other actor's needs and desires. The notion of interpersonal exchange must be conceived and negotiation seen as both possible and necessary. Level II is marked by increasing awareness of the interests of others: The needs of the other are recognized as different from those of the self. But there is not as yet an identification that interests can be recognized as mutual. Balances are achieved by trading which at times involves allowing the other's interests to be met. When absolutely necessary, both parties may compromise (Haan et al., 1985).

Assimilation of the interest of the self to others' interests into the common interest characterizes Level III. An increased awareness that one is isolated from others if their interests are not also taken into account is the main reason for the transition to Level III. Harmony is sought through mutuality, though the self's interests are differentiated from those of others. There is an emphasis on maintaining relations involving good faith. The interests of all parties—self and others—are thought to be identical. Others are categorized as either good or bad (Haan et al., 1985).

It is clear from these brief descriptions that levels of interactional morality involve different concepts of self, self-esteem, and group. The levels are differentiated by the amount of egocentricity, the awareness of the other, and the role of mutuality.

Accommodation of self interests to common interests is the central characteristic of Level IV. The transition to Level IV is marked by an inability to maintain a belief in the goodness of the self and of others in the face of mounting evidence that at times some others act with bad faith. The self is seen as one object amongst other objects. At times announced as such, balances are compromises in which all participate. Interactions of groups are structured and systematized. It is assumed that anyone may at times behave badly. Understanding and, if appropriate, disapproval are directed more at the behavior than at the person (Haan et al., 1985).

Level IV behavior accepts that others sometimes act in bad faith. Also, the transition to Level V depends partly on admitting one's own guilt. Common practice is no longer adequate for solving moral dilemmas well enough to meet the needs of the self and of others. At Level V, self, other, and mutual interests are balanced. The differences between the interests are recognized and taken into consideration. Self and other are equal. Equilibrium is preferably achieved through mutual interests, but if that cannot be brought about, compromises are effected or a decision is taken to choose the least disruptive solution (Haan et al., 1985).

It is clear from these brief descriptions that levels of interactional morality involve different concepts of self, self-esteem, and group. The levels are differentiated by the amount of egocentricity, the awareness of the other, and the role of mutuality. There is a gradual progression towards more specific skills and towards an increased ability to bring about balance among an increasing number of forces. Morality is also not only individual. The level of interactional morality depends increasingly on the other actors and on the specifics of the situation. However, since interactional morality is *action*, it is not correct to say that a person is at a given level. The levels are used to differentiate performances. A person may function at several levels depending on a number of factors, including importantly the characteristics of the other people involved in a specific situation.

Affective Reactions. That individuals and groups interact morally at different levels is inevitable. The basic form of that moral action is dialogue (Haan, 1978). All dialogue involves emotion. This is particularly the case when the dialogue has to do with conflicting needs. How people in a group deal with the emotions aroused depends partly on the levels of interactional morality in their repertoire. But dealing with conflict is also a personal activity. It is an activity which has an effect on others, but which is also in some instances private, intrapersonal. As a result, moral behavior is not consistent across the board (Haan et al., 1985). Haan posited the existence of a metering function in human beings which monitors the necessity for experiencing any disturbing affect (Haan, 1963.) Affect, however, can be threatening, and no cognition is without its feeling component.

In Haan's model, stress is a constant component of all moral problems. Stress arises in a moral situation when the actors' views of themselves as moral beings are brought into question. Moreover, a moral situation challenges the moral identity not only of the actors but also of the group. Whenever a moral problem arises, the group is called upon to be morally functional and sensible (Haan et al., 1985). Individuals and groups may default morally for a range of reasons.

Summary of the Models of Moral Action

Five models of moral action have been presented. James Rest's model identifies four components to moral behavior (Rest, 1986). Each component involves various processes and factors. Interpretation of the particular nature of a situation according to the subject's moral assessment—the first component—is followed by choosing a course of action that is the morally correct one—Component II. Component III involves a decision whether that moral choice really applies to the actor, and whether the moral action choice takes precedence over other desired choices, and raises the issues of motive and value. The final component involves the skills to follow through with, and implement, the moral choice. Rest includes in his components many elements from non-developmental psychologies.

Kohlberg's four-function model involves both a redefinition of his stages of moral judgment to incorporate two substages (Kohlberg, Higgins, Tappan, & Schrader, 1984) and an explication of how moral judgment alone effects moral action (Kohlberg & Candee, 1984). Kohlberg assumes that people at Substage B will intuit an answer to a moral dilemma in agreement with the reasoned and principled answer worked out by the majority of subjects at Stage 5. The four factors Kohlberg included in his model of moral action are interpretation, deontic choice, a judgment of personal responsibility, and follow-through skills. The first three factors are essentially cognitive, and driven by moral judgment.

Carol Gilligan (1982) expanded the concept of morality by identifying a developmental ethic of care and responsibility, mainly found in women. She has found that women's thinking about a moral problem sometimes does not include a clear path of duty (a deontic choice). According to her theory, women also view themselves differently at various developmental moral stages. The self is essentially defined in terms of relationships, and moral judgment is based in needs, care, and on connections. In this sense, moral action is part of everyday experience.

In his theory, Augusto Blasi describes how moral action is affected by moral cognition and moral self image (Blasi, 1983, 1984; Blasi & Oresick, 1986). Truth, according to Blasi, motivates one to action. Self integrity is a central concept. In certain circumstances, Blasi believes, integrity acts as a deciding factor, determining which course of action will be followed. The cognitive structures of moral judgment both define the moral choice and motivate the actor towards moral action. Blasi's concept of the self-as-moral is close to Erik Erikson's (1959, 1968) descriptions of integrity as a polarity of one component of his eight stages.

Finally, new definitions of morality as social dialogue, and of moral behavior as the maintenance of generally acceptable social harmony, characterize the work of Norma Haan (1986). She sketched a five-level scheme of moral behavior. Haan's emphasis was on measuring personal behavior not moral judgement. For her, morality is not thought (reflection, reasoning) but something done (action). The realm of morality is interpersonal interaction. Moral action manifests itself in balancing relations between participants. Determination of a course of moral action comes from engaging in joint evaluations with other affected participants toward a compromise which works for all, not some absolute solution.

Moral concern differs little from childhood to adulthood. Developmental changes do occur in the individual's concepts of the social world, of the self, and of moral interaction. A person may use several levels of interactional morality. Moral skills are acquired with—and depend on—experience. Action, thought, and affect cannot be separated. All three are present in any part of moral behavior.

Moral interaction begins with the identification of the pertinent moral, personal, and affective elements in a situation. This process of identification and awareness continues throughout any subsequent attempt to reestablish or maintain social harmony. The efficacy of the solution—which may be fluid and will probably be temporary—depends on the involvement of all concerned. A solution negotiated in good faith by all actors is more likely to fit the situation than a solution imposed by only some. Participants will be most able to invent satisfactory solutions when they are able to use coping mechanisms and avoid defensive reactions. Moral situations by definition threaten discord and have a strong, stress-producing affective component.

All five models trace a relationship between how subjects apprehend or comprehend the moral world and how they act on that moral understanding. They agree also that cognitive and noncognitive factors are involved in assessment, decision-making, and execution of moral action, though Kohlberg (1958; Kohlberg & Candee, 1984) traced only the cognitive strand. Finally, there is at least an implied agreement that noncognitive developmental psychologies have contributions to make to the study of morality. The theories of moral action sketched in this selective review are in fundamental disagreement about the structure of the morality by which people judge circumstances, about the decision-making processes involved prior to behavior characterized as moral, and about the forms of action that can be called moral. They disagree about the role, existence, and nature of deontic choices. The role of the self also varies from model to model.

References

Blasi, A. (1980). Bridging moral cognition and moral action: A critical review of the literature. *Psychological Bulletin, 88*, 1-45.

Blasi, A. (1983). Moral cognition and moral action: A theoretical perspective. *Developmental Review, 3*, 178-210.

Blasi, A. (1984). Moral identity: Its role in moral functioning. In W. M. Kurtines & J. L. Gewirtz (Eds.), *Morality, moral behavior, and moral development*. New York: John Wiley & Sons.

Blasi, A. (1993). The development of identity: Some implications for moral functioning. In G. G. Noam & T. E. Wren (Eds.), *The moral self*. Cambridge, MA: MIT Press.

Blasi, A., & Oresick, R. J. (1986). Emotions and cognitions in self-inconsistency. In D. J. Bearison & H. Zmiles (Eds.), *Thoughts and emotion: Developmental perspectives*. Hillsdale, NJ: Erlbaum.

Damon, W. (1984). Self-understanding and moral development from childhood to adolescence. In W. M. Kurtines & J. L. Gewirtz (Eds.), *Morality, moral behavior, and moral development*. New York: John Wiley & Sons.

Erikson, E. H. (1959). Identity and the life cycle. *Psychological Issues, 1*.

Erikson, E. H. (1964). *Insight and responsibility*. New York: Norton.

Erikson, E. H. (1968). *Identity, youth, and crisis*. New York: Norton.

Gilligan, C. (1982). *In a different voice: Psychological theory and women's development*. Cambridge, MA: Harvard University Press.

Haan, N. (1963). Proposed models of ego functioning: Coping and defense mechanisms in relationship to I.Q. change. *Psychological Monographs, 77, 8*.

Haan, N. (1977). *Coping and defending: Processes of self-environment organization*. New York: Academic Press.

Haan, N. (1978). Two moralities in action contexts: Relationships to thought, ego regulation, and development. *Journal of Personality and Social Psychology, 36*, 286-305.

Haan, N. (1986). Systematic variability in the quality of moral action, as defined by two formulations. *Journal of Personality and Social Psychology, 50*, 1271-1284.

Haan, N., Aerts, E., & Cooper, B. (1985). *On moral grounds: The search for practical morality.* New York: New York University Press.

Hartshorne, H., & May, M. A. (1928). *Studies in the nature of character: Vol. 1. Studies in deceit.* New York: Macmillan.

Hartshorne, H., May, M. A., & Maller, J. B. (1929). *Studies in the nature of character: Vol. II. Studies in self-control.* New York: Macmillan.

Hartshorne, H., May, M. A., & Shuttleworth, F. K. (1930). *Studies in the nature of character: Vol. III. Studies in the organization of character.* New York: Macmillan.

Kant, I. (1781/1969). *Critique of pure reason.* (N. K. Smith, Ed.). New York: Saint Martin's Press.

Kohlberg, L. (1958). *The development of modes of moral thinking and choice in the years ten to sixteen.* Unpublished doctoral dissertation, University of Chicago.

Kohlberg, L. (1966). Moral education in the school. *School Review, 74,* 1-30.

Kohlberg, L. (1969). Stage and sequence: The cognitive-developmental approach to socialization. In D. A. Goslin (Ed.), *Handbook of socialization theory and research.* Chicago: Rand McNally.

Kohlberg, L. (1971a). Indoctrination versus relativity in value education. *Zygon, 6,* 285-310.

Kohlberg, L. (1971b). Stages of moral development as a basis for moral education. In C. Beck, B. Crittendon, & E. Sullivan (Eds.), *Moral education: Interdisciplinary approaches.* Toronto: University of Toronto Press.

Kohlberg, L. (1984a). The six stages of justice judgment. In L. Kohlberg (Ed.), *Essays on moral development: Vol. II. The psychology of moral development.* San Francisco: Harper and Row.

Kohlberg, L. (1984b). The meaning and measurement of moral judgment. In L. Kohlberg (Ed.), *Essays on moral development: Vol. II. The psychology of moral development.* San Francisco: Harper and Row.

Kohlberg, L., & Candee, D. (1984). The relationship of moral judgment to moral action. In L. Kohlberg (Ed.), *Essays on moral development: Vol. II. The psychology of moral development.* San Francisco: Harper and Row.

Kohlberg, L., & Higgins, A. (1984). Continuities and discontinuities in childhood and adult development revisited - again. In L. Kohlberg (Ed.), *Essays on moral development: Vol. II. The psychology of moral development.* San Francisco: Harper and Row.

Kohlberg, L., & Higgins, A., Tappan, M., & Schrader, D. (1984). From substages to moral types: Heteronomous and autonomous morality. In L. Kohlberg (Ed.), *Essays on moral development: Vol. II. The psychology of moral development.* San Francisco: Harper and Row.

Kohlberg, L., Levine, C., & Hewer, A. (1983). The current formulation of the theory. *Contributions to Human Development, 10,* Basel, Switzerland: S. Karger.

Kohlberg, L., & Turiel, E. (1971). Moral development and moral education. In G. Lesser (Ed.), *Psychology and educational practice.* Glenwood, IL: Scott Foresman.

Kurtines, W., & Greif, E. B. (1974). The development of moral thoughts: Review and evaluation of Kohlberg's approach. *Psychological Bulletin, 81,* 453-470.

Mosher, R. L., (1980). *Moral education: A first generation of research and development.* New York: Praeger.

Mosher, R. L., & Sprinthall, N. (1972). Deliberate psychological education. *The Counseling Psychologist, 2,* 3-82.

Piaget, J. (1932). *The moral judgment of the child.* London: Routledge & Kegan Paul.

Rest, J. R. (1986). *Moral development: Advances in research and theory.* New York: Praeger.

Selman, R. L. (1980). *The growth of interpersonal understanding.* New York: Academic Press.

Simpson, E. L. (1974). Moral development research: A case study of scientific cultural bias. *Human Development, 17,* 81-106.

CHAPTER

FURTHER THEORETICAL
PERSPECTIVES ON MAKING
MORAL CHOICES

Molly Patterson

Some of the most promising work on moral reasoning and moral action in recent years invokes the concept of identity and probes the relationship between moral choice and the concept of self. Identity is a topic currently arousing much interest in a number of disciplines. But what exactly is meant by "identity" remains murky, difficult to specify, and problematic from a methodological viewpoint. The purpose of this chapter, as stated in the Introduction, is to explore the recent research and insights of potentially relevant writing about moral choice and its antecedents from perspectives beyond the original cognitive development paradigm which informed this project.

In order to accomplish its purpose, the chapter is organized into six sections. The first section explores theories of the self and moral identity. In particular, this section draws on the recent work of Kristen Monroe (1996), Anne Colby and William Damon (1992), Augusto Blasi (1993), and Larry Nucci and John Lee (1993). The second section focuses on moral agency, in particular the work of Albert Bandura (1991) who argues for what he calls a social cognitive perspective. Bandura rejects cognitive stage theories. He is interested in the many different factors involved in determining when people will act and think morally and when they will not. A third section looks at the relationship between emotion and moral action. The primary focus in this section is the work of Martin Hoffman (1991). The fourth section examines a contribution from the field of philosophy by Lawrence Blum (1991). The fifth section probes the relationship between these varied approaches, and then discusses the relationship in thinking about moral choice between philosophy and psychology more generally. The sixth section contains very brief concluding thoughts about future directions in research.

Many of the ideas which are being exchanged from an interdisciplinary perspective, in particular between the disciplines of philosophy and psychology, make for rich and interesting conversations. This exchange also introduces some new complications. Most notably, it is challenging to consider how the different perspectives fit together—where do they overlap, how do they conflict with or supplement each other, and how are they describing or concerned with essentially different issues. Because different disciplines are built around different core questions, assumptions, and standards of justification, authors spanning disciplines are frequently involved in multiple conversations at once. This chapter will attempt to bring some clarity to the relationship between the different conversations.

I. Morality, Identity, and the Self

Kristen Monroe: Perspective on Altruism

Monroe's (1996) work stems from her interest in altruism as a challenge to the dominant social science paradigm of rational choice. In *The Heart of Altruism* (1996), Monroe, who was trained as a political economist, examines possible explanations of altruism from different fields, and then explores how those explanations can account for, or fail to account for, evidence of altruism offered by rescuers of Jews from Nazi Germany. The rescuers she interviewed all assisted Jews at great risk or cost to themselves and for no extrinsic reward. Most of the people rescued were not friends or acquaintances prior to the rescue. In addition to the rescuers, Monroe interviews three other categories of people: entrepreneurs, people who have made a great deal of money and who give little, if any of it, away; philanthropists, who give much more than do entrepreneurs but not so much as to jeopardize their own standard of living or that of their family; and heroes, who rescued people they did not know at some risk to themselves. Heroes are distinguished from rescuers by the fact that their heroic acts were single, short-term occurrences, whereas rescuers were involved in altruistic, risk-taking behavior repeatedly and for extended periods of time.

Monroe (1996) argues that rational choice perspectives in the social sciences assume that people will act in their own best interests and choose their actions according to cost/benefit calculations. This approach cannot account for altruism of the sort practiced by rescuers. Rational choice theorists argue that altruists may have a different "utility function" or set of goals and preferences than other people, but that they ultimately behave as they do in order to satisfy their own needs, whether to assure reciprocal behavior in the future or to alleviate their own guilt or pain at seeing another suffer. Still at the core of the rational choice argument is the assumption of a cost/benefit calculation.

Monroe asserts that the rational choice argument works well to explain the behavior of entrepreneurs and even certain philanthropists, but the further one moves down the continuum towards pure altruism, the less "rational actor theory" explains. In particular, altruists do not appear to engage in cost/benefit analyses of weighing the pros and cons of different courses of action. Rather, they simply act on what they perceive to be the need of another human being. The action is understood to be essential and unavoidable, it is not calculated, and there is no perception on the part of the rescuer that a "choice" is involved.

... altruists do not appear to engage in cost/benefit analyses of weighing the pros and cons of different courses of action.... they simply act on what they perceive to be the need of another human being.

In addition to rational actor theory (primarily from economics), Monroe (1996) examines work on altruism in developmental and social psychology, sociobiology, and socialization theory. While she argues that psychology comes closest to providing a satisfying answer, ultimately the available explanations are unsatisfying. What Monroe suggests as an alternative is "perspective":

Perspective conveys the visual idea of locating oneself in a cognitive map, much as locating oneself in a landscape. It contains the idea that we each have a view of the world, a view of ourselves, a view of others, and a view of ourselves in relation to others. This captures what interests me about the importance of world view and identity for altruism. But I also use perspective to imply that each actor has a particular way of seeing the world and constructs this view much as a painter creates a painting. I presume that the perspectives of altruists resemble each other and that they will differ in significant and consistent ways from the perspectives of nonaltruists. (p. 14)

The understanding of oneself (identity) and relationship to other people (world view) delimits the expectations one has of what counts as normal or acceptable behavior in a given situation. If one understands oneself as a human being who is joined with other human beings in a common struggle for the dignity of humanity, then there is no room for cost/benefit calculations of whether to help another person or not. The question is how to help, not whether to help. On the other hand, if there is little perception of being bound to others by a common humanity, if the sense of connection extends only as far as family or close friends or a particular club or community, then the question of whether to help a complete stranger is understood very differently.

Anne Colby and William Damon: Goal Theory

Colby and Damon's (1992) work on goal theory parallels Monroe's (1996) work in that their methods and findings are remarkably similar, although their disciplinary foundations and the orienting questions which appear to guide their theory are different.

Similar to Monroe's (1996) narrative methodology, Colby and Damon (1992) conducted intensive interviews of 23 people who appear to lead extraordinary moral lives (they term their sample "moral exemplars"). Their interviewees were selected from among recommendations Colby and Damon solicited based on a list of criteria developed in consultation with various philosophers, scholars, and religious leaders of different denominations. People they interviewed varied in the kinds of actions to which their moral commitments drew them: helping people who are poor, social justice activism, and attempts to challenge existing social structures. In the article, "The Uniting of Self and Morality in the Development of Extraordinary Moral Commitment," Colby and Damon (1993) describe one interviewee (Virginia) who, as a white woman possessing a deep loyalty to Southern traditions and cultures, nevertheless worked intensively to fight poll taxes, segregation, and the Communist baiting of the 1950s.

Colby and Damon (1993) explore how people deal with conflict between personal and moral goals. They argue that goals are a central component of one's identity (implicit to their theory is the power of identity to motivate action). When morality is central to identity, personal and moral goals become the same, and there is no tension between the two. In this case, the individual is able to be committed fully to moral goals. Not all people experience the fusion of identity and moral beliefs. For these people, identity and morality remain systems that are somewhat separate. Colby and Damon suggest that the content of morality itself does not determine the role of morality in a person's life; rather, the person's sense of self is key.

Individuals with essentially similar moral beliefs may view morality as being more or less central to their sense of self, entailing different levels of commitment to those beliefs. In particular, people for whom morality is a central part of self experience little doubt in their course of action: "Their unity of goals provides a compelling call to engage as well as a sense of certainty about their course of action. Where one's personal choice seems predetermined, there is little room for hesitation or self-doubt" (Colby & Damon, 1993, p. 152). This, of course, is consistent with Monroe's (1996) findings that altruists and heroes do not make "moral choices" in the sense of conducting cost/benefit analyses or weighing the pros and cons. Rather, it is perceived simply as doing what needs to be done, even in the face of great personal risk or cost.

Colby and Damon (1993) probe the path that these 23 moral exemplars took in the development of personal moral goals with particular attention to the dynamic relationship between individuals and social influence. Their model attends to the lifelong process whereby individuals build on their prior experiences; however, it is not a stage developmental theory that specifies particular universal levels that must be passed through in a particular order. They argue that individuals actively engage the social influences to which they are exposed; people are "stimulated and guided" by their social environment, but they are not passive recipients or the "dupes" of social influence.

What remains difficult to specify is why some people continue to develop while others do not and why some people actively engage the challenges and influences of their environment while others do not. This research supports a conception of the unity of personal and moral goals and the central place of those goals in the individual's sense of self.

> The most striking cross-cutting themes are a certainty of belief (a lack of doubt, hesitation, or conflict), a relative lack of concern for possible dangers or negative consequences, the absence of an experience of moral courage (the interviewees do not experience themselves to be extraordinary or unusually courageous), and a positive attitude toward life and deep enjoyment of one's work. (Colby & Damon, 1993, p. 169)

In addition to the interviews they conducted, Colby and Damon (1993) presented their subjects with two dilemmas to determine the subjects' level of development according to Kohlberg's (1969, 1976) developmental model. Subjects spanned the range of Kohlberg's conventional and post-conventional levels. Colby and Damon speculate that there is a relationship between the level of stage development in the Kohlberg system and the kind of activity and moral frame of reference in which the moral exemplars are engaged, with those at the conventional level being more likely to provide direct aid to individuals, while those at the post-conventional level are more likely to be engaged in work oriented towards systematic institutional change.

It cannot be said whether the person's level of development led him/her to particular kinds of activities or whether the particular activities fostered a certain progression in moral development. Further, none of the subjects explained their activities primarily in terms of abstract principles. Even those at Kohlberg's (1969, 1976) post-conventional level, which is defined by abstract principled reasoning, did not rely on abstract principles as the way to justify their work; rather, they used particular events or circumstances to explain themselves.

Colby and Damon's (1993) work is consistent with Monroe's (1996) finding that extraordinary moral action is not necessarily the product of deliberation, of weighing and choosing between different options. This suggests that "moral reasoning," how people adjudicate moral conflict, is only part of the picture. For example, Virginia, the subject described above, went through a period of intense racism in her adolescence and young adult years, even initially refusing to share a table at her college with a student who was Black. As a child, she had friends who were Black, but these relationships were marked by the hierarchy of the deep South (her friends were the children of the nurse employed by her family) and her friendships were largely prohibited by her family. Her attitudes were shaped in part by her experiences at college, but even more strongly by her contact with a friend who was a southerner, like herself, but actively engaged in working against systems of racism. Her goals and sense of self developed through time.

Augusto Blasi (and Erik Erikson): The Development of Moral Identity

The earlier work of Augusto Blasi is discussed in Chapter 5 of this volume. Blasi's (1993) more recent work has moved from a discussion of moral action to an analysis of the development of identity. For Blasi, identity is not a set of personality traits that are separate from cognition. Rather, he is looking at how morality is integrated into the personality and how this works jointly with cognition.

Blasi's (1993) work follows from Erikson's (1968) work on identity. As a Freudian psychotherapist, Erikson developed a theory of identity rooted in Freudian stages of psychosexual development. Erikson starts from the "epigenetic principle" which states that all living, growing things come with a kind of intrinsic master plan for the healthy development of parts into an integrated whole. To achieve a healthy adult identity, the child must navigate a series of stages punctuated by normative crises. When these identity crises are not successfully resolved, they interfere with the adult identity. Successfully navigating the stages in order provides the child the essential elements of a healthy identity: basic trust (sense of well-being), autonomy, initiative, and industry. Failure can bring basic mistrust, shame, self-doubt, guilt, or inferiority.

In adolescence, the healthy personality builds on the elements from these earlier stages to achieve ego-synthesis, "the inner capital accrued from all those experiences of each successive stage, when meaningful identification led to a successful alignment of the individual's basic drives with his endowment and his opportunities" (Erikson, 1968, p. 94). This enables a sense of ego-identity. Erikson describes ego-identity in terms of confidence in one's ability to maintain inner sameness, confidence that one is progressing towards a tangible future, and confidence "that one is developing a personality within a social reality which one understands" (Erikson, 1968, pp. 94-95). Failure to successfully navigate the crisis at this stage results in identity diffusion, which Erikson says is often indicated by the inability to settle on an occupational identity. It is only at this point of adolescence that Erikson would describe a person as having an identity. Development continues throughout adulthood, including stages such as the healthy development of a capacity for intimacy.

> Erikson starts from the "epigenetic principle" which states that all living, growing things come with a kind of intrinsic master plan for the healthy development of parts into an integrated whole.

Blasi (1993) follows somewhat the Eriksonian definition of identity as a special sense of self. He differs in at least three important ways. First, he does not emphasize acceptance of one's culture and cultural roles. Alienation from culture is not, for Blasi, pathological or a failure of identity development. Second, he argues that identity can only be discussed in subjective terms; it is a matter of how one experiences one's self. Third, people may experience their sense of identity differently. These differences are not just a matter of whether one has developed an identity or not (in Erikson's terms) or a matter of the content of the issues around which one has developed the identity. Rather, people who have identities that are organized around similar issues may still relate to those identities differently based upon such things as (a) how central the issue is to their sense of self, (b) whether they see the issue as one that they have chosen and control or as one that is simply a part of them and beyond their control, or (c) whether they see their chosen ideals (and therefore their self) as fragile and requiring protection. Hence, people who have essentially similar moral beliefs may differ in how central those beliefs are to their sense of identity, whether those beliefs have been chosen by them, or how fragile they feel those beliefs to be.

Blasi investigated whether identity can exist in different "modes" and if those modes exist in a developmental relationship to one another. He based his research around four modes of identity described by Loevinger (1976). They are as follows:

- *Social Role Identity.* Here, identity is largely the product of external social forces—relationships to other people (such as family), appearance, and characteristics that garner social approval. There is no sense of core, inner identity.

- *Identity Observed.* One experiences a true, inner self that contrasts with an external, outer self. Self-reflection and self-discovery become more important. The inner self is understood as fixed or given rather than as chosen or constructed by the self.

- *Management of Identity.* Feelings are replaced by ideals, standards and goals as the core of the true self. Identity is experienced as less fixed and more open to change. One is able to improve the self.

- *Identity as Authenticity.* The sense of self is no longer defined by clear sets of goals to be achieved but by relationships to more global concerns and humanity, the discovery of internal conflicts, the affirmation of autonomy in the face of external forces such as stereotypes, and "openness to truth and objectivity in determining one's life and identity" (Blasi, 1993, p. 105).

The last three of these modes—Identity Observed, Management of Identity, and Identity as Authenticity— are all compatible with Erikson's description of achieved identity. Blasi and Milton (1991) designed a method to test whether these modes of identity do indeed occur as distinct clusters of traits within different individuals and if they appear in a developmental sequence. The method consisted of individually interviewing sixth graders and twelfth graders (and in another study twelfth graders and adults) in semi-structured interviews around such topics as the identification of the "real me," the distinction between inner and outer selves, and the desire to change one's self. The interviews were transcribed and used as data for the construction of six self scales, each scale reflecting a dimension of self-experience: real me, private self, self-reflection, sincerity, self-change, and emotional response to self.

Within each dimension, the researchers identified categories which they arranged in developmental sequences. For instance, the scale of "private self" contains five categories ranging from (a) no clear differentiation between an inner psychological self and public self, to (e) inner self is unknowable by other people unless explicitly revealed; desire to keep some aspects of inner self private (Blasi & Milton, 1991). The creation of these scales enabled Blasi and Milton to investigate the extent to which characteristics of self-experience cluster together; for instance, whether a person who is ranked as category (a) or (b) on "real me" also tends to be ranked as category (a) in "private self" and the other areas. If the characteristics do cluster together, it would suggest that the different identity modes as originally outlined by Loevinger do, in fact, describe distinct ways of experiencing identity.

Identity Observed was demonstrated to be prevalent among adolescents, and Identity as Authenticity did not appear until young adulthood. Adults, however, are not necessarily at the level of Identity as Authenticity; many of them appear at levels similar to those of adolescents, consistent with the belief among many developmental psychologists that adults differ widely in the rate at which they develop, as well as whether they continue to develop. Identity develops through time. People may experience their identities very differently. As such, they may also experience the relationship between morality and identity very differently.

Blasi (1993) concludes that moral personality, or the integration of morality and identity, are not necessarily strong predictors of moral action. Further, there may be factors beyond identity that are important predictors. Young children can exhibit a strong sense of what is moral even though they do not have a strong sense of identity. However, Blasi does not conclude from this that moral personality is not an important area of consideration; rather, he suggests that the integration of morality and personality is important and that moral action itself should not serve as the exclusive focus of moral psychology. He suggests that how one conducts one's life over the long run (hence, the need for longitudinal studies) might offer more insight than trying to correlate specific moral beliefs with isolated actions.

Larry Nucci and John Lee: A Domain Approach

Nucci and Lee (1993) are interested in the relationship between autonomy and morality. They argue that this connection exists also in the work of Piaget (1932) and Kohlberg (1969, 1976) (for instance, higher levels of development are associated with autonomously derived moral principles), but little attention is paid to how a sense of personal autonomy develops in children. Nucci and Lee differ from Kohlberg and Piaget by taking a domain approach which suggests that social concepts develop in distinct groupings called domains. Each domain, or partial system, may interact with other domains, but each generally develops in ways that are significantly separate from the others. They hold that there are three basic domains of social knowledge: moral, societal, and psychological. The moral domain has to do with concepts of justice, rights, and welfare; the societal domain orders knowledge of social systems and social organization; and the psychological domain involves emotions, motivations, and the mental states of others, as well as conceptions of the self. This suggests that a child's understanding of social conventions is distinct from the child's understanding of morality. This differs significantly from Kohlberg's and Piaget's argument that it is only at later stages of development that the sense of morality progresses from merely social convention to a more autonomous under-standing.

Nucci and Lee (1993) argue that the idea of "rights" is linked to an understanding of personal autonomy. Areas which are considered "personal" are outside the realm of justifiable social regulation. One has "rights" or personal autonomy with respect to those areas. These conceptions of self or personal autonomy are part of the psychological domain. Individual claims to autonomy and freedom are negotiated with other people and become an understanding of rights. Variations in morality (especially across cultures) can, in part, be explained in terms of the different social understandings of what counts as the realm of the personal.

Individual development can be understood in terms of evolving concepts of the self. Nucci and Lee (1993) tested this idea by interviewing children and adolescents about their sense of the personal. The interviews were semi-structured and based upon actions which the subjects had already identified as personal. The actions were portrayed in hypothetical scenarios. Subjects were asked to explain why the actions ought to remain personal and why it was important that the actor maintain control over those actions.

Based upon these interviews, Nucci and Lee (1993) identified five major levels of development. The first level focuses on concrete, observable, material distinctions between self and other. The second level extends the personal to include notions of personality. The group ceases to be an indistinct other and becomes an evaluator so that one must protect oneself against negative labeling by the group while remaining distinct from the group. At the third level, the personal is extended to included notions of values and ideas; changing values for the group is seen as risking absorption by the group. The fourth level understands the self as an essence around which one's actions must be coordinated; control over one's actions is required to accomplish this. At the fifth level, the self is no longer a stable essence, but rather a constantly evolving project. Control over one's actions is required to carry out the project of creating one's own course of action.

According to Nucci and Lee (1993), the personal and the moral are distinct but interacting cognitive systems. The idea of freedom in the personal realm makes possible the idea of rights in the moral realm. While these are cognitive developmental considerations, they take place within a cultural context. Thus, the development of a sense of freedom and autonomy is done in negotiation with a broader culture. The domain of the personal influences moral development in at least two ways. First, the sense of self is rooted in personal autonomy. Freedom comes to be understood as a psychological necessity. Second, as conceptions of the personal develop, a more complete understanding of the autonomy and subjectivity of others may develop also.

...the personal and the moral are distinct but interacting cognitive systems. The idea of freedom in the personal realm makes possible the idea of rights in the moral realm.

The heart of Nucci and Lee's (1993) conception is the separation of the personal domain from the conventional, as well as the conventional from the moral. They argue that these domains interact and even facilitate development between each other, but that they cannot be collapsed into each other. Further, it is development of autonomy within the personal domain that lays the groundwork for the development of conceptions of rights in the moral domain. The societal domain influences the direction that moral development may take in terms of convention, but the needs of the personal domain may place limits upon the role of the conventional. In this formulation, a conception of rights requires a stable sense of self as bounded and autonomous, and a conception of personal rights is an essential ingredient of psychological health.

The selective review of literature presented in this section by no means exhausts the recent work which is now available on the relationships between conception of identity, the self, and morality. For one thing, all of these theories emphasize what is often called personal identity. The contrast would be a theory of identity which takes more seriously broader social and structural forces such as social roles or social positions. For instance, Tugendhat (1993) argues that moral identity "is not the identity of an individual as such" (p. 9), but as a member of a community. His argument is sympathetic to contractarian philosophy and asserts that one upholds moral rules because one's identity as a member of a particular moral community demands moral behavior.

Other disagreements among theories that employ the concept of identity include which aspects of identity are relevant to morality, how "identity" is to be understood, and the centrality of morality to the self. While disagreements abound and there are many different areas of emphasis, as a group these theories are suggestive of major emerging themes and perspectives.

II. Agency, Responsibility, and Moral Action

The concept of moral agency brings up long-standing interdisciplinary debates about questions of free will and determinism. To speak of people as agents is to invoke a particular conception of personhood that emphasizes autonomy and free will. Philosopher Helen Longino (1996) offers the following rough definition of moral agency:

> I take it that a robust notion of moral agency involves something like decision making or intention formation that is based primarily on values, principles, desires, and beliefs that one endorses as one's own, and that it is effective, that is, results in actions described by the content of the decision, or intention. (p. 282)

This definition captures a way of conceptualizing moral thought that emphasizes choice and deliberation but also a sense of ownership. This would stand in contrast to a theory which emphasizes adherence to cultural norms or values about which one could feel indifferent. Hence, the term moral agency, like identity, can be found in a wide variety of contexts that share little theoretical grounding other than a commitment to the idea that people can generate and control their own actions and intentional states, at least to a significant degree, and that the will or intentions of individuals are an important part of any explanation of moral action.

As a philosopher of science, Longino (1996) demonstrates how different biological theories aimed at making sense of human behavior allow differently for the idea of agency. In the process, she underscores the importance of a notion of agency for moral theory. Longino describes work in neuroendocrinology, especially that of Donald Pfaff (1983) which seeks to correlate later human behavior with prenatal or perinatal exposure to hormones. The idea is that the particular dynamics of hormone exposure during early brain development affect how the brain is organized and this organization sets patterns of how the individual will respond later in life. Similarly, as Longino points out, there are social scientists, such as James Q.

Wilson (1993), who attempt to locate at least some causal explanations for moral behavior in factors such as genetics or the more "primitive" sites of the brain. In such conceptions, ideas of agency or responsibility recede into the background. From this kind of perspective, even though people perceive themselves as self-directed, their thoughts and intentions do not explain as much as the early physiological circumstances which organize the brain and over which people have no control.

In contrast, Longino (1996) points to work in developmental neurobiology which investigates the structure and function of groups of neurons. The aim of that particular line of inquiry is to explain how higher level cognitive activity is possible. Rather than trying to match particular physiological features with specific behavioral outcomes, the theory of neural group selection seeks to explain how self-conscious, self-reflective behavior and learning are possible. Longino argues that this kind of scientific inquiry can potentially add to moral philosophy by creating new ways of understanding. Also, it does not conflict with the fundamental belief of moral philosophy that reflection on moral problems has value because people are, at least to some extent, capable of intentionally directing and redirecting their own behavior.

In a different philosophical project, Michael S. Pritchard (1991) uses the idea of moral agency to point to shortcomings in the theory of utilitarianism by arguing that utilitarianism does not adequately allow for moral agency. "Any theory that holds people morally accountable must find a significant place for moral agents, according them whatever degree of competency that is commensurate with the responsibilities ascribed to them" (Pritchard, 1991, p. 192).

Pritchard (1991) outlines three features of moral accountability:

1. The ability to understand moral concepts—for instance, fairness and promising;

2. Moral sentiments—for instance, feelings of guilt or concern for others; and

3. Participant understanding, which seems to be understanding oneself as a moral agent among other moral agents with whom one shares at least some common understanding, or in Wittgenstein's (1953) language a shared "form of life" which enables people to be intelligible to one another.

Moral sentiments are closely bound up with participant understanding; having moral sentiments ourselves makes it possible to recognize, understand, and appreciate them in others.

The importance of these factors is exemplified by Pritchard's (1991) discussion of children and psychopaths. Psychopaths, he concludes, cannot be considered moral agents because they lack moral sentiments and, consequently, participant understanding. They may have a clear intellectual understanding of moral concepts, but without moral sentiments and participant understanding, they are simply not participating in the same "form of life." This does not mean that psychopaths are therefore excused from behaving appropriately, but it does mean that the same conceptions of accountability simply do not apply. On the other hand, children may also not be regarded as full moral agents, especially when they lack the ability to understand moral concepts. But children are in the process of learning to be moral agents, and, early on, they can exhibit moral sentiments such as conceptions of fairness or friendship. Calling children moral agents does not entirely make sense, but neither does excluding them. Pritchard argues that Kohlberg's (1969, 1976) theory of stage development encourages a condescending attitude towards children by suggesting that they inhabit a very different moral world than adults. Pritchard suggests that even though children do not fit the description of moral agency fully, and do differ significantly from adults, these differences do not need to be characterized in a way that separates children so completely from the adult moral world.

A consideration of Pritchard's (1991) work is valuable for his description of the three features of accountability. In addition, like Helen Longino (1996), he articulates the relationship between moral theory and theories of persons. What people can be held morally accountable for must correspond with a compatible theory of what people are capable of doing intentionally. Moral theory depends upon a conception of human beings which assumes that people are able to be self-reflective and that self-reflection can lead to deliberate choices or changes in action. But while the above theories offer insight into the importance of agency, they do not provide theories of agency. For this, we turn to Albert Bandura, a psychologist.

...children are in the process of learning to be moral agents, and, early on, they can exhibit moral sentiments such as conceptions of fairness or friendship.

Albert Bandura: Social Cognitive Theory and Moral Agency

Bandura's (1989) work builds a conception of what he calls "emergent interactive agency." He differentiates this kind of agency from what he terms "autonomous agency," a theory which would see individuals as completely independent, i.e., not influenced by physiology or environment, and "mechanical agency," which would see the experience of agency as the byproduct of mechanical-like physiological processes (this would be similar to the theory in endocrinology discussed by Longino (1996) in which laws of physiology produce the illusion of self-control). Emergent interactive agency sees affect and cognition as interacting with environmental, physiological, and other factors to produce action. Hence, although how people think does not explain everything about behavior, it is a crucial part of an explanation.

Bandura (1989) identifies the perception of self-efficacy as being the most central aspect of agency. Self-efficacy is the perception that one can, in fact, exercise control and act effectively. When one perceives the ability to control or to create positive outcomes, one imagines or visualizes positive outcomes, feels motivated to attain goals, experiences less stress in the face of adversity, and establishes higher and more challenging goals. When one does not feel the ability to control outcomes, he or she is less motivated, more prone to stress, anxiety, and depression, more likely to establish lower goals, and more prone to feel defeated quickly and easily.

Whether one experiences self-efficacy or self-inefficacy will radically impact the kinds of educational, social, and/or occupational environments one enters, the kinds of challenges one undertakes, and therefore ultimately the kinds of skills and abilities one builds. Self-efficacy and self-inefficacy tend to be self-reinforcing. If one feels in control and competent, one is more persistent and accomplishes more, and this feeds back into the perception of competence. When one experiences high levels of self-doubt and anxiety, one undertakes less, gives up more easily, and ultimately feeds the self-perception of not being capable (Bandura, 1989).

In making the connection to specifically moral behavior, Bandura (1989) explicitly rejects the idea of cognitive stage development (such as suggested by Kohlberg, 1969, 1976), arguing that there is not a single cognitive structure underlying all thought, nor does one make moral decisions according to a single kind of principle that overrides all others. Further, empirical findings attributed to stage development can be adequately explained without a stage-based explanation. In Bandura's view, individuals' moral thinking evolves gradually as they come to adopt new moral principles, discard less complex ones, and choose between assorted principles available to them when making decisions.

Persons are socialized into moral judgment. They are subject to a wide variety of influences including direct instruction, social feedback, and modeling after parents and other people. Socialization involves the interplay of a variety of diverse influences. Individuals take an active role in their own learning; morals are not a matter of simply mimicking parents, as some social learning theorists might suggest (Bandura, 1989).

When people make moral judgments, Bandura (1989) suggests, they combine a number of different factors. In his view an area that needs more research is the means by which people go about weighing, combining, and integrating those factors. His work suggests some of the means by which people regulate their own behavior, or more extensively, how they come to not regulate their behavior according to moral judgments.

A person is motivated to avoid what Bandura (1989) terms "transgressive conduct" by two kinds of sanctions: social sanctions and internalized self-sanctions. Both involve anticipation—the fear of consequences prevents transgressive behavior. Prosocial behavior provides feelings of self-satisfaction and self-respect. Moral conduct is not merely accomplished through reflection upon moral principles or by sheer force of willpower. He identifies three major mechanisms that are used for self-regulation: self-monitoring of behavior, evaluation of conduct in relation to personal and environmental standards, and affective self-reaction. Monitoring one's own behavior is an interpretive act; therefore, it is not just a mechanistic habit of "watching oneself." It is subject to biases of interpretation and affect.

The self is embedded in a social context which also affects the understanding of both oneself and events. Further, the information one gets from self-monitoring is not adequate to predict moral judgment or behavior. Understanding self-regulation is an essential key to understanding moral functioning, but it is only part of the puzzle. One can easily see that self-efficacy should play a role in self-regulation. Self-regulatory influences must be activated in order to work, and there are a number of ways in which they may be disengaged. (Bandura, 1989, cites studies throughout his writing which suggest that the different mechanisms have undergone at least some empirical testing.)

Moral justification is one way that individuals may come to behave in ways that might otherwise violate personal moral sense. Moral justification provides reasons why the behavior in question is morally good (or necessary), rather than morally reprehensible. Military activity is one central example: When killing to serve one's country (or democracy, or God), the otherwise moral imperative against killing becomes a moral imperative to kill. Euphemistic labeling is another way of disengaging self-regulatory mechanisms. Bandura (1989) argues that language provides the thought patterns on which much action is based.

The choice of language can help determine how particular situations might be understood (Bandura, 1989). "Freedom fighting" and "terrorism" can be used to describe the same activities but potentially invoke different moral reactions. "Corporate downsizing" sounds relatively harmless and focuses emphasis away from people that are suddenly rendered unemployed. The recent television labeling system distinguishes (quite questionably, I think) between shows with "violence" and shows with "fantasy violence." It is also possible to construct sentences in the passive voice and through word choice so that the agent—the doer of the action—disappears, removing a sense of responsibility: "The pedestrian was struck from behind by the speeding car," or "The suspect was subdued and removed from the scene."

Bandura (1989) posits that another means for disengaging self-regulatory mechanisms is by comparing the behavior in question favorably with more reprehensible options: "I hit him with a rock, but at least I didn't shoot him." Additional mechanisms include the following:

> Displacement of responsibility (responsibility is displaced onto others; especially effective when there are others involved, especially others who are issuing authoritative orders)

> Diffusion of responsibility (responsibility not easily located with any particular person; especially in cases of group decision making—"The board decided to let 100 workers go")

> Disregard or distortion of consequences (especially possible for mediaries that do not have to witness personally the consequences of their actions)

> Dehumanization (seeing one's adversary as radically different from the self, as not human)

> Attribution of blame (my actions were caused by my victim—"If she had not made me mad, everything would have been okay")

Bandura (1989) states that not every situation is understood by the self to be a morally relevant one. There are a great many factors and a plethora of psychological mechanisms by which ordinary mechanisms can be disengaged which prevent a person from acting in transgressive ways. Such disengagement can happen gradually so that it becomes more difficult to recognize and therefore regulate one's own behavior. The crucial connection between self-regulation and self-efficacy remains to be developed.

III. Integrating Emotion

For a number of the scholars whose work is reviewed in this monograph, a theory of moral reasoning alone cannot provide a complete understanding of moral choice. There is surprisingly little work, however, that seeks to provide a theory linking

The choice of language can help determine how particular situations might be understood ... "Freedom fighting" and "terrorism" can be used to describe the same activities but potentially invoke different moral reactions.

emotion and moral action. This does make some sense: The task would be a daunting one because research (and theory) on emotion is extremely diverse and contradictory. Mary Brabeck and Margaret Gorman (1986) provide a review of psychological theories of emotion that may be relevant to moral theory but end by concluding that emotion is mediated by cognition in the seeming suggestion that cognition remains the more important component. Helen Haste (1990) suggests that intense emotional experiences may provide the impetus for moral understanding and commitment, but the theory of emotion itself is not strongly developed.

Naomi Scheman (1996) suggests that emotions play a central role in how we make sense of a situation (moral perception) and how moral judgments are reached. Scheman, a philosopher, argues that disputes over what kinds of emotional responses are "appropriate" to particular situations are intertwined with disputes about what constitutes right moral judgment in those situations. For instance, whether outrage is justified in response to particular sexual innuendoes is a part of the controversy surrounding what counts as sexual harassment versus morally appropriate treatment of another person. In particular, "outlaw" emotions among people in less socially powerful positions can be important epistemic resources for beginning to recognize and articulate injustice. "Outlaw emotions" is Alison Jaggar's (1989) term for emotions that are deemed inappropriate by the more powerful social group in particular situations—anger rather than humor in response to racially derogatory jokes, for instance. By integrating emotion with perception and epistemology, Scheman indicates a very suggestive direction for the integration of affect and cognition. It remains to be seen how such a theory originating in philosophy might be integrated with psychological theories of emotion.

Martin Hoffman: A Developmental Approach to Empathy

One theory that does begin to develop an account of the role of emotion and which is cited with some frequency in the psychology literature is Hoffman's (1991) work on empathy. Hoffman suggests that empathy is the root of moral motivation. He challenges the primacy that Kohlberg (1969, 1976) assigns to reason by suggesting that understanding alone cannot motivate moral action. He suggests that empathy is a potentially powerful explanation because it is pervasive and because it can be argued to be natural, biologically grounded, and the product of natural selection. An additional strength of empathy as an explanation is the fact that it is "amenable to being shaped by cognition" (Hoffman, 1991, p. 276).

Hoffman (1991) suggests that the capacity for empathy develops throughout childhood. Empathy can be described according to four levels (there is some suggestion that the fourth may actually contain two levels). The first three levels are largely automatic and involuntary; Level Four becomes more cognitively complex. Level One, or global empathy, is evident during the first year of life when the infant may respond with distress when witnessing distress in others. At this point, the infant does not recognize the other as another person but rather reacts as though she herself is being hurt in some way. Level Two, or egocentric empathy, is present between the ages of one and two. At this time, the child identifies internal states in others and responds to the other in ways appropriate to one's own distress. Hoffman gives an example of a child who sought out his own mother to comfort another child when that child's mother was unavailable. As the child moves from Level One to Level Two, she may gain the capacity for sympathy—the desire to make others feel better for their sake, instead of wanting to alleviate others' distress as a way to alleviate one's own distress. Level Three, present through early childhood, involves empathy for another's feelings and the ability to recognize those feelings as being particular to that other person. At this third level, the child described at Level Two would be able to recognize that the child in distress would want his own mother. Level Four involves empathy for another's life condition. This becomes possible in late childhood and enables the child to grasp distress that is chronic, rather than immediate and situational, and to understand distress among a group rather than immediately present individuals.

While later stages are not available to children in earlier stages, earlier stages may be evoked among older children and adults, depending on the situation. An adult may respond with more global-like empathy (including facial expressions and automatic reactions) when confronted by a situation in which the information available is non-verbal and expressive. When the information is available in more complex verbal and symbolic forms, the adult is more likely to respond in the more complex verbal ways consistent with Level Four.

Hoffman (1991) also argues that there are at least five kinds of empathetic affect that can be experienced. These kinds of empathetic affect will be influenced by the kinds of information available and the kinds of causal attributions one makes about the situation.

1. Sympathy. When there is little information about causes available and the victim's distress is immediately evident, the reaction is likely to be only empathetic and sympathetic distress.

2. Anger. When cause can be attributed to a culprit, one may feel both a sympathetic response to the victim and an empathetic sense of being vicariously attacked. In addition, attention may be drawn away from the victim and directed more as rage towards the offending party.

3. Guilt. When one sees oneself as somehow the cause of the distress, there may be an experience of sympathy mixed with self-blame.

4. Empathetic feelings of injustice. This more complex response involves combining information about the victim's plight with some kind of contrasting information, such as information about the victim's overall character or about the broader social context.

5. Complex combination. Any combination of the above is possible, such as empathy with different parties in the situation or varied responses to different aspects of the situation. The foregoing list is based on a simple bystander model, but this provides the basis for further development. For instance, the victim does not have to be physically present; individuals can also respond emotionally to mental representations of the victim or event.

Hoffman (1991) suggests that more mature forms of empathy are responsive to contextual factors and situational subtleties. However, there is also the problem of bias in empathy. He points out that there is evidence to suggest that people tend to be more empathetic towards others who are more similar to themselves. Further, he suggests that people are likely to be more empathetic to immediate situations than to ones that are physically or temporally distant, though such evidence is currently lacking. He argues that such bias is not unique to the concept of empathy and that it can probably be countered through moral education which encourages perceiving a common humanity and which emphasizes the ability to think about situations which are more removed.

A final insight from Hoffman (1991) is the suggestion that affectively "cold" principles, such as justice or equity, may become affectively loaded when associated with empathetic experiences and thereafter stored as "hot" cognitions. When those principles are recalled in the future, they will carry with them their previous affective associations. In this way, moral principles may become emotionally charged.

There is much more to be said about how empathy interacts with other emotions, how it influences judgment, how it develops, why it might not, and whether people might lose their capacity for empathy as they grow older. Certainly, as Hoffman (1991) suggests, the early development of empathy is closely linked to the development of cognitive capacity, but it is not reducible to it. Further, most stages of empathy do not require extensive cognitive complexity, suggesting (as do other theorists) that moral action is importantly accessible to a wider range of people than Kohlberg's (1969, 1976) theory might suggest.

IV. Philosophical Contributions and Insights

There are also important contributions being made to understanding moral choice by philosophers who suggest different ways of framing the issues under consideration or who point out important distinctions that may not be noticed elsewhere.

Lawrence Blum: Moral Judgment and Moral Perspective

Blum (1991) articulates a distinction between moral judgment and moral perception which touches upon Naomi Scheman's (1996) earlier point about the relationship between emotions and moral perception. Moral judgment, according to Blum, is generally understood by people writing in moral psychology as "the faculty which bridges the gap between moral rules (and principles) and particular situations" (p. 702). Moral judgment can be said to encompass both knowing which rules to apply in a given situation and which elements of a situation are morally relevant. These components of moral judgment require more attention from both philosophers and psychologists than they generally receive. Blum suggests that the concept of moral judgment is missing an important element supplied by moral perception which is a complex psychological and moral phenomenon, rather than a singly, unitary capacity.

The concept of moral perception goes beyond moral judgment in three ways. First, moral perception is the capacity to recognize a particular scenario as being morally significant. Simply knowing moral rules or principles is not the same as recognizing situations in which moral rules or principles are called for. Second, moral perception does not necessitate the use of principles or deliberation. Recognizing a situation as morally salient can move a person to act from compassion rather than principled deliberation. Moral perception itself can provide the impetus for action. Finally, moral perception has value in its own right; the very capacity for moral perception is intrinsically desirable. In this respect, moral perception can be tied to character. Moral perception is informed by general values and principles. Whether one notices the discomfort, maltreatment, or needs of others is itself a moral quality (Blum, 1991).

Recognizing moral perception as a complex phenomenon opens the way to investigating how different perceptions are formed and the ways that perception operates in different situations. Different people will perceive different aspects of the same situation as morally salient. Some will see no moral relevance in the same situation. Blum (1991) outlines three aspects of particularity that are relevant to moral perception. The first is the perception of particular situations—the capacity to see individual, specific situations as morally relevant. The second is what he terms the "particularistic attitude"—the recognition that each situation is unique (and therefore an openness to the particular requirements of that situation), even when it shares characteristics with others. The third aspect of particularity is "detail particularity"—attention to the particulars of a situation that require adequate moral response. Some situations afford and require more detailed understandings than others.

When individuals whom one knows well are involved, the potential exists for greater knowledge and understanding of those individuals and their needs than is possible in brief situations involving strangers. Blum's (1991) argument suggests that moral education requires attention to training people's perceptions, and an awareness that perception is multiple and complex, so that one may be more attuned to some kinds of details or situations than to others. Further, it emphasizes the extent to which learning moral principles could not, by itself, provide the capacity to recognize situations in which those principles are called for. Finally, Blum provides a recognition that not all moral action is grounded in principle or deliberation.

V. Finding Relationships Among the Perspectives

This section will examine the collage of ideas about moral thought and action which have been introduced in this chapter for the purpose of determining how these ideas are related, and then present some thoughts on needed interdisciplinary work in moral psychology, in particular the relationship between psychology and philosophy.

A common thread among the first several theories discussed in this chapter is the explicit relationship between morality and identity. Monroe (1996) suggests that persons act in certain situations based on their fundamental sense of themselves in relationship to other people. Such action is less a function of choice (implying deliberation among alternatives) than a reaction to a perceived necessity. What enables one person to perceive the needs of others is the sense of being joined to the other through a common humanity. This perception is what binds altruists together, and it is not noted among entrepreneurs. The findings are important to Monroe because they help refute the widely held belief in social science that all human behavior is motivated by some kind of self-interest.

A common thread among the first several theories discussed in this chapter is the explicit relationship between morality and identity.

Colby and Damon (1992) are similar to Monroe (1996) in that they interview moral exemplars. Many of their moral exemplars do not discuss their work in terms of a choice between alternatives but in terms of meeting needs or doing what must be done. Their work is different in that they talk about morality in terms of goals, and they talk about goals in terms of development and change. Development happens through interaction with the environment but cannot be reduced to external influences. Moral action is possible with the kind of certainty demonstrated by the moral exemplars when one's personal goals and moral goals are the same.

Blasi (1993) also takes a developmental approach to identity, but he lays out more explicit levels or modes of identity. His position that morality is integrated into personality differently for different people implicitly supports Colby and Damon's (1992) contention that moral goals and personal goals are more integrated for some people than for others. His model provides insight into how people might experience their identity differently, and also how people with similar moral ideas may experience their morality differently depending on the relationship between morality and identity.

Nucci and Lee (1993) argue that different kinds of social thinking are organized in different but interacting domains so that a sense of autonomy, a sense of rights, and a sense of social convention are all parts of different domains. A sense of personal autonomy makes possible an understanding of the concept of rights. This challenges Kohlberg's (1969, 1976) and Piaget's (1932) notion that reasoning according to moral principles follows reasoning according to social conventions. This approach by Nucci and Lee neither supports nor contradicts the work of the above theorists. It does, however, provide another way of conceptualizing how people think and learn.

Theories of moral agency are substantially less developed. There are some interesting philosophical insights that indicate the extent to which a theory of agency is implied by any theory which assumes people can deliberately alter their own behavior. In psychology, Bandura (1991) emphasizes the central role that self-efficacy plays in agency, but his discussion of moral action focuses more on other self-regulatory mechanisms. He argues that people weigh and integrate a number of different elements in moral reasoning. He focuses on mechanisms of self-regulation (which generally prevent transgressive behavior), and the means by which these mechanisms can be disengaged, thereby permitting one to engage in behavior that might otherwise seem morally objectionable. His focus on regulating transgressive behavior gives his work a different emphasis than that of other authors.

There are important and suggestive philosophical insights on emotion and morality, in particular Naomi Scheman's (1996) article which links emotion with moral perception, understanding, and judgment. There is little in the way of extensive theory or empirical research; however, Hoffman's (1991) work on empathy as the locus of moral motivation is highly suggestive and merits much empirical testing.

Blum (1991) points to the distinction between moral perception and moral judgment. He argues that much work on moral judgment fails to address explicitly concerns about how individuals know which moral rule or principle to apply in which situation and how to apply it. Further, the concept of moral judgment misses the important idea of moral perception—how it is that one recognizes a situation as morally relevant to begin with.

The authors represented in this chapter as well as in the previous one are using similar terms to theorize. The word "moral" ties them together and lends them a kind of similarity, but it does not mean the same thing for all the theorists represented here at either the conceptual level or at the empirical level of measurement, whether their theory has progressed to actual development of instrumentation or not. Some theorists, such as Kohlberg (1969, 1976), rely on a notion of moral that requires deliberation and choice. Such ideas can be traced to both Immanuel Kant (1785/1964), who suggested an act is moral only when it is performed from conscious, deliberate duty and never reflexively or from habit, and to William James (1890/1950), who argued that a choice is moral only when it is selected from among equally available options. James also emphasized the role of psychological processes, particularly attention, when making such choices. Others, such as Monroe (1996) and Colby and Damon (1992), look at behavior which they identify as morally exemplary but which their subjects identify as ordinary, necessary, and not the product of choice or deliberation. They may regard it as "the right thing to do," but not as a consequence of a perceived moral dilemma or a choice in response to that dilemma. This brings to mind Blum's (1991) argument that moral perception can lead to deliberation among principles, but it may circumvent such deliberation and lead directly to action.

Further, while Monroe (1996) and Colby and Damon (1992) focus on extraordinary sacrifices made by some people on behalf of others, Bandura (1991) attends largely to those mechanisms which keep people from "transgressing" or doing harm. While doing good and doing evil are both important to moral inquiry, it cannot be simply assumed that they are psychologically equivalent. Some attempt is made to argue that similar psychological processes are involved. Bandura suggests that doing good is motivated by the need for positive self-regard and avoiding evil is motivated by the need to avoid negative self-regard. But the work of Monroe and Colby and Damon challenges explanations of altruism that are rooted in self-interest. Looking at morality in relation to identity allows the argument that what one must do because it is a moral imperative and what one cannot do because it is morally unthinkable are both a part of identity: They define one's most essential self (Frankfurt, 1993). However, this may not easily encompass situations which are morally ambiguous and in which the self is torn, or where the dilemmas are less deeply pressing.

Further, an important question is raised for identity theories by the idea of moral agency; in particular, how might agency and identity be compatible or, indeed, incompatible? The extent to which theories of identity can work with theories of moral agency might depend on how much one is able to deliberately shape who one is. Colby and Damon's (1992) work is much more suggestive of development and of an active role in shaping one's own identity than is Monroe's (1996). On the other hand, one could also look at the extraordinary degree of self-efficacy experienced by Monroe's altruists. It could be that if one compared the perceived self-efficacy of rescuers with the perceived self-efficacy of people who did nothing to help, one would conclude that self-efficacy was a central part of the identity of rescuers.

A related complication, as suggested in particular by Bandura's (1991), Scheman's (1996), and Blum's (1991) work, is that decisions may have multiple components, not all of which are moral. Moral reasoning and moral action are often bracketed as though they are a discrete kind of decision making or a separate realm of human activity. How morality is integrated into daily life, as one component among many, needs to receive more theoretical attention. Many of the authors cited above provide useful ways to begin thinking about this question. Thus, not only do theorists use different conceptions of what counts as "moral," but also the events of daily life (in addition to other theorists) suggest that the integration of morality with apparently non-moral considerations requires further explanation. One way of framing this question is to ask what enables people to define "moral decisions" as different from other decisions.

The word "moral" has been a useful descriptive term to designate an area of inquiry, but for scientific investigation to advance, great care and deliberation should be used when establishing what exactly that term encompasses, and how it is linked to other findings which also refer to "moral" thought or action. What is the relationship between moral deliberation and actions which appear to have moral content but that do not involve deliberation? Or what is the relationship between decisions to help another person on one hand, and to do something that might harm someone, however indirectly, on the other? The implication for moral education, then, is the question—education for what? Is moral education raising the level of moral reasoning *à la* Kohlberg (1969, 1976), or is it increasing moral perception *à la* Blum (1991)? Is the goal to build skills for thinking about moral dilemmas, or is the goal to enhance a personality that integrates morality?

> The word "moral" has been a useful descriptive term to designate an area of inquiry, but for scientific investigation to advance, great care and deliberation should be used when establishing what exactly that term encompasses...

A defining issue addressed in this chapter is the relationship between moral philosophy and moral psychology. Most of the work discussed herein is anchored in psychology (cognitive psychology in particular) although it reflects certain philosophical questions and concerns. Some argue that moral philosophy only makes sense if it attends to psychology: How can philosophy make effective prescriptions for behavior if it does not understand how people function (Rorty, 1993; Flanagan & Rorty, 1990)? Others argue that while philosophy should not ignore cognitive psychology, there is no reason to give psychology particular primacy (Held, 1996). The realm of moral philosophy, according to this perspective, ought to remain primarily normative, rather than descriptive. Moral philosophy is concerned with questions that can be addressed by people to the extent that they are capable of being thoughtful, analytical, and self-reflective in the decisions they make about their lives. Descriptions of how people do function, while of some potential interest to philosophy, can not replace, and can only partially impact, considerations of how people ought to function.

To the extent that moral philosophy and moral psychology necessarily overlap, it makes little sense to say that they do not need each other. It seems that no discipline is best served by ignoring the related work of those in other fields. Moral psychology can benefit from careful philosophical distinctions; the social sciences are not always as careful with their theories as they are with their data. In addition, moral psychology is frequently prescriptive in its attempt to be descriptive. This can be seen in the dispute between Kohlberg (1969, 1976) and Gilligan (1982) over what counts as the pinnacle of moral achievement, as well as in Blasi and Milton (1991) who simply arrange categories "in an order that seemed to us approximately developmental" (p. 224). Developmental theories in general run a serious normative risk when ranking what counts as "more" or "less" developed. At the same time, philosophy must recognize that it is frequently in the business of describing how people are in the course of arguing how they ought to be. To the extent that moral philosophers are making empirically verifiable claims, it is worth attending to work that either supports or rejects those claims, if only to challenge and refine one's theory. While this is hardly a complete answer to the question of cooperation among the disciplines, it is at least a suggestion that interdisciplinary work has much to offer without threatening the special expertise of the various domains of theory.

VI. Future Directions

It is probably painfully clear by now that work on the topic of moral action does not constitute an easily identifiable, coherent, or clearly bounded field with a single, traceable genealogy. To the contrary, there are assorted clusters of theorists and researchers across a variety of disciplines and subdisciplines who are sometimes aware of each other's work but often are not. While there are methodological points to be learned from the research reviewed in this article, in particular the use of personal narratives to understand how people make sense of themselves and the trajectory of their lives and Blasi's (1993) scales of identity development, what is most strikingly needed for the future is comprehensive theoretical development in conjunction with methodology. Because "moral action" and its kin are so vaguely and loosely defined, what seems to be missing is a theory which carefully outlines the area of concern, which can at least somewhat articulate its relationship to other existent theories and possible areas of concern, and which can suggest a method of empirically testing appropriate claims. Without further attention to exactly what is being studied and a coherent argument for why that is the thing to be studied, additional empirical research runs the risk of being lost in a growing cacophony of promising but ultimately disjointed work.

References

Bandura, A. (1989). Human agency in social cognitive theory. *American Psychologist, 44*(9), 1175-1184.

Bandura, A. (1991). Social cognitive theory of moral thought and action. In W. M. Kurtines & J. L. Gewirtz (Eds.), *Handbook of moral behavior and development, Vol 1: Theory*. Hillsdale, NJ: Lawrence Erlbaum Associates.

Blasi, A., & Milton, K. (1991). The development of the sense of self in adolescence. *Journal of Personality, 59*(2), 217-242.

Blasi, A. (1993). The development of identity: Some implications for moral functioning. In G. G. Noam & T. E. Wren (Eds.), *The moral self*. Cambridge, MA: MIT Press.

Blum, L (1991). Moral perception and particularity. *Ethics, 101*, 701-725.

Brabeck, M., & Gorman, M. (1986). Emotions and morality. In R. T. Knowles & G. F. McLean (Eds.), *Psychological foundations of moral education and character development*. New York: University Press of America.

Colby, A., & Damon, W. (1992). *Some do care*. New York: The Free Press.

Colby, A., & Damon, W. (1993). The uniting of self and morality in the development of extraordinary moral commitment. In G. G. Noam & T. E. Wren (Eds.), *The moral self.* Cambridge, MA: MIT Press.

Erikson, E. H. (1968). *Identity and the life cycle.* New York: W. W. Norton & Company.

Flanagan, O., & Rorty, A. O. (1990). Introduction. In O. Flanagan & A. O. Rorty (Eds.), *Identity, character, and morality.* Cambridge, MA: MIT Press.

Frankfurt, H. (1993). On the necessity of ideals. In G. G. Noam & T. E. Wren (Eds.), *The moral self.* Cambridge, MA: MIT Press.

Gilligan, C. (1982). *In a different voice: Psychological theory and women's development.* Cambridge, MA: Harvard University Press.

Haste, H. (1990). Moral responsibility and moral commitment: The integration of affect and cognition. In T. E. Wren (Ed.), *The moral domain.* Cambridge, MA: MIT Press.

Held, V. (1996). Whose agenda? Ethics versus cognitive science. In L. May, M. Friedman, & A. Clark (Eds.), *Mind and morals: Essays on cognitive science and ethics.* Cambridge, MA: MIT Press.

Hoffman, M. L. (1991). Empathy, social cognition, and moral action. In W. M. Kurtines & J. L. Gewirtz (Eds.), *Handbook of moral behavior and development, Vol 1: Theory.* Hillsdale, NJ: Lawrence Erlbaum Associates.

Jaggar, A. M. (1989). Love and knowledge: Emotion in feminist epistemology. In A. Garry & M. Pearsall (Eds.). Women, *knowledge and reality: Explorations in feminist epistemology.* Boston: Unwin Hyman.

James, W. (1890/1950). *The principles of psychology (Vol. I).* New York: Dover Publications.

Kant, I. (1785/1964). *Groundwork of the metaphysics of morals.* Trans. H. J. Paton. New York: Harper Torchbooks.

Kohlberg, L. (1969). Stage and sequence: The cognitive-developmental approach to socialization. In D. A. Goslin (Ed.), *Handbook of socialization theory and research.* New York: Rand McNally.

Kohlberg, L. (1976). Moral stages and moralization: The cognitive-developmental approach. In T. Lickona (Ed.), *Moral development and behavior: Theory, research and social issues.* Chicago: Holt, Rinehart and Winston.

Loevinger, J. (1976). *Ego development: Conceptions and theories.* San Francisco: Jossey-Bass.

Longino, H. (1996). Moral agency and responsibility: Cautionary tales from biology. In L. May, M. Friedman, & A. Clark (Eds.), *Mind and morals: Essays on cognitive science and ethics.* Cambridge, MA: MIT Press.

Monroe, K. R. (1996). *The heart of altruism*. Princeton, NJ: Princeton University Press.

Nucci, L., & Lee, J. (1993). Morality and personal autonomy. In G. G. Noam & T. E. Wren (Eds.), *The moral self*. Cambridge, MA: MIT Press.

Pfaff, D. (1983). The neurobiological origins of human values. In D. Pfaff (Ed.), *Ethical questions in brain and behavior: Problems and opportunities*. New York: Springer-Verlag.

Piaget, J. (1932). *The moral development of the child*. Glencoe, IL: Free Press.

Pritchard, M. S. (1991). *On becoming responsible*. Lawrence, KS: University Press of Kansas.

Rorty, A. O. (1993). What it takes to be good. In G. G. Noam & T. E. Wren (Eds.), *The moral self*. Cambridge MA: MIT Press.

Scheman, N. (1996). Feeling our way toward moral objectivity. In L. May, M. Friedman, & A. Clark, (Eds.), *Mind and morals: Essays on cognitive science and ethics*. Cambridge, MA: MIT Press.

Tugendhat, E. (1993). The role of identity in the constitution of morality. In G. G. Noam & T. E. Wren (Eds.), *The moral self*. Cambridge, MA: MIT Press.

Wilson, J. Q. (1993). *The moral sense*. New York: The Free Press.

Wittgenstein, L. (1953). *Philosophical investigations* (G. E. M. Anscombe, Trans.). New York: Macmillan.

S E C T I O N 3

NARRATIVE INSIGHTS INTO MORAL ACTION IN YOUNG ADULTHOOD

The four chapters in Section III comprise the presentation of the results from three different approaches to data collection (see Appendices A, B, and C).

In Chapter 7, Dr. Kathy Kalliel used the Moral Action Interview (Appendix A) which she created. Chapter 7, drafted by Dr. Kalliel, and based originally upon her doctoral dissertation at Boston University, is organized into three parts. The first part categorizes the content of the moral dilemmas shared by the twenty respondents in her sample. This first part is of great importance to the research team, as an earlier concern prior to data collection had been that young adults would choose not to share, or would not be able to share, significant moral dilemmas in their lives.

The second part of Chapter 7 provides extended excerpts from four young adults on quite different topics. These extended excerpts are intended to give the reader a sense of the nature of the actual dilemmas, and a sense of the *context* of the individual lives in which the dilemma occurred. The third part of Chapter 7 is a portion of Dr. Kalliel's assessment of the data she collected. A fuller account is in her doctoral dissertation.

Chapters 8 and 9, drafted by Dr. David Connor, used the Moral Behavior Interview (Appendix B) which he created. Based originally upon his doctoral dissertation, a fuller account of his views is in that source.

The focus of Chapter 8 is on the moral dilemmas which arise in young adulthood from the multi-generational context of their lives: Moral dilemmas arose from all of the interpersonal categories of their lives: with parents and grandparents, with friends and spouses or lovers, and with their own children.

The focus of Chapter 9 is on the moral dilemmas which occur in the workplace. Four types of dilemmas were encountered in the workplace: Superiors in an organization pressuring an employee to act in ways that the employee considered immoral, temptation arising to act in ways not considered to be moral by the young adult, situations occurring where others in the workplace did not act morally, and opportunities arising to act in relation to people in ways which were altruistic, but perhaps at the expense of the employer.

Chapter 10, drafted by Dr. James M. Day, used the Moral Influence Interview (Appendix C) which he created. This chapter reports results from a sub-sample which was interviewed in greater detail. As the process of research unfolded, it had become apparent that there were some former Sierrans who stood out from the rest of the broader sample reported upon in Chapters 7, 8, and 9 on the basis of their ability to describe the wellsprings of their moral action.

On behalf of the research team, Professor Day accepted the challenge of interviewing these "exemplary" Sierrans. The broader purpose of the research reported in Chapter 10 is to contribute to further understanding of what enables some individuals to be relatively more clear in their appraisal of moral dilemmas and decisive in moral action. Such increased understanding is essential information for educators in order to be able to design educational experiences which promote greater moral action.

C H A P T E R

SEVEN

MORAL DILEMMAS FROM
YOUNG ADULTHOOD

The moral dilemmas of 20 young adults from the University of California, Irvine (UCI) classes of 1980, 1981, and 1982, and their thinking about and response to those dilemmas, are the focus of this chapter. At the time they spoke in 1987 with Katherine Kalliel, the interviewer for this chapter, they were in their late 20s or very early 30s.

The chapter is organized into three sections. The first section briefly categorizes the content of the moral dilemmas shared by the young adults. The second section provides extended excerpts from four of the young adults on very different topics: a woman who chose to "blow the whistle" on the actions of a co-worker, a woman who decided not to resume an intimate relationship with a former boyfriend, a man who decided not to continue in an intimate relationship which was not working for him, and a man who was struggling with how a product that he had designed for the defense industry would be used. The third section is Kalliel's view of the meaning of the data she collected for understanding moral action in young adulthood. A more complete representation of Kalliel's analysis is available in her doctoral dissertation.[1]

The instrument Kalliel used in her data collection was the Moral Action Interview (see Appendix A), a structured interview designed to examine individual moral dilemmas and factors associated with moral action. The Moral Action Interview is a series of open-ended and close-ended questions with probes about the subjects' personal moral dilemmas.

The first question in the Moral Action Interview is open-ended, allowing the subjects to choose a moral dilemma and to discuss it thoroughly. Next, standardized follow-up probe questions are included to examine moral decision making from the generalized perspectives of Gilligan (1982), Blasi (1983,1984), Kohlberg (Kohlberg & Candee, 1984) and Rest (1986). The intention of the project was to examine as broadly as possible factors leading young adults to moral action, not to examine

---

[1]Katherine Mary Kalliel. *Moral decisions and actions of young adults in actual dilemmas,* Unpublished doctoral dissertation, Boston University, 1989.

these theories specifically. Also examined by Kalliel were such factors as the role of parents and other significant persons and religious beliefs in choosing how to act in response to moral dilemmas.

> The intention of the project was to examine as broadly as possible factors leading young adults to moral action, not to specifically examine these theories.

The 20 Sierran women and men whose thinking is the basis for this chapter talked about very personal and moving moral dilemmas in their lives. Thus, the researchers' initial concern that the subjects would not reveal themselves at length about such private matters was unfounded. Indeed, the moral dilemmas were presented genuinely, and, at times, very movingly.

I. Content of the Moral Dilemmas

In analyzing the content of the moral dilemmas, the locus of the dilemmas for both females and males was almost evenly divided between work and personal relationships. The content of the dilemmas presented by women was as follows:

Subject 1 decided not to return to an old unfaithful boyfriend.

Subject 4 decided to use disposable paper diapers for her baby, not cloth diapers.

Subject 5 decided not to share course material with her law school classmates.

Subject 7 decided to be faithful to her husband and not have an affair with another man.

Subject 10 decided to give her employer several months notice of her leaving.

Subject 11 decided to let the owner of her company know that a foreman was mistreating the workers.

Subject 12 decided to continue working with a customer who devalued her because she was a minority female.

Subject 13 decided to live with her boyfriend.

Subject 15 decided not to continue having an affair with a married man.

Subject 18 decided not to resume a relationship with an ex-fiancé.

Subject 19 decided to testify in a court custody/sexual abuse case despite her trainee status.

The content of the dilemmas presented by men were as follows:

Subject 2 decided not to tell his mother directly that his brother was homosexual, but to hint that there is something "my brother needs to tell you."

Subject 3 decided to do part-time military-related work which contradicted his beliefs.

Subject 6 tentatively decided not to pursue a romantic relationship with a young woman.

Subject 8 decided not to tell a female friend that her husband, also his friend, was having two affairs.

Subject 9 decided to enforce a fraternity rule to remove a pledge who used drugs.

Subject 14 decided to hint to his parents that his sister was living with her boyfriend.

Subject 16 decided to teach kindergarten in a bilingual format despite a directive from the school administration to the contrary.

Subject 17 decided to change jobs despite a pay reduction which negatively affected his family.

Subject 20 decided to eliminate the power of a business associate in his company.

II. Synopses of Four Moral Dilemmas

The following are extended excerpts from the moral dilemmas of four Sierrans.

Whistle-Blower

A 29-year-old, Hispanic woman described a moral dilemma which occurred at work:

> "I work at a large plant. . .and at least 100% of the men and women out there, they're mainly men, but they're all under this foreman. Now, I would say that 70% of all the workers are illegal, and so they feel very threatened, of course, and they are afraid of losing their jobs. This gives the foreman more power over them and I believe he's a man who uses that consciously or unconsciously; I think he does. An ex-employee that was fired had called me. . .I'm only going by what the termination report I get from the foreman out there and all my payroll records. But I'm not in contact really with the men out there. We had won our case (against him). And so this man who isn't receiving unemployment insurance, he called me to say that he knew he wasn't, but he was going to appeal it. But besides appealing it, which he could do. . .he just wanted to let me know because he knew we weren't aware of the situation, but that he was very unfair. He believed the foreman was very unfair, that every year the employees would be forced to contribute $20 to the boss's Christmas present. The foreman would pocket half the money. The employees made $3.35-$5 an hour for hard work at an assembly table so $20 is a lot of money. The man was threatened for his job on several occasions. Once he wanted to contribute five dollars but the foreman threatened him with his job."

"The foreman ordered the lunch truck for the workers and was getting a kickback. The boss knew that and didn't care. I didn't know it but in this industry everyone did this. But what the owner didn't know was on their half hour lunch break, the workers were forced to go to that one lunch truck. If the employees went to another lunch truck, they were threatened with their jobs and got a verbal notice; and if it happens again the workers would be fired. This man had disobeyed two times and the last time, the man had used another lunch truck since it was cheaper and he was hoping not to get caught. Also, the foreman verbally abused the workers and yelled at them. He used abusive language towards them and spit at them."

"The foreman didn't want the workers to become friends with each other and forced them to buy their lunch from the truck and not bring their lunch from home. The men had to sit at their dirty, greasy work areas for lunch and not talk to friends or anyone."

"I believed this worker and did not want to go talk to the foreman since I was afraid he might convince me not to go to the boss, and he would put doubt in my mind. The owner should be aware of it and work it out. I decided to go tell the owner and then asked if they could notify the court they weren't going to contest the appeal so they could begin to pay unemployment. The boss was really upset about the contribution and conditions about lunch. The owner did not fire him since he is dependent on him. I went with the gut feeling that the man was telling the truth. Even though the foreman was polite and businesslike with us in the office, it was hard, but I believed it was true. I remembered the phone call from two years ago (when a woman called claiming sexual harassment by the foreman). Sometimes when a person comes from a low socioeconomic background and they've been prejudiced against, the minute they get a little power, they use it on someone else."

When asked about her willingness to speak up to the boss despite possible difficulties for herself, she responded:

"I think that I had like an outrage in me in the sense that all this was going on out there and for how long. It was the injustice of how they were being treated. Once I believed that it was just. . . Come on, how much more fortunate I am than they; I can find another job, or I could pay the premiums. How big of a deal is it if the worst thing that could happen happens? I lose my job. Okay. I don't have my insurance anymore. I'll deal with that when it comes. I'm so much better off to start with than these men out there. I guess that gave me and putting it more into perspective and not thinking that the whole world is mean. Or what is going to happen to me."

When asked to whom she felt responsible, she stated emphatically:

"Responsible to the men out there. Because of the language barrier of the man who called, he could not speak English, and I was the only girl in office who could speak Spanish. It was more like a plea. He didn't want to get the men in trouble. But he left it up to me as to what to do. He didn't say, 'Tell the owner that.' I felt responsible to the man. I felt so terrible, especially since he was not receiving unemployment, his wife was pregnant, and he was an illegal so he wasn't able to get another job. If not for the foreman, he would be able to get another job. The termination form said he was fired for coming to work intoxicated. He was not able to be rehired because of the amnesty law, and he could not prove citizenship or authority to work in the U.S. because so much damage was done to him. A lot of damage was done to this man."

She described a cognitive process of moral decision-making:

"When faced with a difficult decision, I think it out. I make the best decision I can, then put it behind me. I consider all choices, look at consequences of each choice. I try to put a perspective on it and look at the very worst that could happen, and it doesn't seem as bad as what is happening to others. That's all one can do in making any decision. I consider anything available, and when I consider all possibilities and look at my gut feelings, I just act. Another choice may seem good, and then you would be wishy-washy and never choose if you debate too long."

"God don't like ugly"

The following moral dilemma about a personal situation was told by a 28-year-old Black woman:

"Recently an old boyfriend has wanted to get back together. We broke up since another woman had his baby when I was dating him two years before. Why not? I'll get him back. I thought of very mean things to do to him. Then I decided, 'God don't like ugly; you'll get yours.' Then a month ago he called me, and I said, 'Yes, I'd go out' to hurt him. The animosity is not gone. Then I decided no. It took too much out of me. It was a strain on me. All the hatred and hurt came back. I was trying to hurt him about when we broke up the first time. I decided not to get back with him since I would do it only to get back at him, which didn't feel right. I had to let go since it wasn't worth all the energy; it took too much out of me. I didn't like the way I was. I thought I was being evil, and that wasn't me; I decided to let it go; I would be lying to him and myself if I got back with him. I would rip him apart and get back at him with words. I wouldn't kiss him goodnight and tried to explain to him my hurt. I think he realizes that I didn't deserve the hurt."

"I decided to be his friend. I decided at first to get back with him to hurt him. I wanted to get back at him but I realized that he had problems. But it just didn't feel right to get back at him. He finally realized he didn't like himself and he said he wants to change. Then I decided to be his friend. I want marriage and commitment, and he wouldn't commit so I was angry at him for that. What bothers me is that now everyone thinks we are back together again, and I have to go through this to convince others that we are not back together again, that we are only friends.

"A part of me would like to get back together with him but I am still angry at him for having the baby. He wasn't honest with me about telling me about the baby until the month it was due, and he had not told me about another woman. He told me the night the baby was born, and the very next day everyone at work knew about it. And that hurt. That really hurt. And my girlfriend said five persons asked her about the baby. I cried. She rushed me to the rest room. Everybody knows. And then he denied telling them. He was disrespectful to me, especially since we worked together. I didn't deserve to be hurt, and I underestimated him. I thought he was just a nerd without friends. He is trying hard to get in my good graces. What hurt me the most about the baby was that he was not faithful to me during our relationship."

She noted that:

"I realized it was a moral decision after considering my behavior towards him [her former boyfriend] and the hurt I was trying to do and how grateful he was for my attention and [hurt disguised as] 'help.'"

She stated that she knew the deontic choice in the situation when she thought about:

"What is that old saying, 'Two wrongs don't make a right'? And then when my brother came in and told me [not to get involved and hurt him]."

The influence of her family was crucial in her decision:

"What bothers me is that now everyone thinks we are back together again, and I have to go through this to convince others that we are not back together again, that we are only friends. Even my Mom. She's like, 'Uh, uh, now you and Tom are back together again.' I'm like, 'No, it's not what you think, we're only friends.' 'Yeah, sure'. I'm like, 'No, listen to me, I said we are only friends, that's it, no more.' But she would not say that she would never agree with it and I would not understand where she was coming from 'cause she would never say until it was over with. She would give me one of those, 'OOO -You're dating Tom again' and grin from ear to ear. I guess she likes it. Why though? She knew what happened and why we broke up. Why would she grin and think it was funny or agree with it. Maybe she was glad I was going with someone she knew. But I know I got my message across that it's not that. And I know my brother didn't like it; he hated it. He would comment to me, 'Are you still trying to get back at that guy? Well, okay, I was going to tell you not to do it anymore. It's been long enough. Stop seeing him. . .' "

She spoke about her keeping herself away from emotional harm in a way that fit with the person she saw herself as being:

"I thought about my right to protect myself the best way I could and at the same time hurt him. An eye for an eye, a tooth for a tooth. I had no shield up the first time but now I did. I felt lousy for hurting him, but I thought I would feel good. I did not want to be the kind of person to hurt someone; it took too much out of me. Over years, my friends told me I was too nice in relationships with men and I would be stepped on. But I didn't like myself the other way—it took too much energy to lie like my friends said I should."

"God, what have I done. I've created a monster."

The following personal dilemma was reported by a 28-year-old, Hispanic man:

114

"Okay, I think it's about this girl I've been seeing for the last two years. The decision is. . .She has a lot of growing up to do. I'm already at a certain stage, and she's at a different stage. She made the decision to say, "Hey, we've been getting together four times already and, uh, we've been hurting each other more and more and we just have to realize we have to do something," but I wasn't willing to let go. And finally at this time right now to make that decision to say, hey, let go and . . . .Basically right now I have to think what I want to do about my own future and her own future, what's beneficial for her. I just got to do my own thing and just live my own life and it's difficult for two years I felt this way about someone that I want to hold on to but it's one of those times when it's not right."

". . . .I think the choice for myself is here—is someone who I feel comfortable with and I enjoy being with and who I've done so many things with the past few years, uh, it's basically, do I let her grow up by herself and learn those things she needs to find out? Sort of like protecting her. I didn't want her to fall. Didn't want her to go through this hard road. And, basically, I was there and basically being almost everything. What's this and what's that? And I realize that I tried to be protective and be there. I can't see her family. There are so many memories. That we've been breaking up so many times her mother and father don't know what is going on. The last time we broke up, I had a real good talk with her Mom and her Dad and said all these years we've been doing things and all the things that have been happening. This is why everything's been changing, and this time I really think we're going to break up. And talking to her on the phone. It was so cold, like all these years didn't mean anything. At the same time, I didn't let go. It's like, sooner or later you're going to realize it, and she said the absolute. I realize there can't be absolutes because you never know what's going to happen. . . but now I have to make the decision: Do I go on with my life and things, keep myself busy? Set other goals and let go? And that's what I have to do. . .She never said that before. All the years we broke up she never said that, 'I don't love you.' She said, 'We shouldn't be seeing each other right now.' Or 'I'm doing other things now.' So we'd just part . There would never be the part of 'I don't love you. I don't care for you.' Other people would say, 'She talks about you all the time.' And then I never let go until she said, 'You can't keep your promises.' And here I am—I can't let go because I made these promises. It's fine. I would never let go until she said, 'You don't have to keep your promises, that's fine.' This time she finally said it. She said, 'The only way we can let go is if we totally let go and know that it will never work.' You know, I go, 'Do you know what you're saying? What about all the times we've been together, what does it mean?' She says, 'I don't know. I guess not.' It just blew me away. You know I'm thinking now about it."

He discussed the process of trying to decide how to act in this situation:

"I weigh consequences of both and go back and forth until I find one that I feel comfortable with or seems right to me. At one point I'll feel so strongly about the decision I will make, and then in a certain amount of time I won't feel as secure about it and will be at the other extreme about what I need to do. And then at another time I'll feel like you're happy, this is the decision you are going to make, better write it down, put it in a tape recorder, remember this decision you've made so the next time you feel depressed or feel you don't know, play it back so you can see the reasons why. So I can see myself in those decisions just swinging back and forth. Now I know when I have a moral dilemma. Other things are logical, but these I swing back and forth. . .It's trying to figure out where the line is drawn and figure out what you owe for something else and what you owe for yourself. I'm beginning to learn. . .[When I talk with others I] use their experiences, what they've gone through, and what they've learned, and try to fit it in my situation and see what actions occurred from the decisions they made and weigh the possible outcome for me. But it doesn't always work though. Still make the same choice. I'm learning to, I don't know yet."

He talked about the influence of his parents on the difficulty to decide in this situation:

"I have a Mom who said, 'Your Dad and I fought so many times, but your Dad never let go. And your father was always there.' And I felt guilty…Well, the choice for me now is that I don't see her, I don't want to see her; I don't see her family. The dream is maybe someday you'll get back together and never go out and look for someone else. My mom is always saying, 'Don't worry, some day it will work out. The dream will come true.' But do you let go and say, 'That is history now' and forget about the two years or whatever and say they don't mean a thing?"

During our conversation, he came to a tentative decision:

"I think what's best for her is for me to leave. I can see that I'm not letting her grow. I'm at the point where she doesn't. See, I'm an adult, and I can understand right and wrong and she doesn't. Like I tell my secretary, it's true she could make me do things that other people shouldn't make people do. I would go out with other girls, and they would never make me do this or say that. She doesn't know any better, and I'm not helping her to morally understand what a relationship is or what's fair to ask or not fair to ask and just getting spoiled. It's getting to the point it's time for me to let her learn and grow up. It's best for her for me to go."

". . .I'm looking for my rights now. Before it was. . .I always did everything for her. I realize that she really didn't care about me. I can understand that because I was spoiling her so much that I didn't care about myself. She said, 'Well, he doesn't care about himself.' I saw her and I said to myself, 'God what have I done. I've created a monster.' I felt responsible in that effect. The last time we broke up I said, 'I feel responsible for all these things we've done together' and I told her I don't believe in those things. It seemed that she was like her mother, you'll be happy if you have a mansion, buy a brand new Porsche."

"It Doesn't Make a Difference; Big Missiles or Little Missiles."

A 28-year-old Caucasian man related the following work dilemma:

"Maybe I avoid decisions—I don't know. I'm trying to think of. . .I'll try to think of any moral decisions I have to make. I can't think of any individual moral decisions or individual. . .I could go back to my work I guess. I was saying that. . .which was never really. . .I guess I've made a decision. I never really. . .maybe if I sat down and thought about it and I'd go because I know the decision I have to make would be unpleasant so I'm not. So. . .When I took the job, it wasn't a job offer, 'Here's your job, and you'll be doing this kind of thing.' I just fell into it, basically. What we do is maybe half military and stuff, half is not, some is medical, some is. . .I don't know. . . .It's hard to explain. But. . .Um. . .Some of the military is basically. . .the type of thing we're doing is not really all that bad. We're just making sure things work like. . .um. . .an electrical connector for a plane to make sure the thing works so the plane doesn't go down because of disconnected brakes or . . .One thing we have which I don't work on, is ah. . .they're switches for missiles, little missiles, it doesn't make a difference big missiles or little missiles, but it's the trigger when it hits, it sets it off. That we do it, that we make sure that there aren't any bad ones in there so they don't premature trigger, so I maybe could look at . . ."

"See, I don't like. . .And I think there is some need for some. I think 'Star Wars' is something I find completely ridiculous. But in the same sense, though, I've done testing for things that go for Star Wars. So. . .when I'm doing it I really don't think much. But when I go home I go, 'What was I doing today?' or something. That doesn't bother me as much as the other people, the people coming in, the customers or something. And listening to them talk. That's what bothers me more."

"We tested, uh, the inflatable decoys for [use with ballistic missiles to confuse the Soviets]. . .if the Soviets had a Star Wars-type [defense] to shoot down missiles. Along with the warheads you have hundreds of decoys. So what we were testing is the decoys, they're balloons, they get up there, and the balloons pop open, and they look like warheads and they go flying. So we were testing those to make sure they survive a lift-off from a rocket. Hoo. Actually, when we were testing it I had no idea what it was. I don't really get involved in the actual testing but just setting up things. But then I had the customers come in. They were saying, 'Well, yeah, this thing gets up there and it does this for five hours and isn't it great. And we have to do this.' And everybody is just is the whole opinion that, 'Yeah we have to do this to the Russians.' And I'm just going. . .There's the real world. I can tell my wife some of the things. And all those people are thinking that way. And I'm thinking what am I doing in the middle of this. . ."

He discussed the benefits of acting in a way that incurred internal conflict but which were supported by his father as a role model:

"Probably the reason I keep doing it is because it's easy. You've got to balance out between how I feel about it and how, um. . .well, you can't even balance it out. It's just ignoring . . .it's the convenience of the job and money and interest versus what I believe in. And right now I guess I ignore that because it doesn't bother me until some days it's like. . .And then I kind of rationalize it. Well, let's see. . .I need another six months and then I can get another job doing something else or something but. . . so my dad has been doing this for about 25 years too. So, it's . . .a military type."

He also expressed confusion concerning a question about his thinking on a moral issue involved in making weapons intended to kill people:

"I'm not sure of the question. . .No, I don't think I consider other people at all. Well, I guess I do.. .their rights to live. These things are meant for killing people. So. I don't think I think of it in those terms. But I mean that's the whole thing. And then you could start tracing it that 90% of the population is doing something, not 90 % but the majority of people somewhere you could connect, uh, I just have a stronger connection. I guess. I would never connect it that way. In the long run. This decision. I don't think about other people's rights consciously but it has to be taken into consideration. . .it has to be there. . .because I wouldn't , if weapons didn't do anything to people, I'd say it's a lot of fun, it's a game. That's the way I think most people consider it. It's a game."

While he reported negative feelings about his career decision, he tempered them with a dismissal of the moral aspect of the dilemma:

"Uh, probably kind of disappointed. It's like. . .there's some pride there, there's a pride in living a perfect, wonderful life and I'm deviating. But I like feel being pulled this way, but eventually I'll swing back. I don't feel like I'm doing a great terrible life. I feel like I'm talking about doing a mass murder or something like that. I feel like I'm dropping the bomb or something. That's why I'm trying to think of some moral decisions and I can't. I'm sure they're there; I just don't recall them unless I'm ignoring them all."

He decided it was all right for him to act the way he did because he was engaging in a 'moral calculus.' Over time he described this as:

"I guess there's a conflict between my idea of the general good and my idea of my personal good. Well, my solution now, and I guess what keeps me going, is eventually my personal good will help the general good and this is just the tool getting there. And in the long run I'd say there is a balance in the long run. And that's why, in the long run, if it doesn't work out that way, then I'll be very disappointed."

> An intrinsic part of many of the work dilemmas was the quality of a relationship or issues involving concern for other persons or themselves.

III. Selected Topics Concerning the Well-Being of the Persons Affected by Moral Decisions

An intrinsic part of many of the work dilemmas was the quality of a relationship or issues involving concern for other persons or themselves (for five out of six for the women, and three out of four for the men). One man, Subject 16, decided to continue teaching kindergarten in a bilingual format, despite a directive from the school administration to the contrary. He discussed his concern for the well-being of the children:

"This is a difficult choice because, uh, being I haven't taught that long but I have developed a certain idea as to what I am doing and how I am educating these children. And I do have very definite beliefs, and one of these beliefs is if you build a child's language ability, that will show as success in reading especially, which is the key to the whole elementary education system. So, uh, the thing now is if you teach them nothing but English and so they're getting lost, and as far as I'm concerned they are losing a great deal of time where they could be learning concepts that would be useful in reading and you would be teaching them in a language they would understand. Now they're missing out just because the district seems to think this is the right thing to do now. So, it's a very difficult choice to make. . .Sure, the children. Ultimately it was them. I think being a teacher and working with children, they are the ultimate focus. . . Ultimate, of ultimate importance and second-arily, now that I think of it, of their parents, too."

The Decision-Making Process Itself

The process used in decision-making on moral dilemmas was presented by most subjects as based on reason: to weigh the consequences of alternative actions logically in order to consider the effects of the outcomes on themselves and/or others. They then chose between alternatives based on either what they thought was "right," or in order to promote the well-being of themselves and others. A few interviewees said that they made moral decisions by determining what *felt* right.

Overall, most of the respondents wanted to show that they carefully thought out their decisions in a sound decision-making process. Few of them stated that they simply performed an action impulsively without much thought. They generally described their decisions as having been made logically, not morally. Deciding what to do seemed a largely secular process little influenced by moral principles or moral codes. The impression given by most of the respondents was that choosing whether to report an unethical foreman or to choose a moral business practice was little different intellectually from choosing what model of car to buy or apartment to rent.

Deciding what to do seemed a largely secular process little influenced by moral principles or moral codes.

None of the subjects in this sample reported a pre-existing philosophical or ethical model specifically for moral decision-making which they consciously applied to real-life situations. When asked to discuss their general process of moral decision making, they used only their reflections upon how they made the decisions in the two dilemmas they reported as part of the Moral Action Interview. They did not discuss either a more general set of guidelines, or a model of principled thought from which their decisions stemmed.

Subject 5, who decided not to share course material with her law school classmates, stated:

> "The process that I would use is, I look at the person, ask myself is it a friend, someone I get along with or someone I can't stand, and I look in the future and see how it affects me, what are the consequences for me. It's kind of like a selfish decision. If it's something I don't care about or won't hurt me, I'll act in one way, if I do, I'll act in another. . . .I look at all the factors and weigh them and decide to look at who's, what's involved, what's going to be affected and reach a just decision, but I don't know how to define 'just'. . . I need to weigh things and think about things. I just can't make snap decisions. I'm so concerned about hurting other people's feelings. That's a factor that plays into decisions. I mean if it's someone I get along with I put in more thought as to, 'Will this person be upset?' But if I don't like them, I don't care what they think."

Influences Reported on the Decision-Making Process

The subjects were equally divided on the issue of whether to ask others what they would do in the same circumstances. Of the six women (out of 11) who talked with others, five reported discussing the dilemma with family members. Of the five men (out of nine) who spoke with others, two reported discussing the dilemma with family members. Only one man mentioned directly discussing a moral dilemma with his father and mother, and one discussed the dilemma with his sister who was also directly involved in the dilemma. None of the other men mentioned discussing their moral dilemmas with family members. The men were more likely to discuss their dilemmas with professional or work-related peers than with family members.

In addition, eight women (out of 11) reported that their families, particularly their mothers, were an indirect resource for them; that is, they considered what their mothers would think or say in the situation, even if they did not ask them directly for input. Only one man reported indirect familial influence.

Little formal moral reasoning was explicitly reported by the group as a whole. The four individuals who reported employing moral principles were two women who used religion as a basis for their deontic choices—one woman who stated that the basis for her deontic choice was the proverb, "Two wrongs don't make a right," and the man who stated that he did not follow the deontic choice indicated by his moral principles. The other 16 Sierrans did not express moral principles or guidelines for their deontic choice.

Self-Perceived Risk to Comfort, Security, or Well-being

Many of the women's dilemmas involved self-perceived risk to their comfort, security, or well-being. When most women analyzed the perceived risk of their choices, they favored their own needs; only two women decided in favor of actions to reduce the risk to other persons, despite potential risk to themselves.

Subject 19, who decided to volunteer to testify in a court custody/sexual abuse case despite her trainee status, stated:

> "First, I thought about what was at risk at a court trial. What types of decisions were going to be made based on evidence presented during the trial. To me what was at risk was the child's well-being. It appeared that the child's court-appointed attorney was heavily biased against the mother and towards the father. . .First, I weighed the risk here and felt the child would be in danger. Second step, I thought: Who was best qualified to present this information to the courts, and was it okay for us to duck that responsibility and leave the kid hanging? I came to the conclusion that it was not morally right for us to duck that responsibility; someone needed to be there to present the information. . .It was either very little evidence, no evidence, or me. I felt I owed it to the child to put in my two cents. "

The Use of the Concept of Personal Rights in Making Moral-Decisions

The concept of personal rights was used typically in making moral decisions, especially when the rights of the respondent were concerned. One woman who reported that she considered others' rights at the expense of her own was Subject 12. She decided to continue to work with a customer who devalued her because she was a minority female:

> "Yes, in a business perspective; what's best for the customer; the customers' rights to receive sufficient service from the company and from me for the best I could provide them with or would someone else do a better job. I decided that given the relationship, I was providing the best I could. My manager understood that. I did that by trying to work through other sources in the company."

Of the four men who reported conflict between their rights and those of others, all decided for their own rights. However, for the four women who noted conflict between their personal rights and those of others, three decided for the others' rights, and one decided for her own.

The Consideration of Responsibility to Self and Others

Most respondents stated that they made their decisions based on feeling responsible to themselves. An example was given by Subject 17, who decided to change jobs despite a pay reduction:

> "Yes, it has a lot to do with what I just mentioned. Inner peace. I was constantly angry at this other place. I was at a level where I think I excelled very quickly at a very early stage in my career. I was promoted once three and a half years into my career, and it usually takes twice that long. So I was able to see the big picture a lot faster than a lot of people. And I got frustrated because I'm a doer, and being a doer I can't stand by and see other people and see a problem and I say, 'Why don't you do something about it?' And I become very vocal. . . .Even though I thought of everybody else, I tried to make everybody happy, and on top of that I knew I would be happy. Yes, I felt I was very responsible to myself."

Feelings for most of the women were an important factor in their moral decision making and their subsequent actions.

The Role of Feelings in Moral Decision Making and Action

Feelings for most of the women were an important factor in their moral decision making and their subsequent actions. On the other hand, feelings were rarely described by men in their narratives, and were not reported to be an influential factor in moral decision making. However, when asked directly about feelings, most women and men reported that they felt distraught or uncomfortable while actually making their decisions.

One subject who reported negative feelings when making a particular moral decision was Subject 10, a 28-year-old Black woman who decided to give her employer several months notice before leaving her employment:

"At first I felt kind of stupid. I felt like, 'What a dork, no one gives an employer this much lead time; you're just opening the door to get cut out of important jobs.' I felt, 'Oh, gosh, you're so Christian, you have to do what's right.' I felt resentful. Why can't I be the old sinner? So at first I felt trapped. I didn't want to do it, but I knew it was the right thing to do. And I started thinking about it and thinking about it and thought it would benefit me if I want to come back and I should be happy about it. So mentally I got myself together."

Deontic Choice (Deciding the Right Course of Action)

Most respondents reported knowing that there was for them one morally right course of action. The one woman who reported no deontic choice never discussed her decision with anyone; she reported feeling "selfish" afterwards. Since most subjects did not articulate firm moral principles or a set of ethical guidelines to help them determine their moral action choice or a deontic choice, they chose as deontic an alternative which, in general, "seemed right" to them based on current circumstances as they appraised them.

The respondents arrived at the deontic choice of a morally right action in various ways, with many reporting an "internal basis" for deciding their choice. Interestingly, three out of the four men with an internal sense of the moral nature of their dilemma did not report a deontic choice; the fourth man did so, but did not follow it.

The man who described an internal basis for his deontic choice was Subject 2, who decided not to tell his mother directly that his brother was homosexual, but to hint that his brother had something to tell her:

"I have a little voice, okay, that tells me what is right and what is wrong. Anyway, that little voice will go ahead and screw me and screw me. It can also make me stressed to the point where I don't eat well or I don't take care of my body; I'll mess up in my job: That little voice can go ahead and cause havoc, can wreak havoc in me. So I've learned to go ahead and follow that little voice. And that's. . .that reaction. I want to say my inner mind; I've never really defined as to exactly what it is. I've heard other people say, 'Well, there's a little voice in me' and I don't know if they are referring to the same type of little voice I'm referring to."

Discerning the deontic choice was a personalized realization which took a varied amount of time. The deontic choice was not quickly or readily apparent for most women and men. Given the complexity of many of the moral dilemmas they reported, this was not surprising. The deontic choice was usually followed by the appropriate action. Most respondents who knew the morally right act were willing and able to follow through with it. The one woman who did not do so reported that she felt "guilty... terrible" about not following what she knew to be the morally right way to act. The one man who reported that he did not follow the deontic choice said he felt "disappointed" about not doing so.

Since the moral dilemmas were self-selected by the Sierrans and were not necessarily a representative sample of their decision-making process and their subsequent actions, it is not possible to generalize and conclude that most subjects always followed through on the right moral course of action. Perhaps many selected dilemmas in which they felt they "did the right thing," and wanted to appear socially or morally "correct" to the investigator. However, it is possible to state that most subjects followed the deontic choice in the dilemmas that they reported.

The Integration of a Sense of Self with the Moral Decision

Even when the process reflected negatively on themselves, most subjects reported that their decisions were consistent with their personalities and how they perceived themselves. One woman who described how her decision was consistent with her personality was Subject 4, who decided to use disposable paper diapers for her baby, not cloth diapers:

> "I don't like my life disrupted. I like doing new things but on my own terms. All I kept thinking was, 'Oh no, I have to sit in the house. Oh no, how am I going to work. Oh no, my breasts are going to hurt. I'm going to get fat during pregnancy.' How my life will be disrupted. So [I'm] selfish and that's all you've got. I like doing new experiences, new things, but I like to come and go from them and don't like to be strapped down, and here's an obligation that will never go away, and that was a decision I knew I had to make. You don't just leave it if you don't like it."

Only in a few cases did the respondents report that they were consciously aware that they had acted to preserve their sense of self. Thus, did they act to retain their own sense of personal moral integrity? In most cases there was little mention in their narratives of needing to act to support their personal moral integrity, even if that was occurring. Their actions did not, by and large, stem from consistently conscious and pre-planned principled decision making.

References

Blasi, A. (1983). Moral cognition and moral action: A theoretical perspective. *Developmental Review, 3,* 178-210.

Blasi, A. (1984). Moral identity: Its role in moral functioning. In W. M. Kurtines & J. L. Gewirtz (Eds.), *Morality, moral behavior and moral development.* New York: John Wiley & Sons.

Gilligan, C. (1982). *In a different voice: Psychological theory and women's development.* Cambridge, MA: Harvard University Press.

Kohlberg, L., & Candee, D. (1984) The relationship of moral judgment to moral action In L. Kohlberg (Ed.), *Essays on moral development: Vol. II. The psychology of moral development.* San Francisco: Harper and Row.

Rest, J. R. (1986). *Moral Development: Advances in research and theory.* New York: Praeger.

C H A P T E R

EIGHT

MORAL DILEMMAS IN
INTERPERSONAL RELATIONSHIPS

The focus of this chapter is on moral dilemmas in multi-generational interpersonal relationships. The subjects are 14 young adults (different individuals from those reported on in Chapter 7) from the 1980, 1981, and 1982 classes at the University of California, Irvine. At the time of the interviews in 1987 with David Connor, they were in their late 20s or early 30s. Connor used as an interview guide the Moral Behavior Interview (see Appendix B)[1] which he created.

The multi-generational relationships that provide the context for this chapter were also multi-directional. Some of the young adults were dealing with issues relating to their parents and grandparents, others were concerned about matters having to do with peers and spouses or lovers, and still others were themselves parents and were experiencing moral questions affecting their own children or whether or not to have an abortion.

> The multi-generational relationships that provide the context for this chapter were also multi-directional.

Kim and her husband provide a clear example of the complexity of some of the moral dilemmas. They had wanted to invest the Thanksgiving celebration with meaning relevant to them and to focus attention on the range of life experiences which caused them to feel gratitude. The desire to do so was in keeping with their attempt to give a spiritual content to all the major rituals of their lives. Kim's parents traditionally had been the hosts for a family gathering at Thanksgiving, but Kim's mother had recently been ill and had wanted to avoid the stress of being in charge of a large celebration. Kim therefore invited family members to her own table, along with personal friends of her and her husband. Kim's parents welcomed the change in plans. It was explained to everyone that a new Thanksgiving ritual would be established and that guests would be asked to speak briefly about their reasons for being grateful.

---

[1] Dr. Connor's Ph.D. dissertation contains a fuller description of his research methodology and an extended report of his findings. *The moral behavior of young adults: Interviews and analyses.* Unpublished doctoral dissertation, Boston University, 1989.

Kim was attempting to bring together both her original family and new friends, to establish a new Thanksgiving tradition with more personal meaning, and, incidentally, to give her and her husband a chance to take over a new role in the family. Then her maternal grandmother also fell ill:

> "It gets about one month away from Thanksgiving, and we had taken all the people we knew who didn't have family, and we'd invited 19 people to come over for dinner, and we explained to everybody up front that each person was going to go around and talk about what they were thankful for, and that it was going to be in what was considered to be in the spirit of the holiday. My grandmother had a stroke. And my mother got very, very: 'Oh my God, this might be the last Thanksgiving we have together,' and called us up and insisted that we come and that we call everyone who was coming to our house and cancel, and that we couldn't possibly not be there for this family gathering."

The grandmother's illness caused Kim's mother to want to experience ritual once more: the symbol of family unity. Kim, out of loyalty to her own invited guests, wanted to continue with plans to celebrate gratitude in a different circle with people who, otherwise, would have had no fellowship on Thanksgiving. A conflict resulted:

> "The bottom line was that my parents couldn't accept our decision, and continually, for about four months after Thanksgiving was over, kept bringing it up how we ruined their dinner and what an irresponsible child I was, and that we'd better never do anything like this to them again. The next Thanksgiving, we'd better be there, and on and on."

The result of the conflict was a power struggle, an appeal by the father and mother to filial duty, an attempt to re-establish the older hierarchy in the family. The reaction was impassioned:

> "My husband was so upset about the whole thing. My husband said: 'I will never have Thanksgiving dinner at their house again because they refuse to treat us like adults.'"

Kim was planning to attempt a reconciliation shortly after the interview, but was not, however, going to plan her future Thanksgiving around her parents. She ascribed her decision to a newly acquired attitude:

> "My attitude is my parents are not going to change. My parents are going to have their belief system, behave the way they want to behave."

It was a source of satisfaction to Kim that she had been honest about her views and had expressed her feelings. She was not optimistic that any satisfactory final answer could be found to the complicated dilemma. Duty to her parents clashed with duty to her new friends. Other issues for Kim were consideration of everyone's feelings and following through on obligations. As a consequence of the controversy, she had come to a new recognition that she and her husband had to take their own needs into consideration more often. She felt that broaching the subject with her parents again, however, would not lead to any change in their understanding of her feelings.

"My new attitude that I'm working on is that we should do it for ourselves, to express the way my husband and I feel, and that if they can't accept that, that's tough, but at least we tried and we, like, said our piece."

The step to keep *her* new Thanksgiving ritual was going to be on her own terms.

This lengthy account of Kim's dilemma serves to illustrate a common problem between the young adults and their parents around the mutual adjustments necessary to change old definitions of relationships and roles. Not all the struggles were as complicated as Kim's, but a sense emerged that some years of effort had gone into tussles and disagreements around one point or another of "appropriate" behavior.

Barry, for example, had lived at home with his parents for several years, and both sides had to make adjustments along the way. He cited two areas of recent disagreement, one with each parent. One of Barry's ambitions was to save enough money to buy a house. He was therefore cutting down on unnecessary expenses, including restaurant or cafeteria lunches. Instead, his mother made his lunch on a daily basis. She did so in exchange for his promising to take her out to dinner once a month. In this way, a reciprocal agreement was struck which yielded an advantage to each. Discord arose when he did not regularly keep his side of the bargain. He would then accede to her reminders.

> ...Kim's dilemma serves to illustrate a common problem between the young adults and their parents around the mutual adjustments necessary to change old definitions of relationships and roles.

Barry's exuberance around the house was the source of friction with his father. Barry worked with other members of the family to mollify the father's annoyance and therefore reined in his enthusiasm to some degree. What emerged from Barry's description of conflict within the family was a picture of a family group involved in an ongoing effort to work out arrangements which would take into account each other's needs and expectations, adjust those expectations as required, and allow roles to shift and change as the need arose.

Paul also lived at home. Sometimes Paul's definition of caring for his parents had led him to lie to them. This choice was made in order to spare them what he perceived as harm while at the same time allowing him the freedom to date young women of a different ethnic background without his parents' knowledge. In order to cover his tracks, he would use alibis:

"I got to be a fairly good liar to them as far as that's concerned."

He was acting out of what he considered to be a double obligation: to himself and to them and their expectations. If to avoid hurting them he needed to lie, he would lie. Being successful at lying to his parents was a source of pride, since he reasoned he was shielding them from knowing his choice of dating partners:

"I'll tell them of the dates I have if I go out with some girl [of the same ethnic background], and that's it. It keeps them happy."

He had been encouraging his sister to lie also in order to cut down on domestic upheaval within the family.

Not all of the subjects, however, were either living at home or unmarried. Some of them were themselves parents, and had to deal with different moral issues. Alice, who was separated from her husband and was the mother of two children under age three, described her duties in compelling terms:

> "When you think about your role as a parent, it's such an important role to me. . .When I had gotten pregnant with Robert, and I wasn't married, and I really felt such an obligation to be everything, to really provide a stimulating environment, to be the mother, to be the father, so that he wouldn't have anything that would be lacking, and then when I got married, and it was three or four months into the marriage that I got pregnant, and it was like 'I can't be a mother to both of two children.' I didn't feel like I could. It's been difficult for me to . . . Because I had given him so much by myself, it was like how could I give another human being the same kind of love and the same kind of attention and to do all those kind of things for the new baby?"

For Alice, the tasks of motherhood were daunting, involving responsibility for the care and well-being of one and then two small children in addition to full time employment with responsibility for the welfare of abused and neglected children. For a while, she considered not having the second child:

> "Why would I go through this a second time when I'm really not sure?"

To deal with the dilemma of whether or not to have an abortion, she involved many other people from both families and from her church. In other areas of her life, such broad consultation was not Alice's usual decision-making process:

> "On the professional level I don't need anybody to make a decision. I just make 'em and so be it, you just go on."

When asked why she had behaved differently in this personal dilemma compared to her much more autonomous, confident decisions when facing difficult professional questions, she expressed the opinion that the difference might have to do with lack of confidence in her multiple roles in the family. She indicated that, in retrospect, the decision to involve so many people had not been good:

> "Then you get the input of your family, and your in-laws, and this kind of thing, and they really cloud things for me, and I end up in hindsight to be making the wrong decision, because I have tried to involve too many people in the decision-making process."

In hindsight, she now felt that the only two people who had a direct right to be involved in the abortion decision were herself and her now separated husband. Instead, she had allowed many others to be involved, both inside and outside the two families. All who were invited to comment expressed opinions on whether or not she should have the baby. Now that the baby had been born, no one took responsibility for its care except her.

Thinking back to the time when she was deciding whether or not to give birth to the child, it was not at all clear to Alice why she had involved so many people in the first place:

Interviewer: "If you hadn't talked to (all of those people), how would you have felt? Would you have felt bad about not involving them?"

Alice: "No. I wouldn't have felt bad."

Interviewer: "Did they have any rights?"

Alice: "I guess my husband had some rights. But they didn't have any rights, and his parents didn't have any rights, but [pause]. Now that we're separated and [my husband] has moved [elsewhere], it's like his grandmother will call, and it's like 'I have the right to visit.' I'm like, "What right do you have?" Just by virtue that you're a relative, does that give some rights?"

Alice was feeling that she was perhaps the one person involved who was without rights. She felt tied by obligation to all:

Interviewer: "If you gave yourself some rights, what would they be?"

Alice: "The right to say 'no' without an explanation for everything that you do. Not being accountable for absolutely every decision, every action, every movement. That would be my right, to just say 'no,' and it be 'no' because."

In the process of involving all of the others, Alice had lost the opportunity to pay attention to herself.

Alice's dilemma provided a poignant depiction of an inter-generational conflict. She was responsible for those younger than she—namely, her two children. She was responsible to those older—namely, both her parents, the parents and grandparents of her husband, and to the extended community from her church as well. Despite her wishes, there was little time left to care for her own needs, a matter about which she was amply conscious.

It was not surprising, therefore, that she described herself as someone at a crossroads in life. As a social worker responsible for abused and exploited children, she cared deeply about the level of her job performance at work. How she acted in her professional life had basic implications for the well-being of the many children assigned to her. In her career she experienced pride for a job well done. In her role as separated wife and single mother, she was conscientiously taking care of two demanding children. When asked how she would define herself, she did so mainly in terms of her two major roles:

Interview: "How would you define yourself now? What are you like?"

Alice: "Physically?"

Interviewer: "Anything. Describe yourself. Who would you say you are?"

Alice: "*Who* am I or *what* am I?"

Interviewer: "Both."

Alice: "I'm just a young woman trying to, to, to survive, I guess. I don't know . . . I guess right now as far as a person and those kind of things, I'm really at a crossroads in my life as far as . . . really trying to determine . . . to make a transition from that real independent type of person . . . that was really career oriented and really success-driven . . . that kind of person, to really a domesticated kind of person, and . . . the children and the home and all those kind of things, and that's where I am right now. And I'm not doing that very easily, either because I still feel like that . . . there are successes that I want to know, in life, and it's like you have to put them on the back burners now because you have children and . . . I was married, and all those kind of things . . . . *who* I am and *what* I am right now is really in a transition type of period for me."

For Alice, both major roles in her life were moral roles which were carried out with moral intentions—that of the ambitious, hard-working social worker at pains to do a satisfactory job, and that of the attentive, if weary, mother seeking to provide for the well-being of two children. Living a moral life for Alice was not easy, particularly when she was subject to the judgments/criteria/norms of so many others.

Cynthia, too, was facing a divorce. Though her children were a few years older than Alice's, caring for their needs was a demanding task. She prided herself on the conscientious way she fulfilled her role of parent: "I'm a working mother, I can provide for my kids." Her UCI education was a source of deep pride for Cynthia. When asked what made her feel good, she replied:

"My children and my education."

The theme of experiencing satisfaction when her children were successful occurred several times in her interview:

"I was real proud my children did well in their exams. . . . I just want to learn as much as I can so I can pass it on to my kids. I was real proud my children did real well in their exams. They scored real high. . . . My son got a reading reward and that made me feel good because I helped him. I read to him and I read to him."

She worked hard to advance her children's education, teaching them both subject matter content and what she considered moral knowledge, such as finishing tasks, applying one's efforts fully, and trying as hard as one could. The achievements of her children validated Cynthia's own sense of self-worth.

Cynthia's career was also in education, a choice she had made because she wanted to improve the lot of pupils in the local schools:

"I wanted to be a *good* teacher, where I grew up, because I saw so many bad ones, coming through the LA city schools. I wanted, my goal was, to replace one bad one."

The interview took place during the summer months when schools were not in session. Cynthia was concerned that some resolution be found to the marital separation before the start of the school year so that she would have available the emotional energy necessary to get her new class off to a good start.

In the midst of the dual challenges to care for her own children and her school children, Cynthia knew that she also needed to consider her own personal needs:

> "I like myself. I don't like what's happening right now [pause]. I like the way my children are growing and the way they're developing. I like the way *I'm* developing. I make time for myself. I like myself enough to make time to work out and to continue going to school and to buy nice clothes."

She took pride in the changes she was bringing about, and she made sure that her own development continued and that her needs were being met, at least partially.

Linda was still responsible for the support of a family, helping her widowed mother and a sibling financially. Her boyfriend was in need of a loan at the time of the interview. Linda therefore found herself in a three-fold conflict. She needed to save money herself in order to realize her ambition to own her own business, her family was dependent upon her financial contributions, and her boyfriend indicated that he had to have help if he was to complete his own professional training:

> "I *could* give him the money, but it seems to me, 'Don't you have family you could go ask?' I'm trying to help support two other people. Anyway it came up last night, it seems anytime we get together, it's a month now, in some kind of way he slides it on in there. 'I've got to finish school.' He may not directly ask me but it's insinuated: 'I don't know how I'm going to make it. I need four thousand dollars by September.'"

Linda was clearly hearing two messages—that he needed money to complete his education, and that she was being asked to provide the necessary financial aid. Both the appeal from the boyfriend and her obligation to her family were consistent with her moral values: It was right and proper to strive, to achieve as much education as one can, and it was a moral duty to help others if one could:

> "I go home, go to sleep, and will sit there and dream how can I help this brother get his money? Should I give him the $4,000? Nooo, that's not, don't do that. But the guilt. I will feel guilty, about not giving to somebody who needs help."

The dilemma involved a decision between what she experienced as two different calls of duty:

> "There's two rights. I seem to favor the right that says don't do it, you are right in not giving him the money, but then again there's the other right that says you could help this person out if they are, they are in need, but *are* they in need? All those little questions keep popping up."

At the time of the interview, she was leaning toward not lending him the money. Her expectation was that the boyfriend ought to take more initiative toward finding the money he needed:

> "This person's, they're responsible. . . . Maybe if he finds out all the other alternatives, there's got to be somebody else he can turn to."

Not helping him with the money directly was hard, however:

> "Person could die tomorrow and I'll be saying: 'I could have helped so and so. I could have helped but I didn't and they're dead now.'"

Linda's dilemma is a clear example of what young adults present as the complexity of everyday moral choices as they experience them. One of her choices was either to fund her boyfriend's last semester of education, or not to do so. Funding him would mean not having the money which she herself would need to start a business, money that might be a key to helping the rest of her immediate family to achieve more financial security. Not loaning him money would result in her experiencing guilt, and perhaps reassessing her image of herself. Favoring one actor—her boyfriend—would potentially affect the well-being of her immediate family, and conceivably of herself.

Moreover, each relationship that Linda was involved in—whether with her mother, her siblings, her boyfriend, or with herself—had a history which influenced her feelings. For example, earlier in her life she had stood next to a fellow pupil who had been shot in high school. This traumatic experience subsequently had an effect on her sense of ambition for her siblings. She had seen her father beaten in a riot, another traumatic experience which affected her relationship with her mother. Her father's subsequent death further affected her sense of responsibility toward her mother. In turn, each element of her history and each relationship was potentially interwoven with others when it came to making moral choices as she experienced them.

That moral decisions take place within a personal historical context was also illustrated by two dilemmas Barry had experienced in deciding whether or not to enter into a sexual relationship. One dilemma had taken place while he was in college; the other was occurring concurrently with the interview. Taken together, the two dilemmas indicate that each had raised different issues for Barry.

The first moral decision was whether or not to have sex with a particular young woman while in college. Barry experienced a balancing act between morality (abstaining) and selfishness (having sexual intercourse). Having sexual intercourse won out:

> **Interviewer:** "Why was it 'selfishness'? Why was it 'morality'?"
>
> **Barry:** "Well, in a situation of sexuality you have a person who you have 18 years of saying 'no,' it's not that, it's not a good thing, and you have your physical desires, and at some point you say well, I'm not going to marry this person, but I need this person at this particular point, and looking back, it probably wasn't the greatest decision, but I don't regret it."

At the start of the college experience, the choice for Barry was between (a) sexual pleasure and (b) following a received moral precept that sexual intercourse was wrong outside of marriage or with someone he did not intend to marry. The only hint of Barry's having looked at the needs and perspective of the young woman involved is in his using the word *selfishness* to describe his action.

He said that he made the decision to have sex using a balance system (this was a recurrent symbol in Barry's description of his deliberations). The weight on one side of the balance was also influenced by the fact that the young woman came from a different ethnic and religious background:

> "That's quite a bit different from what your parents want you to do, and so you, at some point, *you decide* that you at this particular moment in time, it's advantageous of you to pursue an activity and you go through with it [pause]. It's just two things at that point: whether or not *it's right or wrong*, and you weigh all those *factors* as much as balance on the balanced order of facts and you just make that decision."

What he called "selfishness" apparently outweighed other considerations, and he decided not to follow the path that his parents and the conventions of his morality would have dictated:

> **Interviewer:** "Was part of the process thinking about her?"
>
> **Barry:** "At that time, no, but subsequently I have put that a lot more into the equation than I used to."

As an adolescent, Barry's perspective-taking had been more limited than when he became a young adult. He illustrated this by recounting a recent similar quandary involving an older woman with whom he had several interests in common and with whom he had spent some extended time on dates. He found her quite physically attractive:

> "I've recently had a girlfriend who was 38, and had I been in a different mind, say if I'd been in college, I would have gone through with it, but now she's 38, and I'm not going to get married to her and so I told her. I said, 'We can't possibly get married. You're too old.' And she has other factors that I'm not interested in, but I'm very sexually attracted to her, but at this point it was to her best interest not to pursue it. We've gone out together a couple of times as friends but it's sour now."

On this occasion, Barry took what he assumed to be the woman's best interests into consideration. He assumed that she would, like him, not be in favor of engaging in sexual intercourse with someone who could not later be a potential marriage partner. His reasons for ruling her out as a future wife were that she was 11 years older than he and that she was some $8,000 in debt. She did not share his views:

> "But the funny thing is she said to me, 'you know, you really shouldn't have told me that, you should have just gone ahead and gone through with it.' I think that's hilarious (laughter). But that's from her point of view."

His feelings were decidedly mixed at the time of the interview. He had chosen the path he thought was right, and that was a source of somewhat hesitant pride:

> "But I think I feel better about myself for having done it, having disclosed that and then again . . . she's an extremely sweet person, she's a real nice girl, you know, and I just felt like it would be hurtful to her, and it turns out from *her* point of view, that's maybe what she wanted, you know, she wanted to be, to go ahead and do what you want and you know, she'll accept the consequences afterwards."

Barry said that he suspected telling her about his attitude about marriage would change the relationship, but he felt that having weighed the pluses and the minuses, she did not meet his criteria. This time his moral code overrode his physical desire. He also assumed that the potential sexual partner shared the same perspective, which turned out not to be the case.

Other unmarried subjects spoke of similar sexual dilemmas with a moral dimension: One involved a sexual attraction to the wife of a close friend, and another involved the realization that many of the subject's relationships exploited his partners, and did not take their perspective into consideration. The other major interpersonal problems with a moral dimension involved working out living arrangements with non-romantic roommates. A recurrent theme in these dilemmas was discovering that not all young adults share the same moral values or, for that matter, have the same moral perspective on a situation.

> A recurrent theme in these dilemmas was discovering that not all young adults share the same moral values or, for that matter, have the same moral perspective on a situation.

The moral dilemmas of the young adults interviewed were overwhelmingly concerned with interpersonal relationships. This was as predicted by most of the theoretical writing on young adulthood. Typical young adult roles can involve interaction with more than one generation. The moral choices the subjects reported had to do with their roles as offspring, as parents themselves, and as spouses, friends, and peers. The range of complexity of the factors involved in the resolution of the dilemmas was wide, partly reflecting differences in their assessment of the moral elements of a situation.

C H A P T E R

MORAL DILEMMAS IN THE WORKPLACE

The focus of this chapter is on moral dilemmas in the workplace. The subjects are the same 14 young adults whose moral dilemmas in multi-interpersonal relationships appeared in Chapter 8. They were in their late 20s or very early 30s at the time of their interviews with David Connor and were from the University of California, Irvine Classes of 1980, 1981, and 1982. The instrument used was the Moral Behavior Interview (see Appendix B).

Moral dilemmas in the workplace centered on four different themes. The first theme was the employee being pressured by superiors to act in ways the employee considered immoral; the second was the employee feeling temptation to act in ways which were not moral. A third theme was other people in the workplace not acting morally; a fourth was being presented with opportunities through the workplace to act in ways which were intentionally altruistic.

> Almost all of the subjects talked of the workplace as a major arena for moral dilemmas.

Almost all of the subjects talked of the workplace as a major arena for moral dilemmas. Two who were currently unemployed but had recently completed professional training referred to earlier employment or to internships to illustrate the role of the workplace in their moral lives, as did a young woman who had resigned from her job in order to have a baby. Clearly for all of these young adults, issues of moral challenge were closely connected with work.

Interestingly, however, some subjects frequently referred to differences between their behavior at work and their behavior in the rest of their lives. Some even suggested that they used different processes of decision making (or even different skills) depending upon whether the moral dilemma was work-related or related to their personal life. Still others seemed to indicate that they acted in the same ways wherever they were. Some of the subjects reported that they had been asked by their superiors to perform acts during their employment which they considered wrong. The pressure was usually to perform in ways that were either less than safe or less than honest. Barry, for example, was a technical writer responsible for producing the written instructions for handling complex machinery. He was pressured to produce work according to a timetable, not according to a standard of excellence:

"There are situations at work where there's a time factor, and you have to get this book out even though it's not perfect, and you do your best to make it— my goal in that area is to make it so it's not unsafe, no matter what. Even if I have to cut certain areas out, it'll be areas where there's not a safety factor involved. That's how I make that sort of decision. My goal is to make it perfect. But if I don't have the time, if I'm forced to. . ."

The pressure came in the form of having to declare prematurely that a job was finished whether or not the results were good or even safe. Barry tried to avoid working on manuals which could result in the transmission of unsafe procedures.

Elizabeth was asked to falsify records while working for a private company on a government contract in a defense-related industry :

"There was one thing I was asked to do that I would not do, and I told my manager if she wanted that done she could do it because I wasn't going to do it. . . I wouldn't do it because that number was not a number that was calculated by the computer. It was a number that was being put in there by a person that was painting a prettier picture than was really there, and that's why I wouldn't do it."

In a closely related dilemma related by Joanne, she was provided with a choice between producing an honest set of data, or following her supervisor's demands to falsify the record. She refused to falsify the data.

All three young adults experienced a conflict between what they were asked to do and what they felt was the right thing to do. The stakes involved were more than guilt or satisfaction and pride. For each, acceding to the supervisor's request was seen not only as wrong, but also as dangerous, since they could then be held responsible for any errors. In Barry's case, the overall process called for a verification procedure involving field trials of the machinery and of his instructions. When asked whether his reluctance to produce a timely but imperfect product had to do with thinking about the people ultimately using the product, he replied:

Barry: "I do do that. That isn't a concern for my coordinator for some reason."

Interviewer: "Why is it a concern for you?"

Barry: "I see the guy out there doing the job for one, and from a selfish point of view, I'll be participating in the verification, so when it's not right they're going to look at me and say, 'Well, you validated this and where are those steps?'"

The safety of the user was one issue for Barry. Another issue was his own security in the position he held. If he took shortcuts, other people might suffer and so might Barry in the resulting inquiry. He spoke in the interview more about job security considerations than about the safety of the user.

Jane reported an ethical dilemma at her workplace related to being asked to violate the license of a computer software agreement. She was concerned that the unauthorized use might be discovered, and that she ran the risk of being fired:

136

"And you've got to look at it, too, as it might be your job in the end if you get caught at it, so there's probably a little more incentive than a few of the things that you could do wrong at work than using somebody's, that's part of it."

For Barry, Elizabeth, Joanne, and Jane the issue of losing one's job was a major concern in making a moral decision in the workplace. In their comments there was also a discernible sense that a decision which could cost one a job was, in and of itself, a decision of a different order, not so much a harder or a more complicated decision, but a choice which was governed by its own set of rules. It is also possible that for some people, moral action on a work dilemma is a decision about the cost of the proposed solution: Losing one's job may be so strong a concern that the person feels relieved of responsibility to follow the deontic choice.

Elizabeth, when employed in another position which involved migrant workers (many of whom were in the United State illegally), had been struck by the injustice of their treatment at the hands of their immediate supervisors. The migrant workers, all of whom were Mexican, were being charged by their foremen for facilities which the employers were providing for free. On top of this, the foremen extracted other fees:

> "The field supervisors make them pay to get a job. Then once they've got a job they have to pay part of the check to their supervisors for letting them keep their job."

Faced with the second layer of injustice, Elizabeth reacted mainly with compassion for the workers and at first talked openly at her workplace about the situation, not yet realizing that apparently everyone above the foremen knew what was going on. She stopped making comments in public when she realized that her job was on the line:

> "With all this stuff going on at work now, first I kinda would say things, but then I realized I'd better not say anything, or I may not have a job, and that it's better not to say anything and just to try to help them as much as you can without saying, 'I think that's wrong.' I mean everybody knows that the supervisors are charging for the labor camps and they're cutting them a check, and all the company officers and the owners know they give labor camps free but they all know they don't do anything, and I don't, I still can't understand. I could never ask; I know I would be fired if I ever said anything so at first I would say things and then I realized I'm going to get myself in trouble saying things."

In the face of a work environment where the authority figures apparently condoned what Elizabeth saw as unjust behavior, she looked for some way to improve the lot of the fieldhands, and at the same time retain her job:

> "Now it's just like I do little things that I think can help them. You know, if it's translating stuff in English into Spanish or if it's just little things."

Though her job did not call for her to provide assistance to the fieldhands, she offered help with the process of gaining legal alien status and went out of her way to treat the workers with caring and respect. During the interview, she expressed the belief that keeping her job was an overriding and self-explanatory consideration.

It is also possible that for some people, moral action on a work dilemma is a decision about the cost of the proposed solution: Losing one's job may be so strong a concern that the person feels relieved of responsibility to follow the deontic choice.

The concept of a separate hierarchy of moral values in a work situation was clearly expressed by Barry:

> "Most moral decisions [pause] I haven't had to make a heavy moral decision in a long time because I don't steal, I don't know what other morality things come up? I don't kill anybody, I don't go as far as using the Lord's name in vain, I don't even think about that one way or the other, let's see, what other Commandments are there? Adultery—I don't participate in sex with other people's wives, that doesn't interest me at all, so I don't know if I have a lot of moral decisions that I have to make. Now at work, there're ethical decisions."

Barry implied that the rules by which he judged himself or that guided his behavior, including the Ten Commandments, did not apply in the context of work. At work what was involved was not morality, but ethics. He used the word "moral" in the interview to describe certain work-place decisions. He summed up the difference for him between "trying to do the right thing" and self-preservation:

> "I don't want to be faced with the fact that I could be put out of a job if it's wrong. It's not just moral; it's saving one's buns."

Barry seemed to be implying by this statement that the addition of the danger of losing a job changed the entire basis of the calculation: The situation was no longer "just moral," not just another factor in the resolution of a moral dilemma.

Kim, who held an executive supervisory sales level position in a service industry, was clear also that she had different standards of acceptable behavior at work and in the rest of her activities. She had decided that in her job it was necessary for her to lie. She would have preferred not to be in a position where lying was called for, even though sometimes her lying might be a way of at least not harming others:

She had decided that in her job it was necessary for her to lie.

> "I want to be in a business where I'm not put in that position. But because I've made the choice to be here and to be doing this, then within those parameters of having made the choice, then telling a lie is something I have to accept and deal with. I don't like it, but it was, I guess, something of a known factor going in when I decided to do this."

She saw her choice of a particular sales position as inevitably carrying with it a requirement that she be dishonest. Having made that choice, she was under an obligation to follow the rules of her workplace, whatever the personal cost.

That there was a cost to Kim became apparent when she spoke of the standards she held for her life. Her behavior at work was different from her behavior outside of work:

> "I try really hard outside of this because I do have to tell lies in my work; I try really hard in my personal life not to do that."

By implication, while lying *per se* was morally wrong in her estimation, it was permissible under the duress of work-related situations. The workplace exerted a moral normative power in and of itself.

Other subjects also spoke of a difference in their behavior away from the workplace and on the job. Julie, for example, spoke of difficulties in being honest about her feelings with friends and acquaintances. On the other hand, in her professional dealings with others, she had had fewer problems with honesty:

> "At work, especially as the more confident I became in my area, you speak to managers and to other higher people, and that kind of momentum always tends to carry over into the personal life, and so I've been a lot more honest being a professional person; it just spilled over to my personal life, and I have found now that I have started to be honest and that it does, it benefits you I'm finding out."

Thus, one of the skills that can be important in action of any kind—the assertiveness to be honest about her own feelings and desires, both to herself and to others—had been fostered in the workplace and was being applied subsequently in other domains of her life.

As she expressed when describing another dilemma, however, not all the habits Julie found necessary in her professional life had been transferred yet to her private domain. When asked whether there were ways she behaved that she would not want the people at work to know, she replied:

> "I wouldn't want the people at work to know I don't cook. [pause] I'm an absolute slob. [pause] I guess my lack of detail, my lack of attention, my, I won't even let them see my car, my car is like a purse, it has everything in it."

The question was intended to elicit a response about actions around which the subject experienced guilt, and, in fact, Julie did imply at least some guilt about her desire to keep her private behaviors away from the judging gaze of others. She frequently found herself forced to lie about the road-worthiness of her automobile when it was her turn to drive a group of co-workers to lunch or to a meeting.

On a much more serious plane, Alice, too, experienced a dichotomy between her ability and style in the workplace and in her private life. As a caseworker dealing with abused and exploited children she was in contact with critical situations on an almost daily basis. Many of her co-workers, presumably worn down by the size of their caseloads and the stressful nature of their responsibilities, could sometimes be somewhat lackadaisical in their work performance. Not so Alice:

> "I can't go 50-50. I have to go a 100."

The daily temptation for Alice was not to become too involved with the suffering of children in their often chaotic family situations. Instead, she did try to keep in close contact with the children, monitoring their safety and well-being. Decisions made about case disposition were of basic importance to the child's health and well-being:

> "It's really moral. I think all the times I think of some of the moral questions we were presented with in Sierra, and you think about judgmental types of things that you have to deal with on the job. Is it better to remove a child from an abusive parent and cause the child the stress of being separated, or is it best to leave the child in that environment and then try to, you know, do some other things to enhance the environment

that the child is in rather than remove it? So, you know, there's no right or wrong, it's basically a gut feeling kind of thing that you have to deal with on an hourly basis."

Her professional life as she saw it was full of moral decisions. How she decided them had a profound effect on the welfare of other people involved. She described herself as making those decisions with a certain amount of self assurance. In her personal life, however, she lacked both total control over the situation and the autonomy she experienced at work.

Alice had two small children, one whom she was nursing and one who was a toddler, and Alice was separated from her husband. She took the role of mother very seriously. When making decisions in her short married life, she had taken into consideration the opinions of both extended families. Alice experienced a sharp dichotomy between work decisions and personal decisions:

"I'm the kind of person that when decisions, just like professional and business and those kind of decisions, I can make those kind of decisions, I guess, more easily than I can personal decisions. Then you get the input of the family and the in-laws and this kind of thing, and they really cloud things for me, and I end up in hindsight making the wrong decisions because I have tried to involve too many people in the decision-making process, where on a professional level I don't need anybody to make a decision. I just make 'em and so be it, you just go on."

The problem, as Alice saw it, was the difficulty of using professional skills and attitudes in her personal life. The social context of the decision changed also. At home she was aware of the points of view of far more people:

"Once I'm at work or once I'm at school, I know I feel that I'm really in control of those kind of situations so I can make decisions and stand by them, and I can't seem to bring that over into the personal side of me. I haven't been able to so far."

Later in the interview Alice returned to the topic of needing to practice different skills in her personal life if she were to avoid the feeling of being so obligated to others that her own needs were not being met.

Other subjects reported situations in the workplace in which they saw opportunities to be moral agents—that is to say, to work for the well being of others without outside pressure forcing them to take steps to help those others. Paul, who sold medical supplies, was part of a company which made a particular medication that could be sold for a high profit:

"We could command our own price, but we're fairly reasonable."

In that company, he sometimes could make decisions about prices that reflected caring about individual circumstances:

"I work sometimes in an area that doesn't have very rich people, and what I would normally charge, say, one person for the same drug, I wouldn't charge the same thing, and I look at how their economic status is and sometimes I'll base it on that."

In situations where pricing policy was under his control, Paul practiced a personal version of fairness, charging each customer according to their ability to pay, not acting to get maximum financial return for his company.

Not all the moral decisions subjects described in the workplace involved either job security or considerable risk to the well being of others. Many involved questions of honesty about using company resources for personal needs, or about reporting expenses. Sandra, for example, spoke of how she decided whether to put in a full eight hours of work every day:

> "Like for example today, I couldn't go to work till ten 'cause I was dead tired. I got to sleep about 1:30 since I got home from Sacramento very late, and maybe I should feel guilty 'cause I left work early for this interview and I got there late, but I don't because I know there have been times when I've worked very late, worked overtime, so they probably owe me time rather than me owing them time."

Her justification for the short work day, then, was based on a perspective that takes into consideration not only the individual day but also her general work record.

A similar scheme was the structure for her justification for inaccuracies in her mileage and expense accounts:

> "I fill out my expense report, and on the miles I try to make it as accurate as possible, but I don't normally remember to write down my mileage every time I go somewhere, so I guess and I think, you know, I did it as best as I could. I tried to be as honest as possible, but there are times you judge, but you know I figure I'm not pushing a time clock, I don't want to be that regimented, and what it basically comes down to is trust, and if I'm doing a good job, what does it matter if I only work seven hours one day 'cause maybe next week I'll work nine hours."

Her obligation to her employer was fulfilled by her working hard and doing a good job, rather than by reporting technically correct eight-hour days. Inaccuracies in her mileage expenses were merely technical issues, she implied, since on the whole her reports were reasonably accurate.

Jane described keeping inaccurate expense accounts that she considered fair, while at the same time maintaining accuracy in filling out her time card:

> "Filling out your expense account when you travel. Do you lie about how much you spend on your meals or do you (pause)? Now they've put in the alcohol column at the bottom, do you lie about how much you drank or not, and that one bothers me every time I do it. [pause] The way the system is set up is what makes it hard, because you get so much money a day to spend so you go out and you spend it. They give you the blocks, and you've got your meal blocks and your driving, and this, and that, and the other thing. They don't count all the other costs that go along with it. There's nowhere to put them, so what do you do? Do you say, 'I spent an extra $10 on my meals' when you didn't really spend it, but I spent an extra $10 that day. One, you know, I had to pay parking tolls. How do you do it? Is a parking toll really [pause] I wouldn't pay a parking toll if I was here and going back and forth

to work, so obviously the company really should pay for it, so where do you put it? I usually try to just come out even so I get back as much as I spent, and you can't make much money at that anyway (laughter). Everybody always tries but you can't make much money at it."

Jane stated that trying to make money filling in inaccurate expense reports was not unusual in the company. In that context, she tried to make the system be just by claiming all of her legitimate out-of-pocket expenses even though the manner in which they were charged to the company was not strictly honest and accurate. Dishonesty was permissible because the results on balance would be fair on balance.

As for filling out her time cards, Jane said she was more accurate than many of her colleagues:

> "And filling in your time card just saying you worked eight hours a day. I see people everyday that come in and leave for two hours and they'll put eight hours on their time card, and you kind of [pause]."

When asked what her own practice was with regards to her time card, Jane replied:

> "That one, I don't really care. My boss knows when I come and go, so he knows some days I work seven and some nine, and just put it down."

When asked why that was permissible, she replied:

> "Because I know I'm telling the truth when I write it out on the time card, and [pause]. There are a lot of implications about lying about what you're putting on your time card if you're not working the hours even if it comes out to 40 in the end, and say like today I worked seven hours and then I came down here."

Interviewer: "Did you put down seven?"

Jane: "Yes."

Interviewer: "So you always keep an accurate one?"

Jane: "Yes. Actually, I do it because then you can go back and say this is when I put in the extra five hours [pause]. Don't tell me I don't stick around when I have to, I do it to keep track of it for me. I know I'll never have trouble getting 40 hours so it doesn't matter if I fudge a little bit."

Her accuracy in recording the number of hours she worked daily was governed by a desire to prove she had indeed worked at least the required number of hours. She was accurate in her reports in order to protect herself.

Barry's honesty in the workplace could also be considered in the service of self. When the interviewer acknowledged that he had on occasion used his employer's copy machine to duplicate a personal document, sometimes considering the action justified, and at other times feeling guilty, Barry explained that he would never do anything of the sort:

"No, I wouldn't. Other people have done that, and I just feel it's a. . .it cheapens the. . .little things like taking pens out of work, I don't do that either, I don't. I suppose now I don't say that's always. I have made a Xerox copy of a personal item but I very rarely do it. [pause] To me, it's so petty, I don't like the pettiness of taking something from work that I can get for myself. I'd rather get it myself. That's the way I am. Makes me feel good about myself that I don't have that pettiness. [pause] When you think about it, it's such an inexpensive. . .and why get caught, it makes you look. . .I don't need that."

There seemed to be two motives at work in Barry's decision about how to act. On the one hand, his honesty had become part of his personal sense of himself. It was a source of personal pride that he was not involved in petty immorality. Also, the cost of being caught was not worth the expense of the item and would lead to a drop in his moral value in his own eyes and in the eyes of others.

All of the subjects reported moral dilemmas in the workplace. The examples they cited were of four kinds: being asked by a supervisor to act in a way the employee considered immoral; being tempted to act in a way that he or she considered immoral; other people being immoral; or being presented with an opportunity to be of service to others.

There was some suggestion that dilemmas involving job security presented a different order of moral decision making. Concerns about the cost of moral action in accordance with deontic choice seems to play a part in moral behavior in the workplace. An assessment that a particular action would lead to the loss of one's job seemed to be compelling, and perhaps to have its own moral meaning.

Subjects also reported observing differences in their moral actions in the workplace compared to those in their private lives. In particular, potentially morally useful skills learned in one arena do not necessarily easily transfer to another arena. Finally, the subjects reported that moral dilemmas they experienced in the workplace were not necessarily unusual and important events, but could be daily occurrences.

C H A P T E R

EXEMPLARY SIERRANS: MORAL INFLUENCES

T E N

The focus of this chapter is on three young adults who were from the UCI classes of 1980, 1981, and 1982. They had been selected for interviewing after the research team listened to hundreds of hours of taped interviews from the original data collection by Dr. Kathy Kalliel (Chapter 7) and Dr. David Connor (Chapters 8 and 9). The purpose of selecting a small subsample was to conduct more in-depth interviews on the theme of moral influence. The purpose of the in-depth interviews was "to learn more about what it was that enables some persons to be relatively more clear in their appraisal of moral decisions and their apparent decisiveness in moral action" (Sierra research team minutes, May 1988).

Based on listening to so many hours of interviews, it appeared to the researchers that when challenged by moral dilemmas, most subjects in the larger sample responded in relatively narrow terms either in relationship to others or to themselves. While there were notable exceptions, the individual respondents rarely spoke in terms of formulated principles which governed moral decisions. References were also rare to institutional or communal sources of moral guidance such as the church. As a group, the larger sample of respondents did not rely on identifiable moral heroes or examples. While a number of respondents spoke of seeking the advice of friends, family, and partners, relatively few had talked about more broadly defined "spiritual" or faith contexts for assessing and considering the consequences of their actions. Theories of values and ethics did not figure at all prominently in the discussions of moral dilemmas by the larger sample.

...the individual respondents rarely spoke in terms of formulated principles which governed moral decisions. References were also rare to institutional or communal sources of moral guidance...

As determined by the consensus judgment of the research team, subjects selected from the larger pool of interviewees met four criteria:

1. The subjects had been especially lucid in their articulations of moral thought and action;

2. The subjects had been compelling in describing poignant moral dilemmas;

3. In the moral accounts they told, the subjects had been consistent in the relationship between the actions they took and the principles they had espoused; and

4. The stories the subjects told contained an element of risk to their own welfare which was reflected in their deliberations, as well as considerations which would have promoted the welfare of others.

The criteria for selection of respondents for this chapter did not define a group of subjects whose moral decisions necessarily agreed with what the researchers individually might have hoped to see. The subjects certainly talked about choices that would not have been, in ideal circumstances, our own. It was somewhat gratifying, in fact, that the subjects were perfectly willing to discuss things that were obviously not designed to impress the interviewers. Given the aims of the original Sierra Project, described elsewhere in this volume and in Whiteley and Associates (1982), one might have supposed that the Sierrans would have been circumspect regarding the material they were willing to divulge. In fact, they took the opportunity to share candidly and honestly their moral dilemmas.

Five subjects were identified by the research team as best meeting the four criteria for inclusion in this chapter. All happened to be members of ethnic minority groups. They were representative of the extraordinary diversity at the University of California, Irvine during the time of their enrollment, and of a commitment to the development of an interracial community on the part of the original Sierra Project staff. Of the five potential subjects originally selected, three were women and two were men.

In the spring of 1989, it proved possible to contact readily three of the five candidates for the follow-up interviews. All three agreed to participate. Young adulthood in Southern California, at least, is a time in life of frequent movement. In the limited time frame available for interviewing, the other two potential interviewees could not be located.

One of the young women, Sandy, was a sales account executive. Another young woman, Kim, was a human service professional between jobs. The young man, Curtis, was a successful independent entrepreneur and beginning philanthropist.

The Moral Influence Interview

The interview format imposed a uniform structure (See Appendix C: Moral Influence Interview created by James Day) and was thus intended to be precisely the same in every case with regard to the timing of questions and the unfolding of answers. There were, of course, moments when probes were made that were particular to the contexts of the individual speakers' stories.

The interview contained three sections, each with a particular emphasis. The emphasis in the first section was identifying personal figures of moral influence. This section provided an opportunity to learn about those persons from the subject's immediate experience who had been a source of influence on formulating moral perceptions, developing ideas on right and wrong, learning moral decision making, and taking moral action. Subjects were also given an opportunity to identify personal moral heroes, including those not known to the subject who might have had, in the subjects' views, an impact upon their own moral lives.

The second section of the interview contained questions about the relationship between moral principles and moral conduct. The intent was to understand the subjects' perceptions of the roots of their moral strength. In previous research by the interviewer (Day, 1987), some subjects had identified central, formative moral experiences in their stories of moral development. Following up on that previous research, respondents were asked whether or not they could identify such turning points in their own lives.

The third section of the interview emphasized the relationship of the domain of moral meaning-making to the larger context of meanings in the lives of the interviewees. The interviewees were asked to talk about their world views, and to place their sense of themselves within the broader context(s) established by those views. The Moral Influence Interview provided opportunities to return to the basic questions which guided the research (see the Introduction), and to ask very specifically about areas that followed naturally from the initial interviewing.

Stories of Influence: What the Subjects Said

Despite the effort to adhere to a standard format, the subjects quite spontaneously responded to questions by telling stories on their own terms. Their responses were in the form of historical accounts that had within them clearly definable points of beginning and end. The subjects' responses to the first set of questions in the interview were remarkably uniform in content. All of them identified similar moral examples and heroes in their lives. The figures described by the interviewees were spouses or partners, fathers, and persons each of the subjects referred to as having been "mentors."

> **Curtis:** "My wife, definitely. She understands who I am and where I come from, so she knows the context within which I make the decisions that I do. That, in turn, allows me to respect her input on the dilemmas I face. She tempers my sentiments and makes it more likely that I'm more sensitive and diplomatic with people. Because of her I'm more likely to understand and see the good in others."

> **Sandy:** "He's different from me, but not so much that he can't understand me, and he's the kind of person who is very concerned about his impact on other people, very kind, very fair. Sometimes when I'm less inclined to be that way, I see his efforts and they kind of serve as a corrective to my own."

> **Kris:** "I often look at him and say to myself, wow (!), how did a person get to be like that? I mean, he is the most kind and caring person I ever met. Just being with him makes me want to be good."

Each of the subjects referred to their fathers as having been moral heroes in their lives.

> **Curtis:** "When I think of a hero I think of a person's champion, someone who can better and change the course of another's life toward some good end. For me that person was my father. He made certain that we achieved something in life, when most of our peers made little of themselves. He instilled so much in me that when he passed away I was left with what could sustain me in life: values, education, skills. In all of that, central to all of that, was the

message, his insistence, that there is good and bad, a right and a wrong way to live, a way to succeed and a way to fail, and that it takes discipline to really make something of yourself and to be of any value to others."

Sandy: "You know, my father, I guess he fits that term for me, of a hero. He was always an individual and yet at the same time not so much so that he ignored or didn't care for others. He was willing to go his own way even when that was different from the way other people wanted him to go, and he was willing to let me do the same. He didn't always like what I did, but he was willing to talk things through with me. He definitely sharpened my skills of discussion along the way and helped me to see the value of respecting other people's points of view."

Kim: "A lot of the other families in our neighborhood, the fathers went out drinking or were working all the time or simply just weren't around. But when we were growing up our father was always there, regardless of whether he was doing well in his career or having a lot of problems. He definitely cared for us. I remember afternoons, after school and on the weekends, when my father would be involved in art projects in our house and all of the other kids in the neighborhood would come over and be involved. From him I learned that you don't have to gravitate to the lowest common denominator in order to get along with people. You can stand for something better and even if you're different from most of the people around you someone will respect you for what you do and will be better off for it."

Curtis, Sandy, and Kim, also talked about "mentors" in their lives. Moreover, they selected mentors they had met during their student years at UCI. Sandy said of one of the Sierra counselors:

"So many times I say to myself, 'I can't imagine who I'd be if it hadn't been for Nancy. Nancy really took the time and energy to know me and to challenge me to live up to my potential; to go beyond the automatic response and to really think about things from other perspectives. Through our interactions I learned that I could be accepted for being me and at the same time go beyond who that was to become even more. I definitely became wiser and a lot more sensitive in the process."

Kim: "Really, it was a combination of things that changed me. It was the timing—I was ripe for things to happen—then there was the climate, in which we were encouraged to become conscious of ourselves in relation to the other people in the community, and then the person, who was really perfect for me. I remember very clearly some of the things she said to me, often in the form of the notebooks that we turned in and that were returned to us with comments. She would take the simplest sentence and see so many possibilities in it. And I would think, but, that's what I believe; I'm sure that's true. And then, because I respected her and I respected the way that she interacted with me, I would say, well, maybe there is more than one way to see the situation. And eventually I would understand that there was more than just one way. So I moved from a right and wrong universe to one far more complex; at once more frightening and more satisfying because of the reality, and the wideness of the world that there was to live in."

Curtis: "This guy selected me at a critical point, I mean, it was either be part of his world and be part of him or just throw in the towel and be one more failure case. But he did select me and push me and care for me and I didn't fail, because I figured that if I was good enough for him I was good enough to make something successful of myself, too."

Strength of Character

All subjects selected for the "influence" interview were chosen in part because of their consistency between stated principles and subsequent actions as reflected in the stories that the research team had listened to on tape. The second section of the interview concerned itself with an effort to understand the genesis of that consistency, and to explore the explanations that the respondents might give for it. The subjects' answers were once again very consistent with one another. They voiced their replies in two ways. They said that they were consistent in their thinking and action because such consistency was necessary for their own sense of themselves. They said that such consistency was necessary in order to continue to hold their place in the world of relationships which mattered to them.

Each of the interviewees took a similar tack in the process of her or his reply to the questions from the interviewer in this second section of the interview. Each one told a story that recalled a situation in which s/he had acted in accord with her/his principles where a moral dilemma had been concerned. Each subject then summarized the situation and pronounced a kind of judgment or interpretation upon it. "Basically I was able to do that because that's the kind of person I am. I couldn't have done otherwise and still have been myself," said Kim. Curtis observed "It's pretty simple really: You do what you do in order to continue to be yourself, in order to live with yourself at night." Sandy said "It was more important to me to be able to live with myself than to do the 'easier' thing. When that's the issue the other thing really isn't any easier to do."

Each of the interviewees was quick to assert that the personal self with whom they wanted to continue to be able to live was a very concrete self, related to other selves. On first consideration, this proved to be an interesting paradox. The subjects recalled situations in which they had defied the opinions of those around them in favor of being able to live with their own point-of-view. At the same time they said that they had not acted alone. As the subjects recounted their stories, it became clear that each one was thinking of her/himself in terms of a small, core *audience* before which his or her actions would be viewed and perhaps evaluated. Sandy put it this way:

> "Well, no, the other people in the situation, I mean the immediate situation, their opinions didn't much matter to me, at least not to the degree that I would have changed the sense of self I had in my actions in order to satisfy them. There will always be some people who approve of or criticize behavior. That doesn't mean, though, that I wasn't aware of how some people close to me, and in my mind, would think of my actions. I think a lot about certain other people in those kind of moments. I want to do the kinds of things that I could share with them and of which, if they knew, they would approve, or even be proud of."

The third section of the interview provided an opportunity for the subjects to discuss their broader views of the world including their senses of religiosity and spirituality. This section of the interview also provided an opportunity for reflection upon the place of morality in relation to other aspects of their lives. The stories of the three subjects' diverged here. In part, this was because the stories they told became larger stories that encompassed prior ones. None of the subjects considered her/himself to be conventionally religious. Instead, each provided personal definitions of religion, and then distinguished what that was from spirituality, which in turn was embraced by each of the informants. Said one of them:

> "Religion is organized, dogmatic, and social. Spirituality is individual, intimate, personal. Religion tells you what is good or true and tells you who is favored and who is not. Spirituality is developed. You have to work at it and you have to be conscious about it and take time for it. Sometimes, in order to grow spiritually, you have to go beyond or even against religious doctrine."

Each of the informants could articulate a set of fundamental beliefs about the way things are, ultimately, and each one quite spontaneously described the place of their personal morality within that broader scope.

> **Curtis:** "There is a way of things that dictates the workings of the world. What one needs to do is to figure out that way and act in accordance with what it demands in particular situations. The solutions to moral dilemmas lie in the situations themselves. The other parties involved will act in a certain way and will, by their conduct, dictate what one does in one's own role. My father showed me the way. He was the teacher of that. Later my mentor added to my knowledge and helped me to be more skillful in applying it. Moral growth, for me, involves becoming more clear, which in turn makes me more resolute in the way I act."

> **Kim:** " I can't say I have one organizing belief that puts everything else in its place. It's more like I'm questioning that and that several tried and true beliefs are there, meanwhile, that I've gotten from experience. Always be honest. When you're not then you injure not only others but yourself. Life is for learning, and one should always try to learn from what happens. It's possible, ultimately, to be so pure in one's being and one's motivations that one spontaneously does what is right. That's a spiritual condition that one can attain, and one ought to strive for that. To grow means to refine, more and more, what is pure within oneself, so that one's actions reflect that goodness and that purity of what one is. At that point being yourself and being good are the same thing. That's how I would like to be."

> **Sandy:** "I believe that everything happens for a reason. The purpose of life is learning, and everything that occurs happens in such a way as to provide opportunities for learning. When I have a rotten experience it's because I'm supposed to learn something from it. Being of service to others is a way to grow. It is, ultimately, satisfying in its own right. The good that one does comes back and enhances the experience of the doer. It's possible though for one to change in the way one thinks about what 'good' means. What is good

in my view isn't exactly what it was some years ago or even, in some matters, some months ago. Learning often or perhaps always means that you see the same thing from an increasing number of perspectives, all of which have some truth in them. Those perspectives, in turn, become an increasing number of possibilities, or resources, for action. One may not have exhausted all the possibilities for doing good in a situation just because the number of perspectives has increased, but one has at least minimized the possibility that because of not thinking, one has acted rashly in the wrong. I've grown because of circumstances in which I've had to encounter perspectives other than my own and because of the fact that I've actually had to get along with the people who held the other points of view. Actually negotiating day to day interactions in the midst of such conflicts in perspective meant that somehow not only the perspectives had to be understood, but the people, too. My perspectives now are much more inclusive than they once were. I'm at once more humble and more confident. I know that my own attitudes are not the only ones, and that, where differences occur, I'm capable of finding ways to reconcile and learn from them. That means to me that I've grown and that continued growth is possible."

What the Subjects Said: A Summary

One could summarize the content of responses offered by the "exemplary" Sierrans and say something of importance, but to do so apart from the *form* in which the subjects spoke would be to miss an important component of what they had to say. This summary, and the commentary that follows it, will focus on both the *form* and *content* of what they said, and will also address the critical relationship between the two.

What is most important here is at once terribly simple and, at the same time, crucially complex: This subsample of Sierrans told *stories*. Their stories expressed and examined moral experiences. Their stories also provided an opportunity to share moral definitions of their psychological communities of partners, parents, and mentors, and the moral aspirations that were intimately connected to their deepest held convictions about the meanings of life.

Second, all three young adults said that moral thinking and theorizing was, on their parts, inextricably woven together with recollections of actual experiences, of struggles with and constructions of who they were as people, with images of relationships, and with fundamental sentiments of fear, hope, indignation, and longing. Moral thought was embedded in the larger reality of personal and interpersonal identity, and was recounted in the form of presenting and commenting upon experiences that were filled with remembered feelings.

Third, moral heroes for all three subjects were local ones, persons intimately bound up in the daily routines of life. Fathers were the moral heroes first mentioned in the lives of these subjects. It would appear that these subjects have taken the morality of mothers to be a natural occurrence. It is a given, or at least expected, in the role of a mother.

What is most important here is at once terribly simple and, at the same time, crucially complex: This subsample of Sierrans told *stories.*

151

Each one of the informants naturally and quickly identified moral mentors in their discussion of moral heroes. The mentors were, by example and direct contact, tremendous influences. Mentors were persons with whom the subjects very clearly identified, whose acceptance was crucial to a sense of well-being, and whose own character appeared to be better, but attainably better, than the subjects' perceptions of their own characters. Thus, when mentors critically interacted with the Sierrans, challenging assumptions and introducing alternative points of view, their acceptance, credibility of character, and desirable station in relation to the Sierrans established a foundation for venturing out, and in the subjects' views, venturing forward in the moral domain.

Fourth, for the three respondents, immediate moral dilemmas were related to ultimate meanings, to what Tillich (1963) called "ultimate concern." Ultimate, even "cosmic," pictures are described in terms of neighborhood and domestic ones. The drama of moral life is in the everyday, the ultimate in the stories of the mundane. The stories they told were all the more powerful because they were told by young adults who were confronting daily challenges of living, but in the context of a personal moral perspective.

Fifth, these subjects described the critical nature of the relationship that, for them, exists between independence and audience. Their "independence" of behavior, the degree to which they had appeared to others to stand out from their peers because of the exemplary ways in which they had consistently moved from thought to action *despite* others, was, they insisted, a mirage. When asked about aspects of the moral life that might have appeared from some perspectives to be derivative from a capacity for independence (of thought, or action, or both), the subjects told stories of *relationship*. In particular they told stories in which they imagined themselves before audiences before, during, and after the conduct in question. Usually there were three constituencies in the audiences. First was the portion of the audience most affected, in the subject's view, by the subject's actions. This was often the person on whose behalf the subject had chosen to act in making the choice of the "right thing to do." Second was the portion of the audience defined by other parties in the immediate surroundings where the conduct occurred. The role of that group proved to be of some, but not great, importance. Third, and most crucial to the interviewees, was a fairly constant, often silent, very powerful audience composed of those whom the subject loved. This third constituency was composed of the dead, the absent, the imaginary, as well as the recognizable, dear, and intimately familiar ones in whom the person of the actor was vested.

Moral action, for these three informants, was a function of the audience which existed in their minds. This core moral audience is the central reference point in their moral lives.

Commentary

Some of the most formative experiences identified by the three "exemplary" former Sierrans occurred during their years in the Sierra Project community as college freshmen. The Sierrans described those experiences in such a way as to make clear that their moral development had been profoundly enhanced by what happened in the Sierra community. When elaborating upon exactly what it was that was so stimulating to their own conceptions of moral growth, they described the presence of persons on the Sierra staff who were good listeners. Said one of the Sierrans: "In her there was something different. *I could tell my story to her* in such a way as to include the whole truth of my experience. . ." This remark says explicitly what Tappan and Brown (1989) propose as a potent medium for the development of morality; namely, the telling of moral stories, combined with the presence of a very attentive and not immediately judgmental listener.

The irony is, of course, that the Sierrans spoke of a "narrative" kind of development that occurred in a community informed by cognitive-developmental aims. (Whiteley & Associates, 1982) One would do an injustice to both the interviewees and the context from which they spoke if the contribution were ignored of cognitive-developmental theory and practice to the moral authorship and moral development of the subjects in this study. The fact is that another part of the story told by the "exemplary" Sierrans strongly emphasizes the importance of a crucial ingredient of the cognitive-developmental model; namely, role-taking (Jennings, Kilkenny, and Kohlberg 1983; Day 1987).

For these three Sierrans, a foundational part of developmental experience was the presence of a listener who was capable of hearing, and at the same time, of reframing the authors' stories. Such listeners, referred to by all of the "exemplary" informants, were seen as more capable, and more desirable in the moral life by the examples they set for hearing and knowing. The sharing of stories occurred in a community (also stressed in the cognitive-developmental perspective) where there were opportunities *not only to be heard, but to hear.*

The Sierrans were heard, and their authorship was developed, in the context of hearing the stories of others with whom they lived, studied, dined, and worked. Thus, the narratives of the subjects in this study suggest that aspects of perspective-taking and community which were provided for in the Sierra experiment are crucial to the formation and promotion of moral authority and moral responsibility.

The fundamental interplay of two types of theory, and two modes of interpretation, should be noted here. The interviewees stated that part of the power of the Sierra community's impact on moral growth is attributable to what Tappan and Brown (1989) have described as a proposed "narrative" way of encouraging growth. As Day (1987) has suggested elsewhere narrative data is imperative if we are able to know not only that something has happened, but how, and in what meaningful way it has occurred (Day, 1991; Day and Tappan, 1995; and Day and Tappan, 1996).

On the basis of these interviews, the term *"core moral audience"* is used to describe something that each interviewee discussed when they balked at the notion of moral independence. For them, their moral actions always occurred in relationship to other persons. Consistency of moral action for them had much to do with the consistency of the audience before which such actions were performed. Moral principles were developed in relation to the parties who composed the audience, and moral actions prospectively were mentally rehearsed before them. Moral actions were then retrospectively analyzed and evaluated in terms of the perspective of the same audience, with moral action imbedded in a larger, socially constructed identity.

References

Day, J. (1987). Moral development in laboratory learning groups. Unpublished doctoral dissertation, University of Pennsylvania. *Dissertation Abstracts International,* 1987 September, v 48 (N3-A): 600.

Day, J. M. (1991). Narrative, psychology and moral education. *American Psychologist, 46,* 167-168.

Day, J. M., & Tappan M. B. (1995). Identity, voice, and the psycho/dialogical perspectives from moral psychology. *American Psychologist, 50(2),* 47-48.

Day, J. M., & Tappan, M. B. (1996). The narrative approach to moral development from the epistemic subject to dialogical selves. *Human Development, 39,* 67-82.

Jennings, W., Kilkenny, R., & Kohlberg, L. (1983). Moral development theory and practice for youthful and adult offenders. In W. Laufer. & J. Day (Eds.), *Personality theory, moral development, and criminal behavior,* Lexington, MA: D.C. Heath-Lexington Books.

Tappan, M. B., & Brown L. M. (1989). Stories told and lesson learned: Toward a narrative approach to moral development and moral education, *Harvard Education Review, 5(2),* 182-205.

Tillich, P. (1963). *Morality and beyond.* New York: Harper & Row.

Whiteley, J., & Associates. (1982). *Character development in college students, Vol. I: The freshman year.* Schenectady, NY: Character Research Press.

S E C T I O N 4

RESEARCH CONCLUSIONS AND FUTURE DIRECTIONS FOR PROMOTING MORAL ACTION

Section IV was undertaken with two specific purposes: to answer in theoretical context the six organizing research questions around which the Sierrans Revisited Project was organized, and to consider the implications of those answers for the broader educational challenge of designing educational experiences to promote positive moral action. With these two specific purposes, Section IV is organized as follows:

Chapter 11, "Moral Dilemmas of Everyday Life: Voices of the Sierrans" answers the first four research questions:

> Question 1: Will young adults talk about intimate moral issues in their lives?

> Question 2: What actual dilemmas do these young adults identify as characteristic of their work and personal lives?

> Question 3: What are the factors which the subjects identify as influencing their action in response to moral dilemmas?

> Question 4: Does the stage of moral reasoning relate to moral action?

Chapter 12, "Exceptional Moral Behavior," answers the fifth research question in the context of relevant research on moral commitment and altruism:

> Question 5: Are there young people with exceptional characteristics whose moral behavior is exemplary? If yes, what can be learned about how they got that way?

Chapter 13, "Strength of Character and Moral Agency," answers the sixth research question in the framework of four promising theoretical approaches: identity and moral motivation, emotions in moral action, capacity for empathy and moral action, and social cognitive theory and moral agency:

> Question 6: Is it possible to identify a composite of factors/influences which correlate with outstanding strength of character and powerful moral agency?

Chapter 14, "Toward Promoting Moral Action in Young Adulthood," begins by retracing the directions which guided the original curricular development initiative to promote the character education of college freshmen. The next section of Chapter 14 focuses specifically on considerations involved in designing the next generation of curricula to promote moral action in response to moral dilemmas. The third and concluding section of the chapter recapitulates the basic themes which animated the original Sierra Project and this subsequent Sierrans Revisited Project.

C H A P T E R

Eleven

MORAL DILEMMAS OF EVERYDAY LIFE: VOICES OF THE SIERRANS

The rationale and objectives of this research on moral action in young adulthood were introduced in the Foreword and in the Introduction to this volume. They merit brief recapitulation before turning to an analysis of the principal findings. At the time this Sierrans Revisited research began in 1987, over a decade had passed since the first of the sample had been entering college freshmen living in Sierra Hall. The work of the original Sierra Project had ended with the graduation from UCI of the Classes of 1980, 1981, and 1982. It seemed logical, indeed fortuitous, to locate as many of these graduates as feasible for a study of their further development as young adults.

All of the original Sierra Project students were nearly "thirty something," and indeed some of them were even over thirty. Most of the developmental psychologists whose work is reviewed in Chapter 4 concur that some form of critical transition is characteristic for most men and women in the several years preceding and following age 30. Do the ex-Sierrans evidence further maturation in their understanding of themselves and their social-moral world? Did their growth plateau upon leaving college?

A determination was made by the research team for the Sierrans Revisited Project (Mosher, Connor, Day, Kalliel, Porter, Yokota, and Whiteley) to focus this study of the further development of Sierrans on an examination of the "real" (as opposed to hypothetical) moral dilemmas they had experienced, and the moral actions they had taken in their personal relationships and in their work lives. Such knowledge gathering was developmental research. Yet the potential application to character education seemed promising. Many writers in the field (Kohlberg & Candee, 1984; Rest, 1986; Gilligan, 1982; Blasi, 1980) had anticipated such study as the next logical step in the effort to understand why people act morally.

At the beginning of the Sierrans Revisited Project in 1987 (and indeed at its end with the publication of this volume), the voyage into moral action research did seem a logical next step. As was stated in the Introduction, there was no expectation that one initial study would resolve the inherent complexity of the puzzle of why some people respond to a moral dilemma with a moral action and

...there was no expectation that one initial study would resolve the inherent complexity of the puzzle of why some people respond to a moral dilemma with a moral action and others do not.

others do not. It was also beyond the scope of this initial study to attempt to understand whether elements in the moral action process differ from age to age or by gender, race, education, social class, cultural group, or economic circumstance. While this was an ethnically diverse sample, it was quite homogenous with respect to age, geography (almost all from Southern California), educational background, and psychological measures of the components of character (moral maturity, principled thinking, and ego development). Social class status and cultural group membership were diverse as reflects the composition of graduates of a relatively large public research university.

The principal approach of this research was to utilize personal narratives as the core for a series of individual case studies. The focus of inquiry and analysis was on understanding the internal dynamics and anatomy of moral action in response to the moral dilemmas of everyday life. And it merits repeating that an ultimate aim of such developmental research is to understand more fully the origins of moral action so that it may be educated for more effectively. The roots of this research are, after all, in a character education project.

The Introduction to this volume identified a series of six research questions that would be investigated in this Sierrans Revisited Project. This discussion will now turn to a systematic consideration of the first four of these questions.

Question 1: Will Young Adults Talk about Intimate Moral Issues in Their Lives?

The Sierrans, almost without exception, described moral issues they were facing in their personal or work lives and the associated actions they took. An original concern of the researchers had been that the subjects might be reluctant to tell the stories of the moral dilemmas in their lives. This concern proved to be unfounded. Even though all the participants in this research had been in the Sierra Project, we cannot ascribe their relative ease in talking about "real life" moral dilemmas and actions to earlier participation in the moral discussions of the freshman year. There was no control group interviewed. Nor can we assert that there was an effect of the original Sierra Project on the forthcoming way in which the subjects responded to questions.

The personal narrative approach did yield very rich accounts of moral action. The moral conceptions of the young adults which emerged from the three approaches to data collection taken by the interviewers (Appendices A, B, and C) is holistic and evocative of their lived moral lives. Paul Vitz's (1990) timely article in the *American Psychologist*, "The Use of Stories in Moral Development: New Psychological Reasons for an Old Educational Method," provides further theoretical and practical support for this personal narrative approach, as does Robert Coles' accounts of children's narratives (Coles, 1986) and the treatises by Tappan and Brown (1989) and Day and Tappan (1996) which reference many other investigations using this methodology.

To generate the data reported in this book, the contact with each of the former residents of Sierra Hall took less than a day. That is manifestly little time every ten years to satisfy the investigative curiosity of a researcher about the complexity of moral action. Suffice it to say, however, that this research was not constrained by the unwillingness of the subjects to explore and share their private world of morality. The problem became how to synthesize a wealth of self-reported data.

Question 2: What Actual Dilemmas do these Young Adults Identify as Characteristics of Their Work and Personal Lives?

The Sierrans described more than 80 moral dilemmas in their personal and work lives. A partial taxonomy of those real life challenges and their actual moral solutions based on Kalliel's sub-sample is presented in Chapter 7. The richness of the data shared by the respondents has been summarized in Chapters 7, 8, 9, and 10. The complexity of the reasons they cited for acting in the way they did in response to the dilemmas is equally rich:

> A 27 year old woman who refused to go out with a handsome co-worker, her reasons being her spiritual life; "it's just not right to do that to your spouse and it would hurt my husband terribly. I know he loves me."

> A 33 year old woman who made the decision not to have an extramarital affair, she being the unmarried party. She initially dated the man, had "a few physical encounters," then began to feel guilty and frustrated at the situation. The couple became the butt of many negative, snide remarks from people who knew them. Embarrassed, she broke off the affair.

> A 30 year old man who decided to remove a business partner from a jointly owned company. "Don't rub me wrong and don't the hell get in my way or threaten the business because even if you are my brother or sister, I will mow you down. If I feel something is a certain way, I will mow you down."

This latter subject was one of the "Exemplary" Sierrans discussed by Professor Day in Chapter 10.

What is to be said about our subjects and the moral dilemmas they face? First, their stories are of everyday happenings ("affairs" is not a suitable term here although there seem to have been a number of them as well). However familiar and commonplace the dilemmas may seem to the reader, they were profound experiences for those who faced them. And the moral lives of these young adults are sharply, unavoidably drawn, and explicit. The good guys wear white hats. The bad guys wear nothing at all.

One might be tempted to dismiss some of these stories as the stuff of "As the World Turns." Indeed, it may be that soap operas have the wide appeal they do primarily because sometimes they actually raise profound personal and moral issues. Perhaps, by way of continued digression, the "soaps" are one of the most widely generalized forces for adult moral education available since, in global context, the audience is phenomenal. "Soaps" are characterized in international perspective partially in jest, because we are concerned not to trivialize the pain, the victories and the defeats, most importantly the moral and human profundity, of these real dilemmas for our subjects. Every man's (and every woman's) moral life is constituted of these dilemmas.

And that leads to another trivialization as stated. When you have heard one person's moral dilemma, or one theorist's paradigm of moral action, you most certainly have not heard them all. Classic moral "voices" on issues of evil and good, justice and injustice, compassion and non-caring, courage, fear, truth and so on reoccur even in our small sample. But they are new and perplexing and painful to these young adult individuals experiencing them for the first time. And they are filled with reality (a great relief incidentally, from Heinz, his dying wife, and an obdurate druggist).

One of our observations is that it is necessary to study subjects with more time spent with each respondent. A minimum of four hours per Sierran every ten years was, and is, not enough time. The richness of description and character insight possible from the longer, more elaborate story of the moral is increasingly recognized (Coles, 1986; Gilligan, 1982; Vitz, 1990; Day & Tappan, 1996; Tappan & Brown, 1989). Embedded in such in-depth studies of character lies a key to a broader, overarching theory of moral thinking and its relationship to action, and ultimately to education.

One other observation comes from examining the content of the moral dilemmas faced by the women from Sierra. Many of the dilemmas they encountered are consequences of women's steady but so slow "progress" toward equity in the world of work. The Sierran women were in the workplace for a great variety of reasons, but all could be sources of potential moral dilemmas: because they want equity and personal fulfillment in work; because of the economic necessity to support children when no father is present; because of continuing to sustain a two-income family lifestyle and the amenities of the American middle class; or because of the enhanced access to superior public education and to the professional and industrial job market education permits. All of these women were graduates of arguably one of the best public universities in America, and they were "next door" to some of the wealthiest and most rapidly growing areas in America. And the growth of the region is not without its economic dislocations. Even Orange County, the county which is host to the University of California, Irvine, declared bankruptcy in 1994.

> One other observation comes from examining the content of the moral dilemmas faced by the women from Sierra. Many of the dilemmas they encountered are consequences of women's steady but so slow "progress" toward equity in the world of work.

The point is that these women have considerable equity vis à vis the work place. They work in a region of the country which, despite ups and downs, has a low rate of unemployment. The content of their work-related moral dilemmas is not all that different from the kind which were facing the men in the Sierrans Revisited population. Whether the increasing similarities of work experiences and character formation may lead to a stillness of women's voice of caring and the men's voice of justice is a problematic and nagging concern.

Question 3: What are the Factors Which the Subjects Identify as Influencing Their Action in Response to Moral Dilemmas?

A relatively wide and diverse array of factors were reported by the Sierrans as influencing their action in response to moral dilemmas. They included, in no order of priority:

1. Consideration of *one's own well being and that of affected others*. For example, a woman law student who initially loaned her detailed lecture notes to a friend, only to see the friend score higher on a torts examination, subsequently changed her behavior. Because of the cut throat competition for grades and election to the *Law Review*, she decided not to help further. "I don't like it but that's how it is." For another example, a married woman

considering an affair with a co-worker: "I feel responsible to my husband, I know he loves me and I knew immediately I should say 'no.' That's what I did."

2. The influence of *the family*. The mother was especially influential in the moral decisions and actions of the women (much less so of the men). Mothers were persons with whom to talk, role models for decision making, and explicit/implicit sources of standards by which to live. Approximately 80% of the women subjects talked through particular moral dilemmas with family members: the mother, sister, less often brothers. Father was rarely mentioned. However, there was a notable exception with the three "Exemplary" Sierrans reported in Chapter 10 where fathers had a significant role. And some members of extended families including mentors are likely to be part of the "moral audience" described in Chapter 10.

3. Other people and the quality of the *interpersonal relations* involved. Whether it seemed possible to repair a relationship and re-establish trust or to continue to care when hurt by another person figured prominently in the moral dilemmas of the women; for example, with boyfriends, present, potential, and in particular with ex-boyfriends or ex-husbands.

4. The influence of *religion*. Across the sample as a whole, religion was relatively unimportant, but it was *very* influential for those subjects (10 to 15%) who were actively religious. "Then my boyfriend moved in. I felt I had let myself down. I had a standard to follow: the rules of the church and I set it for myself and said, "'There it goes!'" Religion varied in the Sierran's experience from norms or commandments to a mature spiritual faith (See Chapter 10 for an assessment of the influence of the spiritual in the lives of some of the Sierrans).

5. The influence of *society and its norms* were not widely reported. One example was the following: "I decided it was a moral decision when in my Lamaze class, the teacher brought up diaper choices (cloth versus disposable diapers) and then said: `You know, they're not really disposable' and the whole class said, 'What?' First, it is against the law to throw the disposable diaper out and this is what the industry meant for you to do with the disposable diaper [but] they are really not biodegradable . . ."

6. The influence of particular *codes* (religious, business, and professional norms) were cited.

    a. *Marriage vows:* ". . . It's just not right to do that to your spouse and it would hurt my husband terribly. I know he loves me."

    b. *Professional ethics:* ". . . I believe [even as a beginning social worker] that I need to do everything I can to help and protect others." (By a social worker who decides to testify in a court custody/sexual abuse case despite her trainee status).

    c. *Business decision:* "I decided to continue my account with this client even if he was both racist and sexist toward me as a minority woman. `The customer is always right.'" In the work place, *generally*, morality beyond self-interest and self-protection was temporized at the point one's job or livelihood were at risk. For a number of what were termed "everyday heroes" (Chapter 10), however, dilemmas involving injustice, the immorality of war-work, or abuse of workers evoked clear moral actions in response.

7. The influence of one or more personal (i.e., internalized) moral *norms* or *virtues.* "I don't think it's right to lie . . . that would have been deceitful."

8. The influence of *personal moral principles.*

    a. Consideration of one's own *rights* as well as those of others (voices of justice and caring);

    b. Considering the *well-being* of others and oneself (altruism and caring);

    c. "My most basic moral concern is to *oppose racial inequality* wherever I can."

9. The influence of *feelings.* The Sierrans Revisited case studies underscore the importance of *feelings* in association with moral actions. This was particularly evident in the case of the women, much less so in the men. The feelings of the Sierrans associated with moral dilemmas were negative, neutral, positive, or sometimes mixed. They changed in character sometimes from before the moral action to after the action occurred. What was apparent in the case studies was that feelings have different meanings, individual to individual (or in the same person over time), and possess different power to affect moral action. The individual case studies contain an extensive catalogue of feelings. A few excerpts are included by way of illustration. The feeling categories could be used to begin to quantify several aspects of the relationship between affect and action. They are presented here without any necessary order of their salience to individual moral actions. They are ordered roughly from negative affects to positive affects. Negative feelings are presented first:

    a. *Fear.* Anxiety for one's self or the well-being of others involved in the dilemma.

        "Yes, I had to decide, literally, will it make me go crazy? Is he going to put me in a depression state again? I know my future was at stake."

        "To me, what was at risk was a child's well-being. It appears that the attorney was heavily biased against the mother and toward the father. The court was sick of the case and wanted to put an end to it, to focus the blame and pathology solely on the mother and mandate that sole custody be given to the father. In my work with the child I felt that it would be an unhealthy and a dangerous situation for him to be in. (She suspected child abuse). First, I weighed the risk here and felt the child would be in danger."

    b. *Guilt.* "Then my boyfriend moved in. I felt I had let myself down. I had a standard to follow: the rules of the church and I set it for myself and said, 'There it goes!'"

c. *Shame.* "I had a Catholic upbringing through my mother which said you should not live with someone before marriage. I felt ashamed and wondered why it bothered me so."

d. *Anger.* "I find it very irritating when people quote me the Bible for life guidance."

e. *Righteous anger.* "I had an outrage in me in the same sense that all this was going on out there in the shop [which rebuilt automobile engines] and for how long? It was the injustice of how they [the workers] were being treated." This Sierran speaks in the "voices" of both justice and caring.

f. *Pride and self esteem/respect.* "I'm a working mother. I can provide for my kids; I'm real proud of their achievements at school. They scored real high in the exams . . . I just want to learn as much as I can so I can pass it on to my kids." Again, the "voice" of a caring, proud mother is expressed.

g. *Personal integrity:*

   🐚 "I felt compelled to do what I felt was the right thing . . . I have very high moral standards."

   🐚 "It makes me feel good about myself that I don't have that pettiness (e.g., stealing supplies from my workplace) that I can afford to get for myself."

   🐚 "I need to feel good about myself—to be true to myself."

h. *Empathy/caring/compassion for others' well-being.* "Seventy per cent of all the workers are illegal, so they feel very threatened, of course they are afraid of losing their jobs. This gives the foreman more power over them and I believe he's a man who uses that power against them. . . . Also, the foreman verbally abused the workers and yelled at them. He used abusive language toward them and spit at them. The foreman didn't want the workers to become friends with each other . . . the men had to sit at the dirty, greasy work areas for lunch and not talk to friends or anyone . . . I went (to the owner) with the gut feeling that the (fired worker) was telling the truth. Even though the foreman was polite and business-like with us in the office, I believed it was true (the fired worker's charges of the foreman's corruption, cruelty and sexual abuse of the women workers). So I decided to go tell the owner. Maybe the owner would fire me instead of the foreman but I had an outrage in me about how they were being treated. And I said to myself, Come on, worry about a job? How much more fortunate I am than they are . . . I can find another job. I can pay the premium for medical insurance. I'm so much better off to start with than they are. I guess that helped me in putting it into perspective: The whole world doesn't have to be mean . . . or worrying about what is going to happen to me if I report the foreman."

A separate but very similar case study also involved illegal aliens as workers, subject to exploitation, abuse and many other injustices by the company which employs both them and Elizabeth, the former Sierran. Elizabeth began commenting on these injustices but upon realizing her job was at risk, she stopped. The voice of justice was stilled by the same threat (being fired) used against the illegal workers. But her empathy and caring for the workers and her assessment that the situation was unjust were not resolved. As a result Elizabeth went out of her way to treat the workers with respect, to translate official notices for them and to help them get verification of their previous employment: "So that's why I kind of help them because they're getting the short end of the stick all around. I don't like what I see out there, so that's why I'm all for getting them legalized because they're here and aren't going to go away.... Better they should be legal and not exploited." In this compromise her voice of caring was acted upon while her voice of justice was muted.

i. *Responsibility to act.* (Rest's Component 3; Kohlberg's Function 3). "First, I weighed the risk here and felt the child would be in danger (of parental abuse). The second step, I thought who was best qualified to present the information to the court, and was it okay for us to duck the responsibility and leave the kid hanging? I came to the conclusion that it was not morally right for us to duck the responsibility; someone needed to be there to present the information. The third step was deciding who, me or my supervisor, would make the presentation? I felt angry towards my supervisor for being so warm and sympathetic on the surface, but given his unwillingness to present to the court, we had to decide the best person to present the evidence was the supervisor in terms of being credible and an experienced expert in the field; but given his refusal to act, the responsibility fell with me. There was very little evidence, no evidence, or me. I felt I owed it to the child to put in my two cents worth. I decided to contact a lawyer and have a subpoena issued."

j. *Love.* "I know my husband loves me and I love him. It (an affair proposed by a male colleague) just wouldn't be the right thing to do, it would hurt him so deeply."

Kalliel (1989) asked her 20 subjects how they felt *after* making a decision to act morally. Emotion seemed to be "front-loaded" in most moral decisions. Sixty-three percent reported positive feelings: "I felt real good," "awesome," "glad I made the decision I did," "comfortable," "I felt it was morally right and I acted on that," "at peace with myself." By comparison, 27% reported negative or mixed feelings: "I know I sound selfish (in not sharing law school notes with other students). It was just the environment with the stress and the competition." Mixed feelings: "good feelings about what I thought was right to do; anxious about what was to come and frustration because neither the supervisor nor the legal counsel were helpful in preparing me to testify in court."

This sample of emotions and the associated moral action suggest again the multiple determinations of the moral act itself. Based on the data from this Sierrans Revisited research, feelings are clearly present in some moral actions. A solely cognitive, rational model for the emergence of moral action does not square with the reports of our respondents any more than would a claim that emotions are omnipresent influences on moral behavior. The Sierran men, less frequently than the Sierran women, refer to feelings as associated with their moral actions. This is consistent with a developmental picture of men as emotionally less responsive on the feeling dimension. So men's moral deafness to the different voice of women may be simply a subset of their overall disability in responding to affects. Our view, not surprisingly, is that more study is needed of the relation of emotion to moral acts.

The rough taxonomy of feelings outlined above needs refinement. Are these categories of emotions also arranged in a hierarchical stage order or in a progressive manner? For example, is empathy a more complex emotion in relation to moral action and more evocative of moral action than righteous anger? Do subjects at lower stages of moral reasoning also evidence less complex feelings? And what comes first: the feeling or the action? It seems likely that one can *act* oneself into more complex feelings just as he or she may *feel* the way to more complex actions. That an individual Sierran's actions may be more moral than either his or her reasoning or emotions also seems possible to us.

Question 4: Does the Stage of Moral Reasoning Relate to Moral Action?

The data available to the Sierrans Revisited researchers does not allow an informed answer to this question as it was originally framed. The reasons for this are several—some related to the research design itself, some related to the relative homogeneity of the sample, and some related to the sequence with which the research was conducted.

> A solely cognitive, rational model for the emergence of moral action does not square with the reports of our respondents any more than would a claim that emotions are omnipresent influences on moral behavior.

As research projects unfold over time, it becomes apparent that it is not possible to study every interesting question which arises without impacting the focus of the undertaking as a whole. The principal focus of the Sierrans Revisited research became the data from interviews with young adults employing three different instruments: The Moral Action Interview, the Moral Behavior Interview, and the Moral Influence Interview. At the time (1987-1989) when the interviews were conducted following the formats of the Moral Action Interview and the Moral Behavior Interview, three different tests were administered:

1. The Moral Judgment Interview (MJI), the Kohlberg group's measure of moral maturity;

2. The Defining Issues Test (DIT), Rest's measure of principled thinking; and

3. The Washington University Sentence Completion Test (WUSCT), Loevinger's measure of ego development.

With respect to the timing of research procedures, the three tests were not scored until 1990. This was nearly a year after analysis had been completed of the data from the Moral Action Interview (Chapter 7 of this book as drafted by Kalliel and for her doctoral dissertation, Kalliel, 1989), from the Moral Judgment Interview (Chapters 8 and 9 of this book as drafted by Connor and for his doctoral dissertation, Connor, 1989), and from the Moral Influence Interview (Chapter 10 of this book as drafted by Day). The primary reason for separating the scoring and analysis of the empirical measures of moral maturity, principled thinking, and ego development from the analysis of the interview data was so that interpretations of the interview data would not be confounded by knowledge of the test results. A secondary reason for separating the analysis of the test data from the interview data was that the personal narrative approach to interviewing ended up generating such rich data that analyzing it became a much larger task than anticipated at the start of the project.

Table 9

Averaged Scores in College on the DIT, MJI, and WUSCT of Three "Exemplary" Sierrans and their Scores from Retesting part of the Sierrans Revisited Project

| | Subject 11 Whistle Blower on Dishonest Foreman | | Subject 19 Testified in a Child Abuse/Custody Case | | Subject 16 Taught Students Bilingually | |
	Averaged Scores in College	Sierrans Revisited Scores	Averaged Scores in College	Sierrans Revisited Scores	Averaged Scores in College	Sierrans Revisited Scores
DIT	57.86	70.00	51.00	51.00	25.57	36.00
MJI	300.00	350.00	347.25	350.00	306.50	350.00
WUSCT	5.75	6.00	5.25	6.00	3.66	4.00

This tabular presentation of numerical results requires elaboration before moving to the meaning of the data itself.

Porter (1991) utilized the empirical data which had been collected in the Sierrans Revisited Project to address the effects of the Sierra moral education curriculum, not to relate his research specifically to the broader purposes of this Sierrans Revisited moral action research to focus on choice in response to the everyday moral dilemmas encountered in young adulthood. He undertook a retrospective examination of three of the five subjects identified by the research team as "Exemplary" Sierrans in terms of their absolute scores on the measures of moral maturity, principled thinking, and ego development. Porter (1991) summarized these data in Table 6 (p. 78) of his doctoral dissertation. It is presented here in adapted form as Table 9.

First, the research design of the original Sierra Project called for the administration of the DIT, the MJI, and the WUSCT at the start and at the end of the freshman year, and at the end of the senior year (See Chapter 3). This table averages the available scores from the three college administrations, and presents this information as the "Averaged Scores in College." The "Sierrans Revisited Score" is from the same time period that the interviews were conducted.

Second, Porter presented the averages for the Sierrans Revisited sample where there were both complete college scores as well as scores from this data collection. There were not complete college scores for two of the five "Exemplary" Sierrans. The three subjects in the table above are not the same three subjects interviewed by Professor

Day for Chapter 10. All three whose scores are presented in the previous table, however, do appear prominently in Chapter 7.

Porter (1991) also did a comparison of the averaged college scores of the Sierrans Revisited sample as a whole with the scores they received as part of the testing associated with the interviews.

Moral Maturity

Comparing the scores of the larger Sierrans Revisited sample with the "Exemplary" Sierrans, it is apparent that all three "Exemplary" Sierrans had scores at the average of the sample as a whole on the moral maturity measure from the Moral Judgment Interview. Perhaps more importantly, the "Exemplary" Sierrans were in the middle range of what is called the *conventional* range of the Kohlberg stages of moral reasoning.

Table 10
Averaged Scores in College and Scores from the Sierrans Revisited Testing on the Defining Issues Test, the Moral Judgment Interview, and the Washington University Sentence Completion Test

	Averaged Scores in College	Sierrans Revisited Scores
DIT $n = 14$	40.95	48.69
MJI $n = 32$	307.65	364.84
WUSCT $n = 18$	4.76	4.94

Rest (1979) characterized Stage 3 as the "morality of personal concordance." The central standard for determining moral rights and responsibilities is: "Be considerate, nice, and kind, and you'll get along with people" (p. 129). The concept of fairness is generally limited to an individual's primary group, there being no cognitive structure yet developed for defining fairness beyond it. Stage 3 provides a more stable social environment than does Stage 2, for at Stage 3 morality is defined through a broader set of interpersonal relationships rather than through a limited series of individual personal exchanges.

Rest (1979) characterized Stage 4, law and order, as the "morality of law and duty to the social order." The central standard for determining moral rights and responsibilities is: "Everyone in society is obligated and protected by the law" (p. 129). Fairness at Stage 4 is defined as people doing what is expected of them to accomplish society's goals as manifested in socially derived laws. These same laws are then impersonally and impartially applied to all members of society. The individual comes to view any conflict in terms of how it fits into the existing legal strictures of society. Laws, rather than the opinions of others, become the basis of the definition of *fairness*.

As conceptualized by Kohlberg (1964, 1969, 1971, 1976), the conventional stages are:

Stage 3: The interpersonal concordance, or "good boy-nice girl" orientation

Stage 4: The "law and order" authority and social order maintaining orientation

These stages are labeled *conventional* because a person "is identified with or has internalized the rules and expectations of others, especially those of authorities" (Kohlberg, 1976, p. 33).

The subjects in both the Sierrans Revisited sample and the "Exemplary" Sierrans subsample had moral maturity scores which averaged midway between Stages 3 and 4. As a group they are *not* even beginning to make a transition from the conventional stages to the post-conventional stages (Stages 5 and 6). An individual at the post-conventional stages of 5 and 6 has differentiated himself or herself "from the rules and expectations of others and defines his [or her] values in terms of self-chosen principles" (Kohlberg, 1976, p. 33).

On the measure of moral maturity, both the Sierrans Revisited sample and the "Exemplary" Sierrans subsample are typical of other young adults from this university and from this region of the country. There is a relatively dominant conventional culture in Southern California. The young adults in this sample reflect their cultural context as the dominant culture around them does not encourage or support differentiating oneself from the rules and expectations of others, or adopting self chosen principles. Some of the moral actions of the Sierrans Revisited respondents in response to the everyday moral dilemmas of young adulthood must be thought about in the context of conventional moral maturity. In the Sierrans Revisited sample, utilizing post-conventional thinking of principles for choosing a more just arrangement for individuals within society was the exception rather than the rule.

Ego Development

Two of the three "Exemplary" Sierrans were at a stage higher than the group average on the WUSCT measure of ego development. Subjects 11 and 19 received scores of 6 which equate to Loevinger's I-4 level. Professor Loevinger describes I-4 as the "Conscientious" stage of ego development with the following characteristics:

The conscientious stage is descriptive of individuals who possess elements of adult conscience (goals, capacity for self-criticism, sense of responsibility), a differentiated inner life, and a high degree of conceptual complexity (for example, thinking in terms of a number of polarities). Rather than perceiving the world in broad stereotypes, those at this stage discern individual differences, and concern themselves with their own standards for meeting obligations, setting ideals, developing traits, and achieving. They have an ability to rely on their own rather than external opinion. Norms of external groups are replaced by inner rules (see Whiteley and Associates, 1982, pp. 9-37 for a more extended presentation).

168

Table 11
Loevinger's Characterization of "Conscientious" Stage of Ego Development

Impulse Control/ Character Development	Self-evaluated standards Self-criticism Guilt for consequences Long-term goals and ideals
Interpersonal Style	Intensive, responsible, mutual Concern for communication
Conscious Preoccupations	Differential feelings Motives for behavior Self-respect Achievements Traits Expression
Cognitive Style	Conceptual Complexity Idea of Patterning

(Adapted from Loevinger, J. (1976, pp. 24-25.)

Of particular relevance to this discussion of the ego development characteristics of "Exemplary" Sierrans is Hauser's (1976) description of people at Stage I-4 in terms of how the norms of external groups are replaced by inner rules:

> At this stage a person is his brother's keeper; he feels responsible for other people, at times to the extent of feeling obligated to shape another's life or to prevent him from making errors. Along with the concepts of responsibility and obligations go the correlative concepts of privileges, rights, and fairness. (Hauser, 1976, p. 21).

This description certainly has relevance to understanding individuals who would respond to people in need with appropriate moral action. It should also be noted that on the measure of ego development, the third "Exemplary" Sierran tested at a lower level, Stage (I-3).

Principled Thinking

On Rest's measure of principled thinking from the DIT, one of the "Exemplary" Sierrans received the top score in the Sierrans Revisited sample, a score of 70, and one of the others had one of the third highest scores, a 51. In absolute terms, these are high scores, the 70 being exceptionally high for any sample.

There is a direct relationship between years of formal education and increased scores on the DIT measure of principled thinking. In national norms (see Chapter 3) institutionalized delinquents score an average of 18.9, prison inmates average scores are 23.5, and adults who do not continue their formal education beyond high school average 28.2. Toward the higher end of the scale, average scores were as follows: Sierra Project seniors, 46.51; practicing physicians, 49.5; seminarians in liberal Protestant seminaries, 59.8; and moral philosophy and political science doctoral students, 65.2.

Based on previous research from Rest (1979) and numerous other national studies, there is a direct association between years of formal education and increased scores on the DIT measure of principled thinking. Two of the three "Exemplary" Sierrans had elevated principled thinking scores, and the one with the 70 had tested very high in college as well (57.86 average).

High Moral Action with Low Empirical Scores

The "Exemplary" Sierrans subsample is too small to be more than suggestive of an interesting avenue for future research, particularly when one of the three "Exemplary" Sierrans, Subject 16, scored considerably below the Sierrans Revisited average on both principled thinking (36.00) and ego development (I-3). A principled thinking score of 36 puts him below average adults in general (40.00), and about at the average for Sierra Project freshmen (37.31).

In Loevinger's stages of ego development, I-3 is the conformist stage where the individual identifies his or her own welfare with that of the group, and rules are obeyed for the sake of the group, rather than for fear of punishment or hope of immediate reward. Loevinger (1976) states that: "Disapproval is a potent sanction for the individual at this stage. His moral code defines actions as right or wrong according to compliance with rules rather than according to consequences, which are crucial at higher stages" (p. 18).

Subject 16 chose not to comply with the rules of the school administration concerning bilingual instruction in the classroom, hardly a prototypical I-3 action. Subject 16 himself illuminated how he thought about what he did: "They showed up on me and I was doing a lesson (in Spanish) and 'Isn't this your PVP group?' 'Yes.' 'Why were you conducting the lesson in Spanish?' Well then they would write me up as needing improvement in following district policy or one of the other BS grades which they have which is ultimately their way of getting back at you for not playing the game as they wish you to play it. I suppose obviously the grossness of the error I commit would come into play, they wouldn't fire... I have tenure, for one thing. So that's a certain degree of protection. I have clout because I'm a good teacher. I have the respect of the fellow workers because I'm a good teacher. There are a lot of things going for me and yet... My ego would be bruised, I don't know. Now, (they want to fire me) not for something like this. They would reprimand me and reprimand me and reprimand me again. And say, 'That (Subject 16) he's so unruly.'"

In this real life moral dilemma he did not speak as though he perceived a substantial risk to himself or that he was concerned with the disapproval of the rule makers.

Insights from the Empirical Data

Returning to the substance of Question 4, a consequence of the homogeneity of the sample is that there is an absence of representation of subjects in most of the stages of moral maturity as measured by the MJI, and in most of the stages of ego development as measured by the WUSCT. Therefore it is not possible with these data to relate empirically individuals at different stages of moral reasoning or ego development to moral action.

At the same time, there is insight to be gained from examining the interview data in relation to the empirical data on moral maturity, ego development, and principled thinking. Particularly relevant is the capacity of individuals at the I-4 stage of ego development to be able to see themselves with responsibility and obligation for other people. As Hauser (1976) phrased it, "At this stage a person is his brother's keeper" (p. 21). Two of the three "Exemplary" Sierrans scored at I-4, and were high as well on principled thinking. While generalization to the larger question of understanding the wellsprings of moral action is not possible from such small amounts of data, the implications are intriguing.

There are at least three interrelated issues which call for further investigation. First, there are numerous individuals at post-conventional stages of moral reasoning who choose in any given situation not to take moral action. Second, and conversely, as is reported in the research by Colby and Damon (1992, 1993), there are numerous individuals at conventional stages of moral reasoning who quite consistently take responsible moral action when confronted with moral dilemmas.

Third, the apparently complexity of factors involved in moral action based on the consideration of the first four of the six Sierran Revisited research questions reviewed so far argues for future research designs which are more inclusive of factors to consider rather than less inclusive. Intensive focus on only one factor in isolation, such as the role of moral reasoning alone in moral action, will not provide the richness of data necessary to further understanding of the obvious interrelationship of factors. This line of thinking about the next generation of moral action research will be further explored in Chapters 12 and 13 as the fifth and sixth organizing questions of the Sierrans Revisited research are addressed.

Before turning to an examination of the answers to Question 5 in Chapter 12 and Question 6 in Chapter 13, a recapitulation of the answers to the first four questions is in order. First, young adults proved to be open and forth coming about intimate moral issues in their lives. Second, the moral dilemmas of everyday life revealed by the Sierrans Revisited sample were notable for their richness and emotional complexity in both the work setting and in private life. Third, Sierrans revealed that a wide and diverse range of factors influenced their action in response to moral dilemmas. Fourth, the relative homogeneity of the sample turned out to preclude an empirical contribution to further understanding of the relationship of stage of moral reasoning to moral action.

References

Blasi, A. (1980). Bridging moral cognition and moral action: A critical review of the literature. *Psychological Bulletin, 88*, pp. 1-45.

Colby, A., & Damon, W. (1992). *Some do care: Contemporary lives of moral commitment*. New York: Free Press.

Colby, A., & Damon, W. (1993). The uniting of self and morality in the development of extraordinary moral commitment. In G.G. Noam & T. E. Wren (Eds.), *The moral self*. Cambridge, MA: MIT Press.

Coles, R. (1986). *The moral life of children.* Boston: Houghton Mifflin.

Connor, D. (1989). *The moral behavior of young adults.* Unpublished doctoral dissertation, Boston University.

Day, J. M., & Tappan, M. B. (1996). The narrative approach to moral development from the epistemic subject to dialogical selves. *Human Development, 39,* 67-82.

Gilligan, C. (1982). *In a different voice: Women's conception of self and of morality.* Cambridge, MA: Harvard University Press.

Hauser, S. T. (1976). Loevinger's model and measure of ego development: A critical review. *Psychological Bulletin, 83*(5), 928-955.

Kalliel, K. M. (1989). *Moral decisions and actions of young adults in actual dilemmas.* Unpublished doctoral dissertation, Boston University.

Kohlberg, L. (1964). Development of moral character and moral ideology. In M. L. Hoffman (Ed.), *Review of child development research (Vol. I).* New York: Russell Sage Foundation.

Kohlberg, L. (1969). Stage and sequence: The cognitive-developmental approach to socialization. In D. A. Goslin (Ed.), *Handbook of socialization theory and research.* Chicago: Rand McNally.

Kohlberg, L. (1971). From is to ought: How to commit the naturalistic fallacy and get away with it in the study of moral development. In T. Mischel (Ed.), *Cognitive development and epistemology.* New York: Academic Press.

Kohlberg, L. (1976). Moral stages in moralization: The cognitive-developmental approach. In T. Lickona (Ed.), *Moral development and behavior.* New York: Holt, Rinehart, and Winston.

Kohlberg, L., & Candee, D. (1984). Relationship of moral judgment to moral action. In L. Kohlberg (Ed.), *Essays on moral development: Vol. II. The psychology of moral development.* San Francisco: Harper and Row.

Loevinger, J. (1976). *Ego development: Conceptions and theories.* San Francisco: Jossey-Bass.

Porter, M. R. (1991). *Effects of a moral education curriculum on the development of selected aspects of character.* Unpublished doctoral dissertation, Boston University.

Rest, J. (1979). *Development in judging moral issues.* Minneapolis, MN.: University of Minnesota Press.

Rest, J. (1986). *Moral development: Advances in research and theory,* New York: Praeger.

Tappan, M. B., & Brown L. M. (1989). Stories told and lesson learned: Toward a narrative approach to moral development and moral education, *Harvard Education Review, 5*(2), 182-205.

Vitz, P. (1990). The use of stories in moral development: New psychological reasons for an old educational method. *American Psychologist, 45,* 709-720.

Whiteley, J., & Associates. (1982). *Character development in college students, Vol. I.* Schenectady, NY: Character Research Press.

TWELVE

EXCEPTIONAL
MORAL BEHAVIOR

This chapter explores different conceptions of the individual strengths which are important to positive moral action, and the relationship of those different conceptions to the data from the Sierrans Revisited Project on exceptional moral behavior in everyday situations and to informing future inquiry.

Molly Patterson in Chapter 6 previously introduced research on moral commitment by Colby and Damon (1992, 1993) and on altruism by Monroe (1996). Anne Colby and William Damon interviewed people whose moral commitments led them to devote significant portions of their lives to such activities as helping people who are poor, activism on social justice issues, and attempts to challenge existing social structures which are unfair. Kristen Monroe examined altruism in rescuers of Jews from Nazi Germany. These individuals acted at great risk to themselves and for no extrinsic reward. She also interviewed entrepreneurs who kept most of the money they made, philanthropists who gave generously of some of their wealth, and heroes whose life saving acts were single or short term occurrences.

These two lines of inquiry provide a theoretical context for considering exceptional moral action in everyday situations, and a framework for thinking about the Sierrans Revisited results in relation to Question 5:

Question 5: Are there Young People with Exceptional Characteristics whose Moral Behavior is Exemplary? If Yes, What can be Learned about How They Got that Way?

The brief answer to the question of whether there are young people with exceptional characteristics whose moral behavior is exemplary is an emphatic "Yes!" In selecting from among the larger pool of subjects from the Sierrans Revisited Project included in answering this specific question, the research team used as definition of "exceptional characteristics" the following:

1. The subjects had been especially lucid in their articulations of moral thought and action;

The brief answer to the question of whether there are young people with exceptional characteristics whose moral behavior is exemplary is an emphatic "Yes!"

2. The subjects had been compelling in describing poignant moral dilemmas;

3 In the moral accounts they told, the subjects had been consistent in the relationship between the actions they took and the principles they had espoused; and

4. The stories the subjects told contained an element of risk to their own welfare which was reflected in their deliberations, as well as considerations which would have promoted the welfare of others.

Using that working definition, approximately 10% of the larger pool of the Sierrans Revisited Project qualified, and were the subjects for the specific investigation of this question which was reported in Chapter 10.

Moral Commitment

The research of Colby and Damon (1992, 1993) utilized a very different time in the life span from this Sierrans Revisited focus on young adulthood. Their approach was to examine individuals whose adult lives had been characterized by exemplary moral commitment. Their sample of 23 met the following criteria:

1. Sustained commitment to moral ideals or principles,

2. A disposition to act in accord with one's moral ideals or principles,

3. A willingness to risk one's self-interest for the sake of one's moral values,

4. A tendency to be inspiring to others, and

5. A sense of realistic humility about one's own importance (Colby & Damon, 1993, p. 155).

Their method of data collection was to conduct extended interviews concerning personal experiences and beliefs, events and influences which may have shaped character, crucial life decisions, and feelings and thoughts about those crucial decisions. The researchers called this the life history section of the interview. A second part of the interview consisted of the administration of dilemmas from the Kohlberg Moral Judgment Interview. Interview material from the life-history section was used to try to understand the phenomenology of moral commitment, and "the meaning of these people's activities in relation to their values, beliefs, and the life experiences that seemed most salient to them" (Colby & Damon, 1993, p. 156).

This was a somewhat different research approach than James Day employed in Chapter 10 where there was an emphasis on exemplary behavior in everyday life in young adulthood. Nonetheless, there is similarity in the two lines of inquiry in terms of trying to understand the wellsprings of exemplary moral behavior.

Colby and Damon identified characteristics in their sample which have similarities to our subsample:

1. They do not see following principle as a matter of choice (Frankfurt's, 1993, "essential nature" and "volitional necessity").

2. They do not believe that they were courageous when making and carrying out their moral decisions even though many had placed themselves in danger (Colby & Damon, 1993).

3. Irrespective of stage of moral maturity as measured by the Moral Judgment Interview, the justifications for their behavior were in terms of actions, events, or circumstances rather than on generalizations or abstractions (Colby & Damon, 1993).

4. There were parallels to Haste's (1990) study of moral commitment on dimensions of sense of certainty, level of conviction, and lack of doubt (Colby & Damon, 1993).

Even though they were just at the beginning of their adult lives, the Sierrans Revisited subsample of exemplary young adults clearly exhibits aspects of the four characteristics noted above.

There were also differences between the Sierrans Revisited subsample and Colby and Damon's (1992, 1993) sample. One obvious difference was in scope and duration of activities. The efforts of the Colby and Damon sample were directed toward the resolution of fundamental ethical problems of society. And their activities had persisted over extended periods of a lifetime. The Sierrans Revisited sample was at the start of life and career. Their moral actions were focused on everyday issues.

There were other differences as well. Colby and Damon (1993) reported that their sample could be characterized by "a positive attitude toward life and deep enjoyment of one's work" (p. 169). With respect to enjoyment of work, the Sierrans Revisited sample was in such an early phase of career exploration that it is not possible to characterize their enjoyment of work in any meaningful sense. Their work histories were still characterized by a series of jobs.

The Sierra sample, in contrast to the Colby and Damon (1993) sample, were still too young to have encountered life's tragedies. Almost all of their parents were still alive, and they had not lost children of their own. The former Sierrans were encountering their first divorces, but their state of health still seemed satisfactory. They were too young to have encountered personally the lifestyle maladies of stroke, cancer, and heart disease. This situation made the Colby and Damon sample seem all the more remarkable for their positive attitude as they were well along in life (The remarkable life of one of their sample, Virginia Foster Durr, for example, had begun in 1904. She was 84 at the time of her interview for the moral commitment research in 1988).

Another marked difference between the Colby and Damon (1993) sample and the Sierrans Revisited sample was in moral maturity as measured by the Moral Judgment Interview. The Colby and Damon sample covered "the full range of adult development and levels" (p. 172). The Sierrans Revisited sample were all within the conventional (Stages 3 and 4) level of moral maturity. The Sierrans Revisited design called for the collection of Rest's Defining Issues Test for measuring principled thinking, and for the collection of Loevinger's Sentence Completion Test for measuring ego development. Two of the three exemplary Sierrans had elevated principled thinking scores and were also at Loevinger's I-4 conscientious stage. This data was not collected in the research on moral commitment.

Colby and Damon (1993) portrayed a "close relationship between the exemplar's area of contribution and moral frame of reference" (p. 172). Since the Sierra sample is rooted in Stage 3 and Stage 4, it is useful to recapitulate the meaning Colby and Damon assigned to moral action when taken by people at these conventional stages:

> ...those in our sample who reason at Kohlberg's Stages 3 and 4 are as likely as those who evidence principled moral judgment to have unified personal and moral goals, have a close relationship between their moral convictions and their sense of self, and be deeply certain and free of conflict about their moral beliefs.

> ...we see Stage 3 and 4 moral judgment in the context of lives characterized by selfless devotion to the poor. These exemplars are almost always deeply religious, and it may be that their religious convictions serve as a kind of anchor for them. (Colby & Damon, 1993, p. 172)

The notion that convictions can serve as an anchor for conventional thinkers was presented by Colby and Damon in the context of religious convictions.

The Sierrans Revisited data supports the notion that personal convictions can serve as anchors for moral action, but in the context of anchors stemming from cultural affiliation. An example from Chapter 10 is the school teacher who taught his students bilingually in defiance of a school administration edit forbidding the practice. The teacher had himself come from a home where English was a second language, and he knew from personal experience the burden which children of immigrant parents were under to learn both subject matter and a new language in the same limited time frame. Sharing both ethnic heritage and cultural background with his students, he had an anchor for the convictions he acted upon. He also tested in the conventional range on the DIT and the conformist (I-3) range on the Sentence Completion Test.

> The Sierrans Revisited data supports the notion that personal convictions can serve as anchors for moral action, but in the context of anchors stemming from cultural affiliation.

This leads to two points. First, it is absolutely clear that moral action in the face of moral dilemmas stems from a variety of origins, and moral action is by no means limited to post-conventional thinkers. The wellsprings of the individuality of moral action by conventional thinkers may well be different than that of post-conventional thinkers, and they may or may not choose different arenas for that action. Second, in retrospect we believe it was a positive decision to include all three instruments for assessing aspects of character (Moral Judgment Interview, Defining Issues Test, Washington University Sentence Completion Test) as part of the original research design. As was outlined in detail in Whiteley and Associates (1982), these three measures tap different features of character on a theoretical level, and empirically have relatively low correlation with each other.

Just as Colby and Damon (1992, 1993) made inferences on the stage level of moral maturity from two Kohlberg dilemmas, Blasi (1993) made innovative use of a subset of items from the Sentence Completion Test in his research on identity modes and identity development. The three measures of character are collectively the product of years of careful research and development. Even if different paradigms of analysis are being considered (self, identity, domain, pattern, etc.), there may well be value added to future research by inclusion of all of them in whole or part.

Altruism and Moral Action

Kristen Monroe (1996) investigated the construct of altruism in a unique research population which, within itself, was widely diverse (rescuers of Jews from the Nazis in World War II, heroes, philanthropists, entrepreneurs). It was very dissimilar to the young adults who comprised the Sierrans Revisited research sample. The factors associated with time, place, and circumstance which led to the inclusion of altruists in the Monroe sample were very different from those which resulted in the inclusion of the young adults in the Sierrans Revisited sample. In addition to the actions themselves which led to designation as an altruist, the time frame when they did what they did was different, as was the location for their actions. The actions of the rescuers, for example, occurred over half a century ago. If discovered by accident or betrayal, the outcome would have been either instant death at the hands of the Gestapo, or lingering death if they survived arrest and were instead sent to a concentration camp. In most instances, the rescuers had not known the people they rescued before the circumstances of the rescue.

By the very harrowing circumstances of the act which led to their being designated as heroes by the Carnegie Hero Fund Commission, one-quarter of the recognitions have been conferred posthumously. This is because of the dangerous conditions encountered in the attempt to save the lives of people the hero very seldom knew before the act of heroism. By way of contrast, the moral actions of the Sierrans Revisited group occurred in the context of their everyday lives. The moral dilemmas they reported were almost all with people they knew at home or at work in Southern California.

As with the study of Colby and Damon (1992, 1993), however, there are significant theoretical and methodological opportunities to inform the interpretation of Sierrans Revisited data, and to benefit the next generation of research on moral action from a careful examination of the design of the altruism research, and from the principal findings reported by Monroe in *The Heart of Altruism*. Monroe's (1996) definition of altruism is "action designed to benefit another, even at the risk of significant harm to the actor's own well-being" (p. 4). Her approach was to select a population for study who are unusual exemplars of altruism: hence the choice of rescuers of Jews in the most dangerous of conditions.

Monroe (1996) conducted a systematic examination of the traditional explanations of altruism offered by the disciplines of economics, evolutionary biology, and psychology:

> The particular approaches under scrutiny range from the sociocultural which explains altruism through the altruist's religious or educational background, to more elaborate theoretical concepts, such as kin or group selection in evolutionary biology, role models and social learning in psychology, and reciprocal altruism and psychic utility in economics. (p. 5)

Her conclusion from this examination was that it explained behavior by rational actors but not by altruists.

Monroe conceptualized altruistic behavior as running along a continuum, "with pure self-interest and pure altruism as the two poles and modal or normal behavior, including quasi-altruistic acts, distributed between them" (Monroe, 1996, p. 7). She utilized two research tools in her investigation: narrative interviews, and a traditional survey questionnaire administered after the narrative interviews had been completed. In contrast to the Sierrans Revisited research design, she elected not to include the collection of any of what the Sierra researchers designated as the empirical measures of character.

From the point-of-view of informing the methodology of the research tools for the next generation of moral action research, Monroe's analysis of the narrative and how it differs from other modes of discourse and other modes of organizing experience is instructive. The narrative as a research tool has the following characteristics:

1. It requires *agency*: It involves characters or actors who have a place in the plot.

2. When it emphasizes goal-oriented human action, it provides insight on how different people organize, process, and interpret information, and how they move toward achieving their goals.

3. It suggests the speakers' view of what is canonical. By canonical she refers to what seems "normal and right," and what is discussed matter-of-factly. The unusual and exceptional is only remarked upon in the narrative.

4. The mental organization of the speaker is revealed in the sequence of sentences and the way that events are structured, rather than in the truth or falsity of any of the particular sentences or events recounted.

5. It is the speaker's organization of events to give meaning to them which is important, for it is the process of organization which reveals perspective.

6. The narrative suggests how the speaker organizes experience and the distinctions which are made in everyday life.

7. The speaker draws in what he or she considers to be relevant cultural influences which create a context for the analyst. (Monroe, 1996, p. 19)

Data from the sixth characteristic of the narrative, for example, provided Monroe with the information which allowed her to observe "that where most of us distinguish between how we treat strangers and friends, altruists do not" (Monroe, 1996, p. 19).

In order to provide a very personal context which would allow the reader to understand more fully their analysis of the meaning of significant moral commitment, Colby and Damon (1993) shared details from the life of one of their morally committed subjects. Monroe (1996) took essentially the same approach with an opening section entitled "The Human Face of Altruism." Before turning to the analytical framework she employed to distill meaning from her data, it is useful to introduce Otto and his experiences in order to juxtapose altruists like him with the young adults in the Sierrans Revisited sample.

Otto was an ethnic German living in Prague during World War II. Among the risky activities in which he engaged were the following: he openly married a Jewish woman (thereby protecting her for awhile), he worked in the Austrian underground, and he bribed numerous Gestapo officials and concentration camp guards. He was ultimately arrested himself, and sent to a concentration camp. For Monroe, Otto did not fit into any of the easy categories which social scientists like to employ "to explain away actions by which individuals risk their own welfare, perhaps even their lives, to help others" (Monroe, 1996, p. x).

Otto acknowledged that he had saved many Jewish lives, but insisted that the value of his acts was overestimated, others had done much more (he shared poignant examples), and suggested that what he had done was not really altruistic. Why did he risk his life for others? "One thing is important . . . I had no choice. I never made moral decision to rescue Jews. I just got mad. I felt I had to do it. I came across many things that demanded my compassion" (Monroe, 1996, p. xi).

In Chapter 13, the relevance of emotions to moral action is considered, as well as the role of empathy both as a cognitive and as an affective dimension of human experience. Otto reports that "I just got mad," and "I felt I had to do it." The circumstances he encountered required his "compassion." Under far less extreme circumstances, individuals in the Sierrans Revisited sample recounted moral actions which were encased for them also in an emotional context.

In addressing the task of making meaning from her narrative data, Monroe approached it in some ways which can inform the next generation of research on moral action in young adults. A useful perspective may be gained by working backwards from her principal findings. Altruists insist they have not done anything extraordinary or praiseworthy. The specifics of their ethical belief systems differ little from those of rational actors (one of the poles of the conceptual framework Monroe used to place her data along a continuum). Altruism is a logical outgrowth of sense of self in relation to others. Monroe found one notable characteristic shared by all the altruists she interviewed: "All saw themselves as people strongly bound to others through a common humanity" (Monroe, 1996, p. 202).

This view of a world of common humanity was articulated by a man she called Tony:

> I was to learn to understand that you're part of a whole and that just like cells in your body altogether make up your body, that in our society and in our community that we all are like cells of a community that is very important. Not America; I mean the human race. And you should always treat people as though it is you, and that goes for evil Nazis as well as for Jewish friends who are in trouble. You should always have a very open mind in dealing with other people and always see yourself in those people, for good or for evil both. (Monroe, 1996, p. 205)

Monroe (1996) organized her framework for analysis of the data from the narrative interview and the structured questionnaire around the construct of perspective. Perspective included five concepts relevant to altruism as she investigated it: cognition, world view, canonical expectations, empathy/sympathy, and views of self. Monroe found the construct of perspective useful in several ways:

1. It conveys the idea of locating oneself in a cognitive map.

2. It contains the idea of a view of ourselves in relation to others, a view of others, a view of ourselves, and that each person has a view of the world.

3. It is used to imply that each actor has a particular way of seeing the world.

4. It incorporates world views and identity, and affects the cognitive frameworks used to process new information, make sense of reality, and give meaning to action. (Monroe, 1996, p. 14)

Monroe presumed "that the perspectives of altruists will resemble each other and that they will differ in significant and consistent ways from the perspectives of non-altruists" (Monroe, 1996, p. 14). The construct of perspective for Monroe fulfills some of the explanatory functions for which other theorists considered in the next chapter employ notions of self, identity, and guiding force.

There is potential relevance to the next generation of moral action research of Monroe's decision that for the purpose of data classification she would not treat self-interest and altruism as dichotomous phenomena. Rather, a consequence of considering them as opposite poles of a conceptual continuum allowed her to categorize some altruistic actions as mixed. This approach, if applied to categorization of moral and immoral actions on a continuum, would allow a reflection in the classification of data which fits the reality of moral choice as we observed it in the Sierrans Revisited sample. Analyzing archetypical groups also allowed Monroe to test alternate explanations for altruism from the existing literature and to explore what other factors correlate with behaviors at different points on the continuum (Monroe, 1996). This approach is also applicable to the next generation of research in moral action.

References

Colby, A., & Damon, W. (1992). *Some do care: Contemporary lives of moral commitment.* New York: Free Press.

Colby, A., & Damon, W. (1993). The uniting of self and morality, in the development of extraordinary moral commitment. In G. G. Noam & T. E. Wren (Eds.), *The moral self.* Cambridge, MA: MIT Press.

Monroe, K. R. (1996). *The heart of altruism.* Princeton: Princeton University Press.

STRENGTH OF CHARACTER AND MORAL AGENCY

This chapter explores some of the dimensions involved in moral action which are reflected in conceptions of strength of character and moral agency in the results of the Sierrans Revisited Project, and specifically addresses the complexities of Question 6.

Question 6: Is It Possible to Identify a Composite of Factors/Influences which Correlate with Outstanding Strength of Character and Powerful Moral Agency?

Four promising theoretical approaches provide the framework for thinking about Sierrans Revisited results on Question 6: identity and moral motivation, emotions in moral action, capacity for empathy and moral action, and social cognitive theory and moral agency. Prior to examining the Sierrans Revisited data in the context of those four approaches, some of the dimensions of moral action reflected in the data will be addressed briefly, starting with the role of moral reasoning.

Relationships to Moral Action in the Sierrans Revisited Data

The relationship of moral reasoning to moral action is an area of inquiry where much research remains to be done. Noam (1993) indicated that:

1. A higher degree of consistency exists between moral judgment and moral action as level of moral judgment increases; and

2. Many people at these more mature levels of moral judgment are not acting according to their principles of proclaimed judgments.

The translation of these statements into an empirical research agenda is a significant challenge. For example, Colby and Damon (1992, 1993) report that individuals at both conventional stages (Stages 3-4) and post-conventional stages (Stages 5-6) make highly significant contributions to society based on deliberate moral choices. Likewise, the Sierrans Revisited data indicate the presence of repeated positive moral choices by young adults who are at the conventional level of moral reasoning as assessed by the moral maturity measure from the Moral Judgment Interview.

A major challenge for future research is to identify why some individuals at higher stages of moral reasoning did not choose more positive moral choices. When faced with moral dilemmas from everyday life, for example, the Sierrans Revisited research data indicate that our subjects, from the perspective of conventional moral reasoning, felt more free to act upon their convictions in interpersonal situations than they did in work situations where their employment might be at risk.

Noam (1993) described several dimensions relevant to moral action. Three dimensions will be introduced to provide a context for considering central implications of Sierrans Revisited data:

1. Moral action is typically not blind but a conscious choice for the good of friends or strangers, family or peer groups, or larger social systems. Moral choice usually has as its explicit goal to protect and support others, an activity that involves interest and empathy. (p. 218)

our subjects... felt more free to act upon their convictions in interpersonal situations than they did in work situations where their employment might be at risk.

The Sierrans Revisited research speaks to a number of these issues. Our subjects made conscious choices to act (or agonizingly not to act) on behalf of family, strangers (usually encountered in the course of professional obligations), and former "family" such as former spouses or ex-long term lovers. Their usual choice of moral action was in the category of "to protect and support" others.

One aspect of protecting and supporting others, as Noam (1993) presented it, is an activity which involves interest and empathy. Empathy and the presentation of educational experiences to enhance the capacity for empathy are discussed in the later section of this chapter on Capacity for Empathy and Moral Action. There is an extensive literature usually considered outside the province of moral psychology identified with the pioneering research of Carl R. Rogers (1961, 1975) and his associates. The broader point of this literature is very hopeful from the perspective of promoting moral action: Empathy is a capacity of human beings which can be enhanced through formal instruction.

2. . . . moral action requires choice, it entails decision making. . . Each fundamental choice entails giving up other possibilities, jeopardizing relational bonds or career aspirations, and the like. Moral action closes many doors. . . (Noam, 1993, p. 218)

A recurrent theme in the narratives of the Sierrans Revisited sample was that moral choices could jeopardize relationship bonds, particularly with immediate family and significant others.

The dilemma of one young woman comes immediately to mind. A man in her life needed what for her was a lot of money in order to finish his education. While ordinarily this would be a straightforward personal decision of no major moral consequence, in her case she was also the primary support of her mother and a sibling. Her father was dead, and the sum of money involved, $4,000, was money she used in reserve as security for their welfare. She was also an enterprising person, and she had found an opportunity to invest the $4,000 in herself in a way to enhance her long term income, and therefore provide more adequately for her family.

In the scheme of moral dilemmas encountered in life, this dilemma of whether or not to loan money to the boyfriend was not a major moral choice. But for a young woman just starting her career with the welfare of others to consider as well as that of her own, the dilemma became a moral one of consequence. Saying "no" to the loan could have unforeseen consequences for the relationship with the boyfriend. And if she did loan the money and if the $4,000 were not available if she needed it for her immediate family's welfare, then there could be genuine harm to people significant to her. And of course she had found a use for the money herself in the same time frame that the boyfriend wanted the use of the money.

This type of everyday dilemma is the "stuff" of the moral dilemmas in young adulthood which were facing the Sierrans Revisited sample. Our sample, at least in the time frame we collected data from them, had been spared the life and death ethical choices which accompany catastrophic illness or life-threatening accident. Resolving the moral dilemmas they did face, however, as Noam (1993) states, confronted them with the fact that "moral action closes many doors."

3. Acting morally involves taking a stand, often an unpopular one. Not conforming to one's group or giving up the protection of the prevalent culture is always, even in little ways, an act of courage... To this day, prisons and labor camps throughout the world contain people who have acted out of moral motivations and reasons. But even under less extreme situations, moral action often occurs against the backdrop of social conformity and social sanctions, and thus demands strengths. (Adapted from Noam, 1993)

One of the Sierrans Revisited respondents made a moral choice to testify in court in a difficult child custody case in which the more experienced professional staff in her social welfare agency were not willing to make the time to testify. She was still a trainee in the social welfare agency, a circumstance which could have resulted in a difficult and demeaning cross-examination by the lawyers for either the mother or the father involved, depending on which parent thought her testimony on behalf of the child was hurting his or her respective custody case.

The point is that it does take courage to act on moral convictions. One challenge for the next generation of curriculum developers is to sequence educational experiences to enable students to confront examples of simulated realistic and age-specific moral dilemmas within the classroom and laboratory. A much broader issue for future researchers is to learn more about the genesis of the moral strength in individuals of proven moral commitment such as those studied by Colby and Damon (1992, 1993) and Monroe (1996). Once the genesis of significant moral commitment is more fully understood, it will be possible to develop improved curricula to enhance it.

Identity and Moral Motivation

The Sierrans Revisited research was not designed to address the *origins* of personal concern with taking moral action in response to moral dilemmas. Blasi (1993) considered aspects of this when he posed the question of "how objective morality becomes integrated in one's personality, how it acquires personal value and subjective relevance" (p. 116). The answer to the question Blasi posed is fundamental to the design of college curricula concerned with moral development. After noting the absence of clear empirical data, he indicated that a strong personal concern with morality is "not a necessary by-product of the subjective experience of identity" (p. 117). Further, he did not believe that strong personal concern with morality was "even a certain consequence of more sophisticated forms of understanding moral principles" (p. 117). The issue of how to contribute to the development of strong personal concern with morality, and the subsidiary issue of taking moral action in response to moral dilemmas, are fundamental to the construction of college curricula addressed to moral education, indeed to all moral education curricula.

Blasi speculated that specific life experiences have a role in the development of strong personal concern with morality. This speculation occurred in the context of what he saw as the "most interesting and pregnant finding" of his study of the sense of identity in adulthood (Glodis & Blasi, 1991). This finding was that middle adolescents and young adults differed on the dimension of active commitment and responsibility for the ideals and the characteristics with which one identifies:

> ...while middle adolescents have a clear sense of an individual inner self and relate to it with affective attachment and even care, only when one's sense of self is constructed around active commitments and responsibility for those ideals and characteristics with which one identifies does identity acquire the permanence and continuity that Erikson saw as its trademark. At least in our sample, this development only appears among young adults.
> (Blasi, 1993, pp. 113-114)

The development of active commitments and acceptance of responsibility occurs, when it does occur, during what are usually the college years.

In the general context of a discussion of the acquisition of an identity with "permanence and continuity," Blasi (1993) commented:

> It is possible, and not incompatible with a cognitive-developmental view, that the issues around which one constructs an identity depend on specific life experiences, including the exposure to the views, ideals, and life in general, of one's parents, teachers, and friends. (p. 117)

Reports by the Sierrans Revisited sample are divided on the relative importance of parents, teachers, and friends as influences on how an individual responds to moral dilemmas. The Exemplary Sierrans group described in Chapter 10 spoke of the importance of parents and of teacher/mentors from their freshman year. The rest of the sample reported on in Chapters 7, 8, and 9 described the importance of friends and significant others much more frequently.

Blasi (1993) identified another possible alternative for the time in one's life when strong personal concern with morality begins:

> It is also possible that the choice (if one can speak of choice) is made relatively early, even before one's sense of identity begins to appear, and that one's central concerns remain more or less constant for the rest of one's life. What can change, then, is a person's subjective relationship to the ideals that

anchor his or her identity, the specific meaning that "importance" and "concern" have for the person. (p. 117)

For those individuals who reported on the specific importance of parents or religious beliefs, it is quite possible that these sources of influence were present and influential from an early age. The design of the data collection for the Sierrans Revisited research was such that no effort was made to pinpoint specific time of influence.

For Blasi (1993) the more probable hypothesis is that "specific experiences interact with developmental variables to produce both the contents and the modes of identity" (p. 118). Such a circumstance, if it were found to have empirical support, would have important implications for curriculum development. Educators would need to understand the developmental level of the young people with whom they are working and to organize educational challenges to accommodate that developmental level.

The broader question is the linkage between identity and moral action. Blasi (1993) has cautioned that one could argue the following:

> . . . moral identity is not a more secure predictor of moral action than other forms of moral motivation. It is neither conceptually obvious nor empirically evident that the various reasons for morality to be important to a person have different relations to moral motivation and moral action, at least in the large majority of morally relevant situations. (p. 118)

One of the morally relevant situations which fits this characterization may be when acting on one's beliefs is difficult because of especially negative consequences. The Sierrans Revisited sample reported such an area of difficulty in the workplace when one's contemplated moral action could have resulted in the loss of one's job.

Some in the Sierrans Revisited sample chose to take moral actions which involved considerable risk to themselves. Frankfurt (1993) used the concept of "volitional necessity" to address the circumstance where certain actions would be *unthinkable* for an individual (p. 20). In a section on "Volitional Necessity and Identity," Frankfurt went on to address the characteristics of a person without which he or she "cannot be what it is" (p. 22). Volitional necessity constrains the person by limiting the possible choices which are available:

> The idea that the identity of a thing is to be understood in terms of conditions essential for its existence is one of the oldest and most compelling of the philosophical principles that guide our effort to clarify our thought. To grasp what a thing is, we must grasp its essence, namely, those characteristics without which it cannot be what it is. Thus the notions of necessity and identity are intimately related. (Frankfurt, 1993, p. 22)

Taken together, the linkage of volitional necessity and moral identity represents a way of thinking about the Sierrans Revisited subsample and the morally committed individuals in the study by Colby and Damon (1992, 1993). A characteristic of philosopher Frankfurt's way of conceptualizing such individuals would be their capacity to "guide [their] conduct is in accordance with what [they] really care about" (Frankfurt, 1993, p. 23). Such persons simply cannot help willing certain actions:

> These necessities [from the volitional necessities concept] substantially affect the actual course and character of his life. But they affect not only what he does: they limit the possibilities that are open to his will, that is, they determine what he cannot will and what he cannot help willing. Now the character of a person's will constitutes what he most centrally is. . .The boundaries of his will define his shape as a person. (Frankfurt, 1993, p. 24)

In attempting to understand those special individuals whose lives are characterized variously by moral commitment, there have been attempts to explain them from the perspective of both moral philosophy and moral psychology. The terms used for such characterizations vary with the theoretical orientation of the scholar or empirical researcher. For those individuals who relate themselves to the interests of others through moral ideals, such people have an "essential nature" (Frankfurt, 1993, p. 25). The reasons why such people develop as they do is not a subject of agreement.

One of Blasi's (1993) central conclusions is that people vary with respect to "whether and to what extent a person constructs his or her sense of self around moral concerns" (p. 120). Further, it was not clear to him how "identity modes would help us to predict behavior" (p. 120). Nor was it clear "the different ways in which moral beliefs are integrated in personality" (p. 120). One consequence of conducting the Sierrans Revisited research was the realization that the search for universal modes of thinking by the field of moral psychology has been only a "proximate" search for a more elusive source of interest; namely, predicting moral action. The ultimate answers to questions about the role or roles of moral reasoning and the wellsprings of moral action may not be found within universal conceptions.

Moral action may be more fully understood by adopting variations of two different conceptions of human behavior. The first is the general conception of personality that we are all like everyone else, like some other people, and like no one else. This conception is contrary to universalists' conceptions. It may be found in such works as *Personality in Nature, Society and Culture* (Kluckhohn, Murray, & Schneider, 1953), *Culture and Behavior* (Kluckhohn, 1962) and *Action Theory and the Human Condition* (Parsons, 1978). Applying the concept that we are all like everyone else, like some other people, and like no one else to understanding moral action, it may well be that moral action is one of those domains in which the emphasis is on the more individual, rather than the more general, aspects of understanding people.

Another way to conceptualize moral action theoretically is to consider it analogous to Robert W. White's (1973) basic conception of the healthy personality. When invited to write a treatise on the general topic of the healthy personality, he originally declined, stating that he considered such a concept a block to clear thinking. He urged readers to abandon the concept altogether and instead to look at patterns of functioning which seem to work for different people:

> Perhaps I should warn you that the expression, "healthy personality," is one that I consider illegitimate and a great obstacle to clear thinking. I should have to urge readers to abandon it altogether and reconsider what they do without recourse to confusing medical analogies. This means that the article will not exactly fit the idea of "the components of healthy functioning." I consider any such format too abstract and impersonal, and I tend to think along such lines as workable and unworkable patterns of personality—one man's "healthy components" being another man's poison, and vice versa. But the emphasis

that results on individuality does not have to leave us without guides, and one of the things that causes me to accept your invitation is the chance to work out this idea more than done before. (White, 1973, p. 2)

The treatise subsequently authored by White offered both "workable" and "unworkable" patterns of personality with an emphasis on individuality. At the same time, as he promised, the formulation "did not have to leave us without guides." The direct applicability of this formula to moral action research has not yet been attempted.

Emotions in Moral Action

An intriguing area for future research is the role of emotions in moral action. As was presented in detail in Chapter 11, many of the Sierrans Revisited sample, in recounting the moral dilemma they faced, recalled strong emotions which accompanied the dilemmas. Exploring the role of emotions in moral action was not a formal subject of inquiry in the Sierrans Revisited research. There already is an extensive body of literature, however, exploring aspects of emotion in moral action. In the late 18th century, the philosopher Immanuel Kant argued that since emotions and feelings are transitory and capricious, conduct with its origins in emotions is unreliable and inconsistent. The basic reason is that emotions do not have the universality required for principled, rational morality (Kant, 1785/1959).

Other points of view have proliferated in the many years since Kant's influential position was formulated. Cognitive psychologists, for example, have studied extensively the cognitive core of emotions (Lazarus, Averill, & Opton, 1970), their role in therapy for emotional disorders (Beck, 1976) and their role in personality development (Arnold, 1960). Other areas of exploration on the role of emotions have focused on the development of altruism (Hoffman, 1976; Blum, 1980), and reactions toward disadvantaged and victimized people (Montada & Schneider, 1989).

Montada (1993) investigated what he called "moral emotions" in the context of studying how moral rules are represented psychologically, or what he called "moral oughts." Some emotions indicate the existence of moral oughts:

> Salient emotional reactions to deviations from moral norms include guilt feelings when the subject has violated one of his or her personal moral norms, and moral outrage or resentment when another person has violated a duty that the subject normatively expected that person to meet. (Montada, 1993, p. 294)

Montada (1993) explored the role of emotions in terms of the cognitive models of guilt and resentment. He proposed that by using cognitive models it is possible to suggest hypotheses about antecedents and motivational consequences of emotions as "moral emotions are embedded in a network of antecedents and consequences" (p. 297).

The design of the Sierrans Revisited research did not call for investigation of emotions and their role, if any, in moral action. It became apparent as the research progressed (see Chapter 11) that outrage served as a motivator for taking action in some circumstances, and emotions such as love and caring sometimes influenced the choice of action in response to moral dilemmas. Guilt and shame were reported

It became apparent as the research progressed that outrage served as a motivator for taking action in some circumstances, and emotions such as love and caring sometimes influenced the choice of action in response to moral dilemmas.

as consequences of having chosen one course of action over another. The presence of emotion was so pervasive in the stories of moral dilemmas and moral choice told by the Sierrans Revisited respondents that future researchers are encouraged to investigate the specific circumstances in which emotions trigger action, whether emotions are a factor in making a particular choice, and what emotions are consequences of particular moral choice outcomes.

Capacity for Empathy and Moral Action

Martin L. Hoffman (1991) traces the significance of the role which empathy may occupy in a comprehensive moral theory. Empathy is described as a "reliable, biologically based motive that became part of human nature through the long process of natural selection" (p. 276).

While Hoffman's (1991) argument for the role of empathy in moral action is within the disciplinary framework of moral psychology, he traces the origin of the relationship to the moral philosophy of David Hume in the 18th Century (Hume, 1751/ 1957). Hoffman cites another philosopher, John Stuart Mill (1861/1979), as suggesting that empathic anger, defined as a natural feeling of retaliation, serves as a "guardian of justice." Yet another and more contemporary philosopher, John Rawls (1971), is cited as arguing, in contrast to Hume, that empathy lacks "the situational sensitivity necessary for achieving a rational consensus" (Hoffman, 1991, p. 286). Hoffman himself has responded to the Rawls critique of Hume with a concept of "mature empathy" which has the following characteristics:

> . . . a high degree of situational sensitivity as well as a sensitivity to subtle differences in the severity and quality of the consequences that different actions might have for different people. It thus seems clear that empathy can contribute to sophisticated, informed moral judgments. (Hoffman, 1991, p. 287)

Hoffman (1991) also proposed a resolution of another issue dividing Hume and Rawls, namely that of "empathic bias" (pp. 287-289).

Hoffman (1991) traces a second general rationale for the role of empathy in moral action to the general proposition that there are motivational properties in affect, and to the work of learning theorists in the 1940s and 1950s and their linkage of affect and reinforcement to motivation for action. Drawing also on the psychoanalytic theory of object relations in which individuals are motivated to possess objects (people) that are invested with affect, Hoffman concluded that . . . it seems safe to assume that empathic affect motivates action on behalf of the person with whom one empathizes or toward other people in general" (p. 276).

Since empathy reliably disposes people "to act on behalf of others, it follows that empathic affects must be an important type of moral motive" (Hoffman, 1991, p. 277). In this conception, "emphatic distress" is portrayed as a prosocial moral motive. Hoffman's general line of inquiry (Hoffman, 1975, 1978, 1980, 1984a, 1984b, 1987) defines a moral act in motivational terms rather than in the cognitive-developmental paradigm associated with Lawrence Kohlberg wherein moral action was based on principles of fairness and justice following a cognitive process of moral reasoning and judgment.

One theoretical reason that it is possible to raise the level of empathic understanding is to be found in the conceptualization of empathy as both cognitive and affective. In such a conceptualization, empathy as a cognitive process conveys the ability to observe and make meaning of what other persons are feeling and to make inferences about their emotional state from overall behavioral cues. There is a capacity for connectedness to other people denoted by empathy (Eisenberg, 1986; Batson, 1991). The affective component of empathy manifests itself in emotional arousal toward the plight or other circumstances of people in need.

The concept of empathy was introduced into the original Sierra Project from a different theoretical perspective and rationale. The theoretical rationale was developed from the practice of counseling and psychotherapy of Carl R. Rogers (1961, 1975) and his associates. Empathy is portrayed by the proponents of the Rogerian approach as one of three primary ingredients of therapist behavior in successful psychotherapy, the others being genuineness and unconditional positive regard. From this perspective of the positive role of empathy in successful psychotherapy have been developed a number of straightforward approaches to teaching listening skills and modes of empathic communication. These teaching approaches were variously developed for use with counselors and therapists in training, then extended in scope to the training of other professionals, to paraprofessionals, and to lay persons.

Empathy training, in the form of listening skills instruction, was introduced early in the development of the basic Sierra curricula because individual freshmen complained that other freshmen would not listen to them. The exercises involved were entertaining for the participants. Also, the basic curriculum was developed under the supervision of counseling and clinical psychologists who were involved themselves in the empathy-listening skills paradigm. The Sierra Project experience with teaching empathy skills to freshmen is that it is possible to improve listening and understanding skills in freshmen in a straightforward manner. Empathy is identified as a "capacity" precisely because of our experience that it is possible to raise the level of empathic understanding in a wide variety of circumstances.

With respect to the role of empathy in the Sierrans Revisited research, the design of the data collection did not provide for the systematic collection of data on feelings in general, or of any particular emotions, including capacity for empathy. Since irrespective of specific format the interviews were tape-recorded, listened to extensively, and many were transcribed, it has been possible to form clinical impressions of what the Sierrans were communicating on the dimension of empathy in moral action. Before stating these clinical conclusions, it is useful to clarify further what Hoffman (1991) defined as the empathy involved in moral action:

> My scheme for empathic distress, which is an empathic affective response to another person's distress, starts with a simple innocent by-stander model in which one encounters someone in pain, danger, or deprivation and generates five empathic affects that are mediated by social cognitive development and various causal attributions or inferences. (p. 277)

Three of the five empathic affects are largely automatic and involuntary. The fourth and fifth modes are most relevant to the Sierrans Revisited research:

> The fourth and fifth modes involve language mediation (which enables one to emphasize with another's verbal report of his feelings) putting oneself in the other's place, and thus call on higher-order cognitive processes that are more subject to voluntary control. (Hoffman, 1991, p. 277)

Utilizing Hoffman's definitions of empathic distress and response, there are empathic comments associated with the moral dilemmas encountered in both interpersonal relations and in the workplace. Individual subjects differ greatly in their commentaries which had empathic elements.

The method of Sierrans Revisited data collection simply does not provide evidence for more informed comment about the role of empathy in subsequent moral action. This represents yet another promising area for future inquiry, particularly concerning levels of empathic capacity in relation to the motivation of moral action. Also, it is beyond the scope of this concluding chapter to address the methodology of researching empathy in the context of its role in motivating moral action, or to distinguish the differences in practical conceptions of empathy used by Hoffman (1991) and the proponents of the Rogerian approach to counseling and psychotherapy (Rogers, 1961, 1975).

Social Cognitive Theory and Moral Agency

Bandura's (1991) approach to understanding moral thought and action within the framework of social cognitive theory has significant implications for the content of data to be collected in a study of moral action and for the systems of meaning applied to the data. The system of meaning to be applied to the data begins with the proposition that "Human behavior cannot be fully understood solely in terms of social structural factors or psychological factors. A full understanding requires an integrated perspective in which social influences operate through psychological mechanisms to produce behavior effects" (Bandura, 1995, p. 202). He employs a system of multicausality; in this approach, sociostructural and personal determinants are co-factors within a unified causal structure.

... Sierrans Revisited data collection simply does not provide evidence for more informed comment about the role of empathy in ... moral action. This represents yet another promising area for future inquiry, particularly concerning levels of empathic capacity in relation to the motivation of moral action.

For Bandura (1991), "a comprehensive theory of morality must explain how moral reasoning, in conjunction with other psychosocial factors, governs moral conduct. Moral conduct is motivated and regulated mainly by the ongoing exercise of self-reactive influence" (p. 45). Within the conceptual framework of the cognitive interactionist perspective from social cognitive theory, "personal factors in the form of moral thought and affective self-reactions, moral conduct, and environmental factors all operate as interacting determinants that influence each other bidirectionally" (p. 45).

While it is beyond the scope of this chapter to explore in detail this multicausality model with interacting (interactive) determinants, the general implications for the future research on moral action in young adulthood are several. First, data would need to be systematically collected on each of the various determinants which are hypothesized to interact "bidirectionally": personal factors in moral thought, affective self-reactions, moral conduct, and environmental factors. The Sierrans Revisited design did not approach data collection in this framework. Second, the personal narrative approach which was used in the Sierrans Revisited research would have to be supplemented by more systematic data collection following initial interviewing. There might, of necessity, be fewer subjects who are covered in greater depth and detail. Subsequent structured data collection to augment personal narrative data would make it possible to analyze more fully bi-directionality (mutual influence and interaction among relevant factors) than personal narrative data alone.

In the Bandura (1995) paper on human agency there is a section on moral agency which, in some respects, goes well beyond the Bandura (1991) treatise on the social cognitive theory of moral thought and action. Bandura (1995) is particularly helpful in stimulating thinking about the next generation of research on what the Sierrans Revisited research team called the exemplary Sierrans with his thinking about moral agency. Bandura's concept of moral agency begins with the premise, "In many areas of social and moral behavior the self-regulatory standards have greater stability. People do not change from week to week what they regard as right or wrong or good or bad" (Bandura, 1995, p. 198). Other theorists explored constructs of moral identity or moral self to address, among other phenomena, the consistency of behavior over time such as has been encountered in the case of the exemplary Sierrans reported in this volume or the morally committed sample studied by Colby and Damon (1992, 1993). Bandura introduced notions of "moral agency" and "guiding structure" to address aspects of the consistency and organizing capability of individuals whereas other theorists used concepts like self, perspective, and identity. These concepts are not at all interchangeable. But there is a common attempt among theorists to try to account for and explain a commonly observed capacity for consistency and constancy in some human beings.

For Bandura (1995), "A theory of moral agency must specify the mechanisms by which people come to live in accordance with moral standards" (p. 198). He sees a movement in psychology toward cognitive structures linked to major domains of functioning and away from global cognitive structures. Within developmental psychology he sees a similar movement away from the global structuralism associated with Piaget (and presumably aspects of Kohlberg's work). The concept of moral agency is presented in the context of explaining self-regulation of moral behavior and his view that "It is difficult to conceive of a personality process that is disembodied from a guiding structure" (p. 201). Irrespective of the theoretical perspective, understanding more fully the origins of exemplary, morally committed behavior expressed over time is a crucial agenda item for the next generation of research on moral action.

From the theoretical perspective of social cognitive theory such research might begin with the cognitive structure of moral rules:

> Moral rules represent an enduring cognitive structure for judging the moral status of conduct in situations containing many morally relevant decisional ingredients. One does not have a set of moral standards on Monday, none on Tuesday, and a new set of Wednesday. It is through the cognitive rule

structure that the self-regulatory processes of self-monitoring, self-evaluation, and self-sanctions govern conduct anticipation. (Bandura, 1995, p. 210)

The Sierrans Revisited approach to data collection did not allow exploration of the notions of self-sanction and self-monitoring. Further, the impression from listening to the interviews of the exemplary Sierrans is that they have very high standards for themselves in terms of self-evaluation. In this sense, they are very similar to the types of people Bandura (1995) was referring to as he described people with high efficacy and the role of efficacy belief systems in the exercise of human agency Again, understanding more about the origins and characteristics of such individuals will inform curriculum development in moral education.

References

Arnold, M. B. (Ed.), (1960). *Emotions and personality: Vol. I. Psychological aspects.* New York: Columbia University Press.

Bandura, A. (1991). Social cognitive theory of moral thought and action. In W. M. Kurtines & J. L. Gewirtz (Eds.), *Handbook of moral behavior and development: Vol. I. Theory.* Hillsdale, NJ: Lawrence Erlbaum.

Bandura, A. (1995). Reflections on human agency. In J. Georgas, M. Manthouli, E. Besevegis, & A. Kokkevi (Eds.), *Contemporary psychology in Europe: Theory, research and applications.* Seattle, WA: Hogrofe and Huber.

Batson, C. D. (1991). *The altruism question: Toward a social psychological answer.* Hillsdale, NJ: Lawrence Erlbaum.

Beck, A. T. (1976). *Cognitive therapy and the emotional disorders.* New York: International Universities Press.

Blasi, A (1993). The development of identity: Some implications for moral functioning. In G. G. Noam & T. E. Wren (Eds.), *The moral self.* Cambridge, MA: MIT Press.

Blum, L. A. (1980). *Friendship, altruism, and morality.* London: Routledge and Kegan Paul.

Colby, A., & Damon, W. (1992). *Some do care: Contemporary lives of moral commitment.* New York: Free Press.

Colby, A., & Damon, W. (1993). The uniting of self and morality in the development of extraordinary moral commitment. In G. G. Noam & T. E. Wren (Eds.), *The moral self.* Cambridge, MA: MIT Press.

Eisenberg, N. (1986). *Altruistic emotion, cognition, and behavior.* Hillsdale, NJ: Lawrence Erlbaum.

Frankfurt, H. (1993). On the necessity of ideals. In G. G. Noam & T. E. Wren (Eds.), *The moral self.* Cambridge, MA: MIT Press.

Glodis, K., & Blasi, A. (1991). *The sense of self and identity among adolescents and adults.* Unpublished manuscript, University of Massachusetts, Boston.

Hoffman, M. L. (1975). Developmental synthesis of affect and cognition and its implications for altruistic motivation. *Developmental Psychology, 11,* 607-622.

Hoffman, M. L. (1976). Empathy, role-taking, guilt, and development of altruistic motives. In T. Lickona (Ed.), *Moral development and behavior.* New York: Holt, Rinehart, and Winston.

Hoffman, M. L. (1978). Empathy, its development and prosocial implications. In C. B. Keasey (Ed.), *Nebraska Symposium on Motivation (Vol. 25).* Lincoln: University of Nebraska Press, 169-218.

Hoffman, M. L. (1980). Moral development in adolescence. In J. Adelson (Ed.), *Handbook of adolescent psychology.* New York: Wiley, 295-343.

Hoffman, M. L. (1984a). Interaction of affect and cognition in empathy. In C. Izard, J. Kagan, & R. Zajone (Eds.), *Emotions, cognition and behavior.* New York: Cambridge University Press.

Hoffman, M. L. (1984b). Empathy, its limitations, and its role in a comprehensive moral theory. In J. Gewirtz & W. Kurtines (Eds.), *Morality, moral development and moral behavior,* New York: Wiley.

Hoffman, M. L. (1987). The contribution of empathy to justice and moral judgment. In N. Eisenberg & J. Strayer (Eds.), *Empathy and its development.* New York: Cambridge University Press.

Hoffman, M. L. (1991). Empathy, social cognition, and moral action. In W. M. Kurtines & J. L. Gewirtz (Eds.), *Handbook of moral behavior and development: Vol. I. Theory.* Hillsdale, NJ: Lawrence Erlbaum.

Hume, D. (1751/1957). *An inquiry concerning the principle of morals (Vol. 4).* New York: Liberal Arts Press.

Kant, I. (1785/1959). *Foundations of the metaphysics of morals.* Indianapolis: Liberal Arts Press.

Kluckhohn, C., Murray, H. A., & Schneider, D. (1953). *Personality in nature, society, and culture.* New York: Knopf.

Kluckhohn, R. V. (Ed.). (1962). *Culture and behavior: Collected essays of Clyde Kluckhohn.* New York: The Free Press of Glencoe.

Lazarus, R. S., Averill, J. R., & Opton, E. M., Jr. (1970). Toward a cognitive theory of emotion. In M. B. Arnold (Ed.), *Feelings and emotions.* New York: Academic Press.

Mill, J. S. (1861/1979). *Utilitarianism.* Cambridge, MA: Hackett.

Monroe, K. R. (1996). *The heart of altruism.* Princeton: Princeton University Press.

Montada, L. (1993). Understanding oughts by assessing moral reasoning or moral emotions. In G. G. Noam & T. E. Wren (Eds.), *The moral self*. Cambridge, MA: MIT Press.

Montada, L., & Schneider, A. (1989). Justice beliefs and emotional reactions toward disadvantaged and victimized people, *Social Justice Research, 3*, 313-344.

Noam, G. G. (1993). "Normative vulnerabilities" of self and their transformations in moral action. In G. G. Noam & T. E. Wren (Eds.), *The moral self*. Cambridge, MA: MIT Press.

Parsons, T. (1978). *Action theory and the human condition*. New York: The Free Press.

Rawls, J. (1971). *A theory of justice*. Cambridge, MA: Harvard University Press.

Rogers, C. R. (1961). *On becoming a person*. Boston: Houghton Mifflin.

Rogers, C. R. (1975). Empathic: An unappreciated way of being. *The Counseling Psychologist, 5*(2), 2-10.

White, R. W. (1973). The concept of healthy personality: What do we really mean? *The Counseling Psychologist, 4*(2), 3-12.

TOWARD PROMOTING MORAL ACTION IN YOUNG ADULTHOOD

Chapter 14 is divided into three sections. The first section reviews some of the guiding directions for the original curricular initiative to promote the character education of college freshmen. The second section addresses the next generation of curricula in moral education with a special focus on promoting moral action in response to normative moral dilemmas encountered in interpersonal relationships and the workplace. The third section is a recapitulation of basic themes and directions.

Guiding Directions for the Original Curricular Development Initiative

One of the underlying purposes defined at the beginning of this book was to determine what might be learned from moral philosophy and moral psychology that we could apply to the results of the Sierrans Revisited Research, and that would assist us as we reflected upon the implications of this research for character education. One general contribution of moral philosophy is analyzing "the principles of civic virtue and its most general preconditions" (Rorty, 1993, p. 39).

What are the general preconditions for moral development?

What are the general preconditions for moral action?

Both Chapters 6 and Chapter 13 have addressed some of the preconditions for moral development and for moral action from the perspectives of various philosophical points of view.

One of the broader issues raised by the Sierra Project and this companion Sierrans Revisited initiative is what role can the freshman year in college—and indeed four years of undergraduate study—have in raising the level of moral action in society? A closely related conceptual question is who will provide the primary sources of instruction in moral choice? Will it be the random effects of the self-forming and constantly reforming peer groups, or the cultural norms of the mass media? For how long are parents especially influential? What roles will the institutions of organized religion play? Are there viable roles for educators in educating for moral choice within the traditional roles accorded to school and university by society?

A related approach to raising the level of moral action is to identify the core tasks which must be accomplished. Wren, a philosopher, spoke of the "seemingly impersonal demands of morality (to be fair, keep one's promises, etc.)" as also "deeply personal demands as well" (Wren, 1993, p. 94). The task of moral education in such a conception is to provide learning experiences which will translate the impersonal into the personal. A variation on this idea is Blasi's (1993) linkage of moral action to moral understanding which is in turn related to personal responsibility: ". . . moral understanding more reliably gives rise to moral action if it is translated into a judgment of personal responsibility" (p. 99).

> The task of moral education... is to provide learning experiences which will translate the impersonal into the personal.

The original Sierra Project curriculum was designed to take advantage of the openness to new experiences of entering freshmen, the richness of residence hall living, and the nature of the freshman year requirements. Residents of Sierra Hall, which was home to the Sierra Project, were required to enroll in a four unit course (sixteen units is considered a full academic load) each quarter for the three quarters which comprise the academic year at the University of California, Irvine. Entering students from all of the academic units at UCI were eligible to enroll in Sierra. A majority of freshmen had either declared a major as part of the admissions process or had some sense of general direction for their academic study. Even the undecided students could easily complete their class schedules with general breadth requirements.

The reasons that entering freshmen actually have little flexibility in their academic schedules are easy to understand. First, those who are engineering majors already are encountering a heavily prescribed curriculum. Second, those students who think they want to become physicians have to fit into their schedules all of the prerequisites for such courses as organic chemistry as well as relevant courses in the biological sciences. Third, there are challenging lower-division breadth requirements ranging from mathematics to humanistic inquiry which both have to be met, preferably early in the course of academic study, and are most valuable for the undecided students. Fourth, there are challenging (or oppressive, depending on one's point-of-view) requirements for learning to write through freshman English or a variation depending on level of skill.

The reason for this extended sketch of the pressures related to course choice is to underscore the importance of being able to offer academic credit for initiatives like Sierra. With all of the other pressures they are under, freshman students simply are not going to have the time to engage themselves fully in the tasks of the Sierra curriculum without being able to earn academic credit. Since the inception of the Sierra Project, the pressure for additions to graduation requirements has increased within the university in the form of compelling calls for increased global and multicultural literacy for college graduates, as well as for literacy in computers and broader information technology. The point is that there are clear structural limitations on the amount of academic credit which is available for elective courses in the freshman year. Nevertheless, academic credit is essential in order for students to have the freedom to participate fully in the Sierra experience.

One curricular casualty which was a consequence of time pressure on freshmen (and other factors) was the attempt to provide an opportunity in spring quarter of the freshman year for additional academic credit (two units) for what was called field study. The rationale for field study was straightforward: to provide students with an opportunity to try out the skills they had been learning in Sierra (for example, empathy, assertiveness, conflict resolution, etc.) on selected aspects of significant problems in society by internship placements in community agencies. The School of Social Ecology, which was the academic host for the Sierra Project, already had an established field study program required of graduating seniors. Therefore, there was already in place the set of ongoing relationships with community agencies which are essential to establishing challenging field study placements.

The major problem which accounted for the low participation was that students did not have the time in their schedules to allow them to participate. There were conflicts in scheduling with laboratory sections in the science and engineering courses. There were not enough breaks in the schedule between normally taken freshman classes and their required discussion sections to permit students to leave campus in order to spend meaningful amounts of time at a community agency. Finally, field study required either an automobile or sufficient time to travel into the community by public transportation. Many of our participating freshmen did not have cars on campus since they were living in residence halls.

Also, as the academic year progressed, the participating faculty and students discovered activities within the existing formal context of the Sierra residence hall and the existing formal freshman curriculum which needed additional time. For example, weekend retreats were popular with students as well as strong contributors to the development of a sense of community. In addition to the commitment of Saturday and Sunday, much of Friday before a Sierra retreat would be spent in preparation and travel. The journal writing requirement was another ongoing activity which was more valuable in direct relation to the amount of time which could be put into the initial process of writing, into subsequent reflection on the commentary of the journal reader, and into drafting a response to the reader's comments.

It became apparent to the faculty and staff of the original Sierra Project that the impact of the curriculum on character development would be enhanced it if could be spread over four years of undergraduate studies. The original design of the Sierra Project, however, was to offer an exploratory year in 1975-1976, and then revise the curriculum and repeat it for three years (1976-1977, 1977-1978, and 1978-1979). This determination was made in order to facilitate the systematic study of the development of character over the freshman year, and of the differential effects of the curriculum itself.

At the conclusion of the original period of time for the Sierra Project (1975-1979), the overwhelming sentiment of faculty, staff, student staff, and Sierra alumni was to continue offering the newly created freshman year program. Since the faculty and staff resources which were available to maintain the Sierra initiative were finite, the UCI offerings have remained focused on the freshman year. This is still accepted as a positive determination given the realities of resource constraints.

Developing The Next Generation of Curricula

There now exists a body of theoretical developments and research results to support the creation of the next generation of curricula to build upon the basic structure of

Sierra and to focus on experiences which will promote moral action in response to moral dilemmas. Since the context for creating the next generation of curricula remains the four years of undergraduate study, it is useful to begin with the practicalities of fitting new classes into the challenges of upper-division instruction. An assumption of this presentation is that the moral action component will build upon a previous Sierra-type experience in the freshman year. This is particularly important given what has been learned about the importance of sequencing educational experiences.

The system for the allocation of academic credit and of graduation requirements at UCI is that there is a clear distinction between lower division and what are considered to be usual breadth courses (those designed to contribute to a well educated citizen in society), and the upper division requirements for graduation in a specific major, or for pre-professional training. The original Sierra Project existed within the lower division structure. The academic credit earned (a total of 12 units over three quarters) counted toward the 180 units required for graduation, but not for satisfaction of individual breadth requirements or for the specific requirements of the various majors.

In considering the problems involved in creating an upper-division academic focus on moral action, it is useful to present separately the different opportunities for establishing academic credit, and the outline of some of the basic choices on the content of the curriculum. With respect to the different opportunities for establishing academic credit, the original Sierra Project had been created within the context of an academic school with an interdisciplinary mandate. Further, there had been a policy choice to open the freshman year program to entering students from across the campus. The determination to promote disciplinary diversity, coupled with the multi-ethnic composition of students within Sierra, has always contributed to a broader climate for learning than would, for example, a largely Anglo student body of social science majors.

Recognizing that each college or university will have its own specific procedures for establishing academic credit, there are at least three general choices of direction:

1. Establish courses on moral action at the upper-division level under the auspices of traditional disciplines and departments. Courses established in such a manner usually count as upper-division elective credit toward the satisfaction of requirements for a major in whatever department the course has received sponsorship.

2. Establish courses on moral action at the upper-division level under the auspices of the campus mechanism for granting course credit for interdisciplinary initiatives. From a content point of view, particularly if the course is team taught by instructors conversant with moral action dilemmas originating in their specialties, this approach could be very stimulating for students, and for instructors. Such an offering might not qualify for upper-division credit for the requirements of specific majors. In that case, it would still count as elective units toward the total number needed to earn an undergraduate degree.

3. Include modules within existing courses which will draw the participation of a broader network of instructors than might become involved otherwise, and through them participation of a larger population of students. There are

compelling moral dilemmas associated with most contemporary subject matter without even getting into the moral action dilemmas which abound in history and literature through the ages.

With respect to the content of courses on moral action, there are many domains of human experience which can be tapped. The suggestions which follow are illustrative:

1. Kalliel in Chapter 7 reported a compilation of the moral action dilemmas of young adults. Students could be assigned to compile a parallel inventory of the moral action dilemmas associated with being college freshmen, or with being college students in general. They could also be assigned to utilize some combination of the interview formats for the Sierrans Revisited Project research to investigate what action their contemporaries are taking in response to moral dilemmas. The opportunity being explored here is to involve students in thinking about the dilemmas which exist for their contemporaries and which arise in the culture with which they are most familiar. While most freshmen do not encounter many work place dilemmas in the traditional sense, the university setting abounds with moral dilemmas, as does the interpersonal domain of the student culture.

2. Active participation in learning from the moral dilemmas of the community is an opportunity which we could not make work in the freshman year for a host of reasons. Most of the problems encountered should not be insurmountable for upper division students. Whether the community involvement experience is called field study or some other appropriate descriptor is inconsequential. What is consequential is providing an emphasis on identifying the moral dilemmas involved in the everyday life of the broader community, learning what choices are being made, and who is making them.

3. It is apparent from the work of Colby and Damon (1992, 1993) on moral commitment, and of Monroe (1996) on altruism that there are moral exemplars in all walks of life. These individuals can be interviewed by undergraduates using some version of the personal narrative interview.

These are three example which are representative of feasible and affordable approaches to introducing specifics of moral dilemma content into the college curriculum.

> While most freshmen do not encounter many work place dilemmas in the traditional sense, the university setting abounds with moral dilemmas, as does the interpersonal domain of the student culture.

A Recapitulation

The original Sierra Project had as one of its stated purposes to influence intentionally the moral thinking of the next generation of society's leaders and citizens in the direction of a more morally just society. It was also designed to be a freshman year program which would develop dimensions of character in college students, and a longitudinal study of the growth of character during the freshman year and over four years of undergraduate study.

A program with such fundamental purposes as the Sierra Project raises the basic issue of whether there is a viable role for educators in addressing challenges of moral choice. The basic rationale from the inception of the Sierra Project is valid twenty-five years later:

Rationale One

> Universities have an opportunity through their curricula to develop in students a greater capacity for ethical sensitivity and awareness, an increased regard for equity in human relationships, and the ability to translate this enhanced capacity into a higher standard of fairness and concern for the common good in all realms of their lives. These accomplishments are ultimately self-rewarding.

Rationale Two

> There is a benefit to society of a citizenry whose lives are characterized by principled thinking and moral maturity. Such individuals will be more responsible citizens, leaders, and parents. Society as a whole is therefore a beneficiary of character education for college students.

Rationale Three

> There is an ultimate benefit to participants in terms of greater potential for accomplishment throughout their adult lives. Personal growth and psychological maturity are closely related to many dimensions of accomplishment in adulthood.

Rationale Four

> There is conclusive evidence that properly sequenced educational and psychological experiences raise the level of moral reasoning and ego development of adolescents and young adults. This research is extraordinarily hopeful in its implications: For society, education can make a difference in the moral reasoning of the citizenry.

Rationale Five

> Experiences during the college years provide many opportunities for influencing moral reasoning. The typical college environment contains the opportunity for exposure to, and intellectual confrontation with, diversity in beliefs, lifestyles, and personality types. Since the vast majority of beginning college students reason in a highly conventional manner, their moral referents are those people immediately around them.

Rational Six

> An experience in higher education should provide an opportunity to reflect on the purposes of learning, on the uses to which acquired knowledge is put, and on the ethical dilemmas which confront citizens individually and as members of society collectively. The purposes of a college education include preparation for life and career, as well as personal development. (Loxley & Whiteley, 1986)

The Sierrans Revisited Project began in 1987 as an expansion of the conceptual basis of the original Sierra Project to include an explicit examination of moral action. The conceptual basis of the Sierra Project focused on moral and character development with corresponding empirical measures of moral maturity, principled thinking, and ego development. The sample chosen for the Sierrans Revisited Project research study of moral action was comprised of former participants in the Sierra Project program of academic study and residential living. They are now young adults confronting the moral dilemmas of everyday life in interpersonal relations and in the workplace.

This volume reporting on the Sierrans Revisited Project provides answers to three fundamentally important conceptual questions about character development and moral action:

Are there theories of character and moral development which can inform college educators?

Are there proven curricular approaches to character development and promoting moral action which college educators can adopt?

Are their promising theories and avenues of research which can stimulate original approaches to fostering moral action?

Theories of Character and Moral Development

The answer to this first question concerning relevant theories of character and moral development begins with the original conceptual and empirical definitions of character in the Sierra Project. Character was defined conceptually as having two parts. The first part refers to understanding what is the right, fair, good thing to do in a given circumstance. The second part refers to the ability to do those things (the courage to act in accordance with one's understanding).

The empirical measures of character adopted by the Sierra Project were moral maturity from the Moral Judgment Interview (Kohlberg, 1973; Colby, Gibbs, Kohlberg, Speicher-Dubin, & Candee, 1979), ego development from the Washington University Sentence Completion Test (Loevinger & Wessler, 1970; Loevinger, 1976), and principled thinking from the Defining Issues Test (Rest, 1979). The utilization of these three proven research instruments made it possible to study growth and development in character over the course of the freshman year, and over four years of the college experience.

The work of the original Sierra Project (Whiteley & Associates, 1982; Loxley & Whiteley, 1986) was informed by theories drawn largely from cognitive-developmental psychology. Chapter 5 extends this treatment of character development, moral reasoning, and ego development to include the specific thinking on the origins of moral action as conceived by Norma Haan, Augusto Blasi, James R. Rest, Carol Gilligan, and Lawrence Kohlberg. It was their presentations on theory which heavily influenced the approach to research of the Sierran Revisited Project.

In contrast to the research on components of character in which there were existing "proximate" empirical measures, there were no such comparable measures of moral action. Therefore, the basic method of data collection utilized in the Sierran Revisited research was the interview in three variations of the personal narrative approach (see Chapter 7, 8, 9, and 10).

A final resource relevant to the first question for college educators who wish to work in the area of character research and the furtherance of moral action is the review in

Chapter 4 of different conceptions of the developmental tasks of young adulthood. Compared to theory and research on childhood, adolescence and adulthood, the period of life known as young adulthood has been comparatively understudied.

Curricular Approaches to Character and Moral Action

The second question is whether there are proven curricular approaches to character development and promoting moral action which college educators can adopt. This question can be answered resoundingly in the negative. While there are numerous curricular approaches to character development, few of their advocates would claim that they are "proven." The approach of the original Sierra Project to character development is detailed in Loxley and Whiteley (1986), and summarized in Chapter 3. In Chapter 2, Ralph L. Mosher discusses two methods to promote moral development which were used in the public schools in the 1970s: classroom discussion of moral dilemmas embedded in the academic curriculum, and discussion by students of everyday or "real" moral issues occurring in the life of the classroom or the school.

Mosher goes on to offer a searching critique of the foundations of the Sierra curriculum. The issues he chose to focus upon are valuable to consider by educators contemplating offering curricular initiatives themselves. Phrased in the form of questions, the following are a sampling of some of those issues raised by Mosher :

1. Will the teaching team include a moral psychologist and/or a normative philosopher or ethicist?

2. Are there going to be systematic formal discussions of either abstract moral dilemmas or of those naturally occurring in the residence hall?

3. Will there be a deliberate attempt to provide for diversity among student participants on dimensions ranging from stage of moral reasoning to ethnicity, gender and culture?

4. How broadly defined will be the purposes of the curricular initiative?

5. Is an important objective the building of a strong sense of community among participants?

6. What is the "hidden" moral curriculum of the residence hall or the peer group, and how does the "hidden" curriculum relate to the planned/sanctioned curriculum?

7. Are there benefits derived from embedding the course in a residence hall environment which are commensurate with the added effort?

8. Are there benefits derived from working with a class composed of students from all four years of undergraduate study instead of just freshmen or just seniors?

9. With a curriculum intended to enhance character, what are the feasible approaches to sequencing curricular experiences, particularly with a diverse class?

10. Again with a diverse class of students, what approaches to instruction will compensate for differences in cognitive development?

11. What closely reasoned linkages exist between one or more theories of late adolescence and the curriculum?

The answers provided to the representative questions above, and to others raised by Mosher (see the Foreword and Chapter 2), will shape the nature of the curricular initiative.

Curricula to enhance moral development are not new. Their rationales differ, as do the assumptions they make about the nature of moral development itself and its precursors. The construction of curricula to enhance moral action, however, is a much newer phenomena. This book reviews promising theories which can undergird curriculum development. These reviews are provided in Chapters 5 and 6.

Promising New Theories on Promoting Moral Action

The third and final question is whether there are promising new theories and avenues of research which can stimulate original approaches to fostering moral action. Unlike the answer to the second question, the answer to the third is emphatically "yes."

First, the promising theories presented in this book are of relatively recent origin. In addition to reviewing the theories themselves in Chapters 5 and 6, the discussion of the research results from this Sierrans Revisited Project in Chapters 11, 12 and 13 is informed and framed by those promising theories. Initial planning for the Sierrans Revisited Project on moral action in young adulthood drew on two of the theorists whose empirical measures had been such an integral part of the scientific work of the original Sierra Project: Lawrence Kohlberg and James R. Rest. It was their thinking on the components of moral action plus the thinking of Norma Haan, Carol Gilligan, and Augusto Blasi which informed the design of the Sierrans Revisited research.

The new theories, which have appeared in the years since the Sierrans Revisited Project began in 1987, have their origins primarily in moral philosophy and moral psychology. These theories reflect research programs on such diverse topics as moral identity (Blasi, 1993), altruism (Monroe, 1996), moral commitment (Colby and Damon, 1992, 1993), and moral agency (Bandura, 1991, 1995). These new approaches as well as others are reviewed in Chapter 6, and discussed in relationship to Sierrans Revisited data in Chapters 12 and 13.

Second, the presentation of the theories is organized in terms of a series of categories which are useful for college educators:

Exceptional Moral Behavior. This category addresses the characteristics of individuals with exceptional moral behavior, including individuals whose adult lives are characterized by persisting moral commitment (Colby & Damon, 1992, 1993); in people who rescued Jews from the Nazis under the most harrowing of circumstances (Monroe, 1996); and young adults in the Sierrans Revisited research on moral action in the everyday dilemmas of young adulthood (see Chapter 12).

Strength of Character and Moral Agency. This addresses the complex of factors which are associated with strength of character and powerful moral agency. The discussion of Sierrans Revisited results and recent literature is presented in sections on Identity and Moral Motivation, Emotions in Moral Action, Capacity for Empathy and Moral Action, and Social Cognitive Theory and Moral Action. This section is particularly relevant to the educator who is considering initiating program development on moral action inquiry (see Chapter 13).

Moral Education in the College Years. The first section of this chapter recapitulates some of the guiding directions of the Sierra Project initiative to promote the character education of college freshmen. The founders of the original Sierra Project selected the freshman year as the place to begin a process of reflection on the purposes of higher education and on the ethical challenges which confront citizens individually and as members of society. The second section addresses the next generation of curricula in moral education with a special focus on promoting moral action in response to normative moral dilemmas on two dimensions of personal experience: in interpersonal relations and in the workplace.

Conclusion

The current state of knowledge about promoting moral action is such that it is essential that curriculum development in moral action proceed in parallel with an active research program. There are major unfinished research agendas associated with the five theorists whose work was central to the initial development of the Sierra Project. There are also extensive research agendas associated with the theorists introduced in Chapter 6 whose contributions are singled out for comment in Chapters 12 and 13. Incorporating aspects of these previous investigations provides numerous points of departure for a new generation of basic research into the wellsprings of moral action, and improved curricula to promote it.

References

Bandura, A. (1991). Social cognitive theory of moral thought and action. In W. M. Kurtines & J. L. Gewirtz (Eds.), *Handbook of moral behavior and development: Vol. I. Theory,* Hillsdale, NJ: Lawrence Erlbaum.

Bandura, A. (1995). Reflections on human agency. In J. Georgas, M. Manthouli, E. Besevegis, & A. Kokkevi (Eds.), *Contemporary psychology in Europe: Theory, research and applications.* Seattle, WA: Hogrofe and Huber.

Blasi, A. (1993). The development of identity: Some implications for moral functioning. In G. G. Noam & T. E. Wren (Eds.), *The moral self.* Cambridge, MA: MIT Press.

Colby, A., & Damon, W. (1992). *Some do care: Contemporary lives of moral commitment.* New York: Free Press.

Colby, A., & Damon, W. (1993). The uniting of self and morality in the development of extraordinary moral commitment. In G. G. Noam & T. E. Wren (Eds.), *The moral self.* Cambridge, MA: MIT Press.

Colby, A., Gibbs, J. C., Kohlberg, L., Speicher-Dubin, B., & Candee, D. (1979). *Standard form scoring manual* (Parts 1-4). Cambridge, MA: Harvard University Center for Moral Education.

Kohlberg, L. (1973). Continuities in childhood and adult moral development revisited. In P.R. Baltes & K. W. Schaie (Eds.), *Life-span developmental psychology: Personality and socialization.* New York: Academic Press.

Loevinger, J. (1976). *Ego development: Conceptions and theories.* San Francisco: Jossey-Bass.

Loevinger, J., & Wessler, R. (1970). *Measuring ego development: Vol. I, Construction and use of a sentence completion test.* San Francisco: Jossey-Bass.

Loxley, J. C., & Whiteley, J. M. (1986) *Character development in college students: Vol. II. The curriculum and longitudinal results.* Schenectady, NY: Character Research Press.

Monroe, K. R. (1996). Th*e heart of altruism.* Princeton: Princeton University Press.

Rest, J. R. (1979). *Development in judging moral issues.* Minneapolis, MN: University of Minnesota Press.

Rorty, A. O. (1993). What it takes to be good. In G. G. Noam & T. E. Wren (Eds.), *The moral self.* Cambridge, MA: The MIT Press.

Whiteley, J. M., & Associates. (1982). *Character development in college students: Volume I, The freshman year.* Schenectady, NY: Character Research Press.

Wren, T. E. (1993). The open-textured concepts of morality and the self. In G. G. Noam & T. E. Wren (Eds.), *The moral self.* Cambridge, MA: MIT Press.

APPENDIX A
MORAL ACTION INTERVIEW

Katherine M. Kalliel

1.   Tell me about a moral decision you've made recently or are currently making?

2.   How did you go about making a decision what to do or not to do?

3.   How did you decide this was a moral decision?

4.   When did you decide this was a moral decision?

5.   a.   Did (Will) you make your decision in this situation based on your consideration of other people's rights? By rights I mean what is just or fair or follows a moral authority.

            yes   no   Whose?

            What were their rights?   Anyone else? Explain.

      b.   Did (Will) you make your decision in this situation based on your consideration of your own rights? By rights I mean what is just or fair or follows a moral authority.

            yes   no

            What are your rights?   Explain.

6.   If the rights were in conflict in this situation, how did (would) you decide between them?

7.   Did (Will) you make your decision in this situation based on your feeling responsible to yourself? By responsibility I mean feeling an obligation or a duty to yourself that you had to follow.

            yes   no   Explain.

8.   Did (Will) you make your decision in this situation based on your feeling responsible to others?

            yes   no   Who?

            Anyone else?   Explain.

9.   If the responsibilities were (are) in conflict, how did (would) you decide between them?

10.   Did (Will) you make your decision in this situation based on your feeling responsible to other people's rights?

            yes   no   Explain.

11.   Did (Will) you make your decision in this situation based on any moral principle?

            yes   no   Explain.

12.   Did (Will) you make your decision in this situation based on considering the well-being of anyone?

            yes   no   Whose?   Explain.

13.   a.   How did (do) you feel about making this moral decision?

      b.   How did (do) you feel after making this decision?

14.   Did you ask anyone else what he or she would do in the same circumstances?

            yes   no   Explain.

15.   a.   Was part of this process based on knowing that one course of action was the morally right one?

                yes   no   Explain.

      b.   If yes, what told you this was the morally right course of action?

      c.   If yes, when did you know that this was the morally right course of action to take?

d.   Did you know there was a right moral course of action to take but did not follow that courseof action?

         yes   no   Explain.

e.   If yes, how did you decide it was all right for you to act the way you did and not follow the right moral course of action?

f.   If you did not follow what you know to be a right moral course of action, how did that make you feel?

16.   What gave (would give) you the moral strength to follow through in your decision in this situation?

17.   If this situation comes up again that *(specific situation)*, will the process about making the decision be the same, not whether you would come to the same decision?

         yes   no   Explain.

18.   Was this a typical way for you to make a moral decision?

         yes   no   Explain.

19.   a.   Have you ever been in the same situation and made a different decision?

         yes   no   Explain.

       b.   If yes, why was the decision different?

20.   Have you recently considered doing something that was morally right but did not?

         yes   no   Explain.

If yes, then ask the following questions #22-41:
If no, go back and ask the following questions #22-41 for answer #19a
If no to #19a, and no to #20, then ask 21.

21.   Tell me about another moral decision you've made recently or are currently making?

22.   How did you go about making a decision what to do or not to do?

23. How did you decide this was a moral decision?

24. When did you decide this was a moral decision?

25. a. Did (Will) you make your decision in this situation based on your consideration of other people's rights? By rights I mean what is just or fair or follows a moral authority.

        yes   no   Whose?

        What were their rights?   Anyone else?   Explain.

   b. Did (Will) you make your decision in this situation based on your consideration of your own rights? By rights I mean what is just or fair or follows a moral authority.

        yes   no

        What are your rights?   Explain.

26. If the rights were in conflict in this situation, how did (would) you decide between them?

27. Did (Will) you make your decision in this situation based on your feeling responsible to yourself? By responsibility I mean feeling an obligation or a duty to yourself that you had to follow.

        yes   no   Explain.

28. Did (Will) you make your decision in this situation based on your feeling responsible to others?

        yes   no   Who?

        Anyone else?   Explain.

29. If the responsibilities were (are) in conflict, how did (would) you decide between them?

30. Did (Will) you make your decision in this situation based on your feeling responsible to other people's rights?

        yes   no   Explain.

31. Did (Will) you make your decision in this situation based on any moral principle?

        yes   no   Explain.

32. Did (Will) you make your decision in this situation based on considering the well-being of anyone?

        yes   no   Whose?   Explain.

33. a. How did (do) you feel about making this moral decision?

    b. How did (do) you feel after making this decision?

34. Did you ask anyone else what he or she would do in the same circumstances?

        yes   no   Explain.

35. a. Was part of this process knowing that one course of action was the morally right one?

        yes   no   Explain.

    b. If yes, what told you this was the morally right course of action?

    c. If yes, when did you know that this was the morally right course of action to take?

    d. Did you know there was a right moral course of action to take but did not follow that course of action?

        yes   no   Explain.

    e. If yes, how did you decide it was all right for you to act the way you did and not follow the right moral course of action?

    f. If you did not follow what you know to be a right moral course of action, how did that make you feel?

36. What gave (would give) you the moral strength to follow through in your decision in this situation?

37. If this situation comes up again *(that specific situation)*, will the decision-making process be the same? (Not whether or not you would come to the same decision.)

        yes   no   Explain.

38. Was this a typical way for you to make a moral decision?

        yes   no   Explain.

39   a.   Have you ever been in the same situation and made a different decision?

                  yes   no   Explain.

         b.   If yes, why was the decision different?

40.   After reviewing the two processes of making the above two moral decisions, can you tell me how the way you have made moral decisions fits with who you are as a person? What does that say about you?

41.   Thinking back over the way that you made the two moral decisions we have talked about, can you come up with a theory about how you make moral decisions?

APPENDIX B
MORAL BEHAVIOR INTERVIEW

David Connor

In this part of the interview, we'll be talking more specifically about moral behavior. I'm interested in the decisions you've been making and the thoughts and feelings connected with those decisions.

1.   a.   We're going to be looking just at who you were in college. I'd like to summarize and define who you were in those days. Back then, how would you have described yourself?

     b.   From your current point of view, how do you define yourself then?

     c.   How did you feel about yourself in college?

     d.   When you were in college, what about yourself made you feel good, proud?

     e.   What about yourself made you feel bad?

2.   a.   In terms of beliefs and actions, how were you similar to the people you spent time with?

     b.   In terms of beliefs and actions, how were you different from the people you spent time with?

     c.   How would you describe the beliefs and behaviors of the people you admired, you looked up to, when you were in college?

     d.   In college, what beliefs and behaviors did you dislike when you saw them in other people?

3.   a   In college how did your parents influence what you did and didn't do?

     b.   In college, how did your parents influence how you felt?

     c.   In college, how did your parents influence what you believed?

4.   a.   In college, were there things you did or didn't do that you wouldn't have wanted your fellow students to know about?

                Yes   No   What?

    b.   Were there things you did or didn't do that you wouldn't have wanted your professors to know?

                Yes   No   What?

    c.   Were there things you did or didn't do that you wouldn't have wanted your resident assistant to know?

                Yes   No   What?

    d.   Were there things you did or didn't do that you wouldn't have wanted your girlfriend/ boyfriend to know?

                Yes   No   What?

5.   a   Tell me about a moral decision you made in college.

    b.   Tell me about the process of making a decision -- what to do or not to do in that situation. What were your thoughts and feelings?

6.   How and when did you decide it was a moral situation?

7.   a.   Was part of the process thinking about other people's rights?

                Yes   No

                If yes, whose? Which rights?

    b.   If so, were the rights in conflict?

                Yes   No

                If yes, how did you decide between them?

    c.   In what sort of situation would you typically have considered people's rights?

8.   a.   Was part of the process thinking about responsibilities to yourself and other people?

                Yes   No   If so whose?

                What responsibilities?

b. If so, and the responsibilities were in conflict, how did you decide between them?

c. In those days, in what sort of situation would you typically consider responsibilities to other people?

d. In those days, in what sort of situation would you typically consider responsibility to yourself?

9. What feelings of yours were involved in the process?

10. Was part of the process asking what someone else would do?

       Yes   No   If so, who?

11. Was part of this process knowing that one course of action was the morally right one?

       Yes   No

       What was that course of action?

12. a. If part of the process was knowing there was a morally right action and you didn't follow that course of action, how did you decide that it was all right for you to act the way you did?

b. What feelings did that bring up for you?

13. a. Would you call this process of seeing a moral situation and making a decision typical of you?

       Yes   No

b. Had you been in a similar situation before but made a different decision?

       Yes   No

       If yes, why the change?

c. Have you since been in a similar situation but made a different decision?

       Yes   No

       If yes, describe how you decided differently.

14. a. In college, what were some of the things you did that you felt good about?

b.   In college, what were some of the things you didn't do that you felt good about not doing?

c.   Do you still feel the same way about those behaviors now?

      Yes   No   Why?

15.   a.   In college, what were some of the things you did that caused you a twinge of conscience while you were doing them?

      b.   In college, what were some of the things you didn't do that caused you a twinge of conscience while you were not doing them?

      c.   Were there things you did or didn't do that seemed acceptable in college but caused you a twinge of conscience afterwards?

            Yes   No   If yes, why?

16.   Imagine you had a younger brother/sister or daughter/son. Looking back, what choices did you make that you would like them to decide differently?

Now let's talk about your current life.

17.   a.   What are some of the changes in you since college; how are you different?

      b.   Were any of those changes conscious decisions on your part?

            Yes   No

            If yes, what was the process of that decision?

18.   a.   How would you define yourself now? What are you like?

      b.   How do you feel about yourself now?

      c.   What about yourself makes you feel good, or proud?

      d.   What things about yourself don't make you feel good?

      e.   What behaviors and feelings are so typical of you that if you didn't act or feel that way you just wouldn't be you?

      f.   Do you ever decide in a moral situation to act in a certain way because "That's who I am", or not act in a certain way because "That's not me?"

            Yes   No

            If so, describe those situations.

19. We all make decisions about how to behave, and sometimes after trial and error people develop patterns of habitual moral behavior. In terms of how you treat yourself and other people, what are some of your typical habits with friends, at work, with strangers?

20. a. Who are the significant people in your life now? How are they significant?

    b. I'd like you to think of the people you spend time with, in terms of beliefs and actions. How are you similar?

    c. How are you different from the people you spend time with, in terms of beliefs and actions?

    d. And now think of the people you're the closest to, and their beliefs and actions. How are you similar?

    e. In terms of beliefs and actions, how are you different from the people you're closest to?

    f. What beliefs and behaviors do you dislike when you see them in other people?

    g. What influence do your parents have still on how you act, how you feel, and what you believe?

21. a. Are there ways you behave, things you do or don't do, that you wouldn't want your boss/supervisor to know?

        Yes   No

        If yes, what are they?

    b. Are there ways you behave, things you do or don't do, that you wouldn't like your fellow workers to know?

        Yes   No

        If yes, why?

    c. Are there ways you behave, things you do or don't do, that you wouldn't want your friends to know?

        Yes   No

        If yes, why?

    d. Are there ways you behave, things you do or don't do, that you wouldn't want your husband/wife/lover to know about?

        Yes   No

        If yes, what?

e.   Are there ways you behave, things you do or don't do, that you wouldn't want *me* to know about?

   Yes   No

   If so, what?

22.   Imagine/think of a younger brother/sister or daughter/son. Are there ways in which you'd like him/her to be different from you in what they do or don't do in moral situations?

23.   a.   Tell me about a moral decision you've made recently or are currently making.

   b.   How did you go about making a decision what to do or not to do?

24.   How and when did you decide this was a moral situation?

25.   a.   Was part of the process thinking about people's rights?

   Yes   No

   b.   In what sort of situation would you typically consider other people's rights?

26.   a.   Was part of the process thinking about responsibilities to yourself and to other people ?

   Yes   No

   If yes, whose? What responsibilities?

   b.   If the responsibilities were in conflict, how did you decide between them?

   c.   In what sort of situation do you typically consider responsibilities to other people?

27.   What feelings of yours were involved in the process?

28.   Was part of the process asking what someone else would do in the same circumstance?

   Yes   No

   If yes, who?

29.   a.   Was part of this process knowing that one course of action was the morally right one?

   Yes   No

   If yes, what action did you know was morally right?

220

b. If so, at what part of the process did you know what was morally right? When?

30. a. If you knew there was a moral course of action and didn't follow that course of action, how did you decide it was O.K. for you to act the way you did?

b. What feelings did that bring up for you?

31. a. If this situation comes up again, will the process be the same?

        Yes   No

b. Was this a typical decision process for you?

        Yes   No

c. Have you ever been in the same situation and made a different decision?

        Yes   No

        If yes, describe the process. Why was the outcome different?

d. You've talked about some critically important areas of our research. I've asked you a lot of detailed questions about the parts of your decisions. It would be helpful if you'd take a couple of minutes to tell me now about your whole process in your own words. What was the beginning?

32. a. Can you tell me about a time when you considered doing something that was morally right, but you didn't?

        Yes   No

b. If yes, what was that process like?

33. a. Thinking ahead to the next ten years, what are your hopes and aspirations for yourself?

b. What are some of the things about yourself you may perhaps change in that time? How?

c. What are some of the moral problems you may be facing then? How do you think you'll go about dealing with them?

APPENDIX C
THE MORAL INFLUENCE INTERVIEW

James M. Day

Preamble

Interview

I'd like to thank you for agreeing to this interview, and for taking the time to meet with me. Those of us who are trying to understand moral thinking and behavior are very grateful to you. I'm very grateful now to have some time with you, and to have this opportunity to try to broaden my own understanding.

In this interview, I would like to talk with you about your moral self and how that might relate to other experiences of self you have had; experiences alone or with others—persons you love, friends, family, and with others more generally.

In addition, I'd like to talk with you about how your moral self relates to religious beliefs and experiences you may have or have had at one time. I'd like to know anything about your most deeply held views of, or feelings about the world and how it works, what gives meaning to your life, and how those experiences may be, or have been, connected to your moral being.

Questions: Section I

1. a. To whom are you the closest in your life at this time?

    b. Whom do you care about most deeply?

3. How do the persons you have named relate to your moral life; to the way(s) you think about good and bad, right and wrong, how to get along with other people in the world?

4. a. Are there some people, more than others in the group you've just described, who have or have had a greater moral influence on you than others you know well?

    b. How? In what way?

5. Are there any of the persons about whom we've just been talking whom you see as a moral example; someone who, by their actions, inspires you, makes you want to be a better moral

person, or about whom you think sometimes "Yes, I'd like to be that way, or be that kind of person?"

6. a. Sometimes people select from their environments, from their experiences, other people they don't even know but who inspire them morally. Sometimes that is a real, live person, sometimes an historical figure, sometimes a person from books, or films, from legends, myths, or religious literature.

   b. Is there anyone like that in your life?

   c. Do you have any heroes? How have they affected you and your moral sense of life and self?

7. Are there others to whom you turn for moral guidance when you have a question about what's right or wrong to do?

Section II

8. Are there moral principles or moral habits that you follow in daily life?

9. What helps you to act consistently with your principles, or keeps you from doing so?

10. What would you say have been the roots of your moral strength or character? What sources have most shaped, or otherwise influenced, your sense of moral self?

11. Have there been central moral experiences in your life—experiences that may have dramatically affected your moral self and the ways you have behaved thereafter?

Section III

12. If you were to sum up your view of life, and what it means, what would you say?

13. If I say to you the words, "religion," "religious," and "spiritual," what do they mean? Do "religious" and "spiritual" mean the same thing(s) to you?

14. a. Have you ever had what you would refer to as a religious experience?

    b. A spiritual experience?

    c. What were they like?

15. a. Have those experiences affected your moral life?

    b. In what way(s)?

CONTENT AND AUTHOR INDEXES

The content index is designed to be read in conjunction with the author index. The presence of an author in the content index is in association with either major citations to a moral action theory or aspect of a theory, or a theory of young adulthood. References to other aspects of their work appear in the author index, and are not duplicated in the content index.

There are some topics which are referenced and discussed throughout the book; however, they are only identified in the content index where there is a systematic treatment of them. An example is the relationship of *moral reasoning* to *moral action*. This topic is covered systematically in Chapters 5 and 6 and is the subject of much disagreement among theorists and researchers. The interested reader is directed to those chapters.

The *Sierra Project* and the *Sierrans Revisited Project* are indexed in terms of their basic aspects and implications, but not all descriptive references have been indexed. The same is true for the empirical measures of principled thinking (from the Defining Issues Test), moral maturity (from the Moral Judgment Interview), and ego development (from the Washington University Sentence Completion Test).

Theories of *Young Adulthood* are indexed under Y, but are best treated in the context of their coverage in Chapter 4. In the content index, the theories are listed under the name of the first author. Where co-authors exist, they are included in the author index and in the reference list for Chapter 4.

Content Index

Altruism
   in exceptional moral behavior, xxxii, xxxv,
   84-85, 175, 179-182, 201
   (see Kristen Monroe's theory of altruism)

Autonomy
   and moral action, xxxii, 89-91
   (see Larry Nucci and John Lee's domain
      theory of autonomy in moral action)

Bandura, Albert
   theory of moral agency in moral action,
      xxxii, 192-194
   (see moral agency and social cognitive
      theory)

Blasi, Augusto
   theory of moral action 75-76, 87-89, 185-189

Carolinian creed, xiv

Chambered nautilus
   as visual metaphor for student
      development, v

Character
   conceptual definition, 29, 203
   growth during the freshman year, 31-43

Character development
   defined, 29

Character education
   defined, 29
   rationale for in higher education, xvii-xix

Colby, Anne and William Damon
   theory of moral commitment, xxxv, 85-87,
      176-178, 201

Community
   and moral values in higher education, xxxv,
      1, 3-10
   Sierra Project implications for, 43-48

Ego development, xix
   defined, 29

Ego development (cont.)
   empirical results of Sierra Project, 37-38, 42-43

Emotions in moral action, 160-165, 189-190
   (see Immanel Kant)

Empathy in moral action, 190-192
   (see Martin Hoffman)

Exceptional moral behavior, 205
   see Chapter 10 (145-153), 12 (175-182)
   altruism
   moral commitment

Freshman year
   empirical findings, 38-45
   importance of moral action as outcome of, xi
   University 101, xi

Gilligan, Carol
   theory of moral action, 74-75

Haan, Norma
   theory of moral action, 76-78

Higher education
   conceptual questions about theories of
      character and moral development,
      203-204
   implications of Sierra Project for, 43-48
   obstacles to character development of
      students, 25-31
   purpose of character education in, xvii
   role in education for moral action, xiv
   sense of community and moral
      values on, xxxv, 3-10

Hoffman, Martin
   theory of empathy in moral action, 96-98

Identity, 55-56
   (see Moral Identity, Erik Erikson's theory of
      young adulthood)

Kant, Immanuel
   critique of emotions and feelings in moral
      action, 189
   role of moral judgment in moral conduct,
      xxiii

Kohlberg, Lawrence
    model of moral action, xxix
    philosophical issues in defining morally
        commendable action, xxiii
    theory of moral action, 71-74

Lee, John and Nucci, Larry
    domain approach to autonomy in moral action,
        xxxii, 89-91

Monroe, Kristen
    theory of altruism in moral action, xxxii-xxxiii,
        xxxv, 84-85, 175, 179-182, 201

Moral action theories, xxii-xxiv, xxxi-xxxii,
        69-70, 78-80, 83-84, 205-206
    Augusto Blasi's theory, 75-76, 87-89, 185-189
    Anne Colby and William Damon's theory
        xxxv, 85-87, 176-178, 201
    Carol Gilligan's theory, 74-75
    Norma Haan's theory, 76-78
    in relationship to personality theory, 107-108,
        109
    Lawrence Kohlberg's theory, 71-74
    Kristen Monroe's theory, xxxii-xxxiii, xxxv,
        84-85, 175, 179-182, 201
    Larry Nucci and John Lee's theory, xxxii,
        89-91
    James Rest's theory, 70-71

Moral agency
    Albert Bandura's theory, 93-95
    in strength of character, xxxv, 206
    Helen Longino's theory, 91-92
    Michael Pritchard's theory, 92-93
    (see social cognitive theory and Albert
        Bandura's theory of agency in moral
        action)

Moral commitment
    in exceptional moral behavior, xxxv, 85-87,
        176-178, 201
    (see Anne Colby and William Damon's
        theory of moral commitment

Moral dilemmas in young adults
    consequences of moral decisions, 118-123
    content of dilemmas, 110-118, 125-134,
        135-143, 145-152, 159-160

influences on response to dilemmas, 160-165
organization of Sierrans Revisited research,
    197-199
talking about moral issues 158
use of personal narrative in, 152-153

Moral identity
    in moral action, xxxii, 185-189
        (see Augusto Blasi's moral action theory)
    use in concept of "volitional necessity,"
        187-188

Moral judgment
    Lawrence Blum, 98-99

Moral maturity
    defined, 29
    empirical results of Sierra Project, 35-36

Moral reasoning
    relationship to moral action, xxii-xxiv,
        165-171, 183-185
        (see also moral action theories in Chapter 5
        and 6)

Nucci, Larry and Lee, John
    domain approach to autonomy in moral
        action, xxxii, 89-91

Personal narrative interview, xxxiii-xxxiv,
    152-153, 158, 160

Principled thinking
    defined, 29
    empirical results of Sierra Project, 29, 31-35,
        38-42

Rest, James
    theory of moral action, 70-71

Self theory
    and moral action, xxxii

Sierra Project
    central implications, 2, 43-48
    conceptual and empirical definitions of
        character, xix-xx, 29
    curriculum, 29-30, 197-206
    description of, xvii-xviii, 201

Sierra Project (cont.)
  educational environment of, 9-10
  empirical findings, 2, 31-45
  objectives, xvii-xviii, 201, 206
  rationale for, 2, 26-31, 201-202
  role of moral action, xxxii

Sierrans Revisited Project
  conclusions and directions for future
          research, xxxiv-xxxv, 197-206
  narrative insights into moral action,
      xxxiii-xxxiv
      (see personal narrative interview)
  purpose, xx-xxii, xxiv-xxv, 157-158, 202-203
  research questions of, xxviii
  theoretical underpinnings, xxx-xxxiii,
      203-204
      (see Chapters 4, 5, and 6)

Social cognitive theory
  and moral action, xxxii, 192-194
  (see moral agency and Albert Bandura)

Strength of character, 183, 206

University of South Carolina
  Latin motto, xiii
  University 101, xi

University of California, Irvine
  allocation of academic credit, 200
  curricular restraints, 198-199

Young adulthood
  Charolette Buhler's theory, 56-57
  developmental issues associated with, xxxi,
      64-66
  Erik Erikson's theory, 55-56
  Sigmund Freud's theory, 54
  Carol Gilligan's theory, 63-63
  Roger Gould's theory, 60
  Robert Havighurst's theory, 57-58
  Carl Jung's theory, 54-55
  Lawrence Kohlberg's theory, 63
  Daniel Levinson's theory, 21, 60-61
  Bernice Neugarten's theory, 62

Author Index

Adelson, J., 64
Aerts, E., 69, 76, 77, 78
Allport, G. W., 9
Angyal, A., 5, 9
Arnold, M. B., 189
Averill, J.R., 189

Baltes, P. B., 53
Bandura, A., xxxii, 83, 93-95, 100,101, 192-194, 205
Batson, C.D., 191
Beck, A.T., 189
Bertin, B. D., 26, 31, 44
Blasi, A., xxxi, xxxii, xxxiii, 69, 70, 75-76, 79, 83, 87-89, 100, 102, 103, 109, 157, 185-188
Blum, L.A., 83, 98-99, 100, 101, 102, 189
Bocknek, G., 54
Brabeck, M., 96
Brown L. M., 153, 158, 160
Brown, R., xxi
Buff, S. A., 65
Buhler, C., 56-58
Burris, M. P., 31

Candee, D., xx, xxxiii, 29, 72, 73, 74, 75,78, 79, 109, 157, 203
Cargan, L., 65
Carter, M. W., 40
Colby, A., xx, xxxii, xxxv, 29, 31, 63, 203, 83, 85-86, 99-100, 101,171, 175, 176-178, 183, 185, 187, 201, 205
Coles, R., 160, 158,
Connor, D., xxxiii, xxxiv, 165
Cooper, B., 69, 76, 77, 78

Damon, W., xxxii, xxxv, 76, 83, 85-86, 99-100, 101, 171,175, 176-178, 183, 185, 187, 201, 205
Darrow, C. N., 60, 61, 65
Datan, N., 62
Day, J. M., 147, 153, 158, 160
Deemer, D., 31, 32
Dewey, J., xvii, xxx, 16, 48
Douvan, E., 64
Dupont, H., xxiii

Eisenberg, N., 191
Ellis, A., 18
Erickson, V. L., 26
Erikson E. H., 16, 19, 55-56, 58, 60, 65, 76, 79

Ferrant, B. A., 31, 44
Fischer, J. L., 56
Flanagan, O., 102
Frankfurt, H., 101, 187, 188
Freud, S., 54, 65

Gagnon, J. H., 65
Gamson, W. A., 20, 30
Gans, H. J., 51
Gibbs, J. C., xx, 29, 31, 63, 203
Gilligan, C., xxi, xxxiii, 56, 63-64, 69, 74-75, 79, 102, 109, 157, 160
Glodis, K., 186
Gorman, M., 96
Gould, R., 58-59, 65
Greif, E. B., 70

Haan, N., 69, 76-78, 79
Hareven, T. K., 65
Hartshorne, H., xxii, xxiii, xxxi, 69
Haste, H., 96
Hauser, S. T., 169, 171
Havighurst, R. J., 57-58, 60, 65
Held, V., 102
Hendrix, L. J., 40
Herrnstein, R., xxi
Hewer, A., 72
Higgins, A., 72-73, 78
Hintze, J. L., 40
Hodgson, J. W., 56
Hoffman, M. L., 83, 96-98, 100, 189,190-192
Holmes, O.W., v-vi
Hume, D., 190
Hyde, J. S., 56

Jacobson, E., 20
Jaggar, A. M., 96
James, W., 101
Jennings, J. S., 31
Jennings, W., 153
Jenrich, R., 34
Jung, C. G., 54, 65

Kalliel, K. M. xxxiii, 164
Kant, I., xxiii, 72, 101, 189
Kilkenny, R., 153
Klein, E. B., 60, 61, 65
Kluckhohn, C., 188
Kohlberg, L., xix, xx, xxiii, xxxi, xxxiii, xxiv, 29, 31, 63, 69, 70, 71-74, 75, 78-79, 86, 89, 93, 94, 96, 98, 100, 101, 102, 109, 153, 157, 168, 203
Kurtines, W., 70

Laslett, B., 65
Lazarus, R.S., 189
Lee, J., xxxii, 83, 89-90, 100
Lee, L., 14, 31
Lesser, I. M., 56
Levine, C., 72
Levinson, D. J., xxi,16, 21, 60-61, 65
Levinson, M. H., 60, 61, 65
Lieberman, M., 31, 63
Loevinger, J., xix, xx, 29, 88, 169,203,

229

Longino, H., 91, 92, 93
Loxley, J. C., i, xvii, xx, xxvii, 14, 15, 16, 17, 18, 20, 21, 47, 202, 203, 204

Maller, J. B., xxii, xxiii, 69
Marcia, J. E., 56
Massarik, F., 56
May, M. A., xxii, xxiii, xxxi, 69
McBee, M., 25
McKee, B., 60, 61, 65
Mill, J.S., 190
Milton, K., 88, 89, 102
Monroe, K. R., xxxii, xxxv, 83, 84-85, 99, 101, 175, 179-182, 185, 201, 205, 206
Montada, L., 189
Mosher, R.L., 18, 19, 26, 70
Murray, H. A., 9, 188

Neugarten, B. L., 62, 64
Noam, G. G., 183, 184, 198
Nucci, L., xxxii, 25, 83, 89- 90, 100

Opton, E.M., 189
Oresick, R. J., 75, 76, 79
Orlofsky, J. L., 56

Parsons, T., 188
Pascarella, E. T., 25
Pfaff, D., 91
Piaget, J., 89, 100
Porter, M. R., 166, 167
Prager, K. J., 56
Pritchard, M. S., 92-93

Rawls J., 190
Resnikoff, A., 31
Rest, J., xx, xxxiii, 26, 31, 32, 33, 69, 70-71, 75, 78, 109, 157, 167, 203
Rogers, C.R., 184, 191, 192
Rorty, A. O., 102, 197
Rosen, J. L., 62
Rudolph, F., 25

Sampson, P., 34
Sanford, N., 9, 44
Scharf, P., 26
Scheman, N., 96, 98, 100, 101
Schneider D., 188
Schneider, A., 189
Schrader, D., 73, 78
Selman, R. L., 73
Shuttleworth, F. K., xxii, 69
Simon, W., 65
Simpson, E. L., 70
Speicher-Dubin, B., xx, 29, 203
Sprinthall, N.A., 18, 19, 26, 70

Tappan M. B., 73, 78, 153, 158, 160
Tillich, P., 152
Trudeau, G. B., 28
Tugendhat, E., 91
Turiel, E., 70

Uhlenberg, P., 65

Vaillant, G. E., 60, 65
Verrill, A. H., v
Vitz, P., 158, 160
Vygotskii, L., 15

Weber, C. O., xxiii
Wertheimer, M., 53
Wessler, R., xx, 203
Whiteley, i, xvii, xxvii, xx 1, 10, 14, 15, 16, 17, 18, 20, 21, 26, 28, 31, 44, 46, 47, 153, 168, 202, 203, 204
Wilson, J. Q., 92
Wittgenstein, L., 92
Wolfe, A. 65
Wren, T.E., 198

Yokota, N., xxii, 31, 44